# The Shadow of Victory

## Myrtle Reed

[ZHINGOORA BOOKS]

This edition is published by
Zhingoora Books.

# CONTENTS

# CHAPTER I
# THE PROPHECY

It was a long, low room, with a fireplace, roughly built of limestone, at one end of it. The blazing logs illuminated one corner and sent strange shadows into the others, while the winter wind moaned drearily outside. At the right and left of the fireplace were rude counters, hewn from logs, resting on stumps of unequal height, and behind them were shelves, packed with the sordid miscellany of a frontier trading-post. A closed door on either side seemingly led to other apartments, but there was no sound save the wind and the crackle of the flames. A candle, thrust into the broken neck of a bottle, gave a feeble light to a little space around one end of the counter on which it stood. The rafters were low— so low that a tall man, standing on tiptoe, might easily unhook the smoked hams and sides of bacon that hung there, swaying back and forth when the wind shook the house.

Walls, ceiling, and floor were of logs, cut into a semblance of smoothness. The chinks were plastered with a bluish clay, and the crevices in the floor were filled with a mixture of clay and small chips. At the left of the chimney was a rude ladder which led to the loft through an opening in the ceiling. Fingers of sleet tapped at the glass, swirling phantoms of snow drifted by, pausing for a moment at the windows, as if to look within, and one of the men moved his chair closer to the fire.

"You fed the cattle, didn't you, Chan?" The half-breed grunted assent.

It was the eldest of the three who had spoken. His crouching position in his chair partially concealed his great height, but the firelight shone full upon his iron-grey hair and the deep lines seamed upon his kindly face. His hands were rough and knotted, his fingers straight and square at the tips—hands without beauty, but full of strength.

The hand which rested on the arm of the chair next to him was entirely different. It was fair and smooth and slender, with tapering fingers, and with the outer line of the palm delicately curved; instinct with strength of another sort, yet gentle almost to the point of femininity. The hand accorded ill with the deep, melodious voice of the man, when he said:

"Uncle, you don't know how glad I am to be here with you and Aunt Eleanor. I feel as if I had come home at last, after many wanderings."

"You're welcome, my boy," was the hearty answer. "I'm glad you got through before this storm came, 'cause travellin' 'cross country isn't good in February, as a rule. Things will be closed up now till Spring."

"And then—what?" asked the young man.

"Trains of pack-horses from Rock River and the Illinois. Canoes and a bateau from Milwaukee, in charge of Canadian *engagés*. Then the vessel from Fort Mackinac with goods for the trade, and Indians from all over creation. The busy season begins in the Spring."

Chandonnais, the half-breed, was audibly asleep in his warm corner, and the guest arose to walk nervously about the room. He was clad in rusty black broadcloth, which had seen all of its best days and some of its worst, and clung closely to his tall, lank figure, as though in fear of the ultimate separation. His hair was black and straight, his eyes deep brown and strangely luminous, his mouth sensitive, and his face very pale. He was not more than twenty-five or six, and looked even younger.

John Mackenzie quietly watched him in his uneasy march back and forth. At last he came to the fire, stopped short, and put a questioning finger upon the limestone. "Here's some initials," he said. "J. B. P. D. S.—what does that stand for?"

"Jean Baptiste Pointe de Saible, I reckon," replied Mackenzie. "He built this cabin. The Indians say that the first white man here was a negro."

"P. L. M."—continued the young man. "Who was he?"

"Pierre Le Mai, I guess—the French trader I bought the place from."

"You should put yours here, too, Uncle."

"Not I, my boy. I have come to stay—and my children after me."

"That reminds me of my young charge. Shall we begin to-morrow?"

"As you like. The sooner the better, I suppose. You brought books, didn't you?"

"All that I have; not many, I regret to say."

"Johnny has a spelling-book that came from Mackinac in a chest of green tea, when the vessel touched here last year. He was very anxious then to know what was inside of it, but I don't know how he feels now."

"Have you any special instructions for me?"

"No," answered Mackenzie, rising. He put his hand on the young man's shoulder and looked down into his face. "I never had much book-learning," he said, "'cause I ran away from school, but I want that my son should have it. Teach him everything you know that he can learn; it won't hurt him none. Teach him to tell the truth, to be afraid of nothing but dishonour, and to be kind to women. You look like your mother, boy."

The door opened suddenly, and the gust of wind that came in with it put out the candle and filled the room with the odour of burning tallow. "How!" grunted a stalwart Indian, in general salutation.

"How!" responded Mackenzie. "What is it to-night?"

The savage was more than six feet in height, and looked like the chief that he was. He was dressed from head to foot in buckskin, cunningly embroidered and beaded by a squaw. He wore nothing on his head, but a brilliant blanket was draped over one shoulder. A powder-horn hung at his side and a hunting-knife gleamed in his belt.

The squaw came in behind her lord and master, and shut the door, three grey wolf skins falling to the floor as she did so. "Shaw-ne-aw-kee," commanded the Indian, pointing to Mackenzie.

The woman obediently laid the skins upon the counter, and Black Partridge began to bargain for flour and bacon, speaking his own tongue. An animated conversation ensued, with many gestures on the part of the Indian. Mackenzie answered quietly, in the harsh Pottawattomie dialect, and stood his ground. The chief finally yielded, with a good grace which might or might not have been genuine, and the transfer was accomplished.

The Indian picked up one of the skins and pointed to a blood stain near the top of it, then began to talk rapidly. Mackenzie listened till he had finished speaking, then turned to his nephew.

"Look here, Rob," he said, "this will interest you. He says he had no trap, so he took his last piece of bacon and his hunting-knife and went up into the north woods. He sat down under a tree and waited, with the bacon in his left hand and his knife in his right. Presently the hungry wolf appeared, and, after due investigation, came near enough to stab. He says he waited from midnight till almost sunrise. A white man never could do that."

"Hardly," returned the young man, fingering the skin curiously. "What monumental patience!"

This speech, with a little additional compliment, was translated for the benefit of Black Partridge, whose stolid features gleamed momentarily, then relapsed into impassive bronze.

A cheery whistle was heard outside, then a stamp upon the piazza, a merry and prolonged tapping, reinforced by a kick, at which the door burst open, and a young soldier entered.

"Evening!" he shouted to Mackenzie. He pounded the Indian familiarly on the back, saying, "Hello, Birdie," tweaked the squaw's ear and tickled her under the chin, and reached the fire before any one else had time to speak.

"Ronald," said Mackenzie, "this is my nephew, Robert Forsyth, from Detroit. Mr. Forsyth, Ensign George Ronald, of Fort Dearborn."

Ronald drew his heels together, saluted with mock solemnity, then wrung Forsyth's slender hand in a grip that made him wince. "Proud to know you, sir. Third in command, at your service, sir. Have you come to enlist?"

Chandonnais awoke, muttered an oath, and ran to the door, shutting it noisily. "Your pardon, sir," continued Ronald. "Wind's from the south this evening. Thought I'd let a little warm air in. Never appreciated in this world. Hope I may be in the next. Do I speak to a soldier, sir?"

"No," laughed Forsyth.

"Who's the lady you have with you, Birdie?" asked the Ensign, turning to the Indian. "Am I mistaken in supposing it to be Mrs. B. Partridge?"

"Me no spik Ingleesh," answered the chief, with great dignity.

"Neither do I, Birdie, neither do I," continued the soldier, genially. "Devilish language with all kinds of corners in it to hurt yourself on. I was pitched into it headlong the day of my arrival, and have been at sea ever since. Don't fool with it, Birdie. You're getting on all right with signs and pictures and grunts, and if Mrs. B. P. doesn't speak it, why, so much the better. Vast resources in the language known to women only. What, going? Bye-bye!"

Another breeze from the south entered the room as Black Partridge and the squaw made a stately exit, the woman carrying the provisions for which the wolf skins had been bartered.

"Ronald," began Mackenzie, drawing another chair from behind the counter, "I'd advise you to be more careful with the Indians. They're a treacherous crowd."

"I am careful," answered the Ensign, hurling a very shabby overcoat across the room, and sinking comfortably into Mackenzie's chair. "That's why I asked about Mrs. B. P. You see, I was skating on the river this morning, before this little snow flurry struck us, and I met this lady. She seemed to want to go, so I took her with me. She slid along on her moccasins, hanging on behind, and had a fine time till we struck a snowdrift, just around the bend. The woman tempted me, and I did throw her into it. Lord, how she squalled! It may have been ungallant, but it was fun."

Mackenzie laughed, in spite of his well-meant efforts to keep his face straight, and Forsyth's eyes were bright with new interest. Chandonnais was asleep again.

"It was quite natural to make inquiries, wasn't it?" resumed Ronald. "I wouldn't want tothrow another man's wife into a snowdrift, especially when the gentleman in question is a six-foot savage with a tomahawk, and peculiar ideas about fair play."

"Your manner of speech is not suited to the Indians," said Mackenzie, soberly.

"There you go again—always criticising, always finding fault. Criticism irks me. That's why I left the Fort this evening. Fussy lot, over there."

"What was the matter?" asked Forsyth.

"Nothing at all. Captain and his wife reading last month's papers, and taking no notice of visitors. Lieutenant and his wife writing letters, likewise oblivious of visitors. All inhospitable—nobody asked me to sit down. Barracks asleep. Doc and I played solitaire, because it's the only game he knows—to see who could get through first, and he kicked up a devil of a row because I cheated. Hasn't a man a right to cheat when he's playing solitaire? No law against cheating yourself, is there?"

"That's a mooted question," Forsyth answered.

"Maybe so, maybe so. I mooted it awhile with the Doc, and then quit. Coming over, I managed to get into the hole I broke in the river for this morning's bath, but it was all slush and ice—no harm done."

His garments were steaming in the generous warmth of the fire, and perspiration beaded his forehead. He stood a little over six feet in his stockings, and his superb muscle was evident in every line of his body. His thick, yellow hair was so long that he occasionally shook it back, like a mane. He had the face of a Viking—blue eyes, straight nose, red and white complexion, and a mouth and chin that in some way suggested steel. One felt the dynamic force of the man, his power of instant and permanent decision, and the ability to put that decision into immediate action.

"Sorry you're not going to be a soldier, Mr. Forsyth," he continued. "I knew you weren't, as soon as I saw you—you're altogether too young. The barracks are full of old ladies with the rheumatism. The parade ground is bloody with red flannel when the troops limp out, which is seldom, by the way, the Captain having a tender heart. Me and the other officers are the only ones under the age limit, if there is any age limit. When a man gets too old to be of use in the army, the President says: 'Don't discharge the poor cuss—send him out to Fort Dearborn, where all his old friends are. He'll be well taken care of, and won't have anything to do.' When you see an old man in a tattered uniform, bent and wrinkled and gummy-eyed, who puts his hand up to his ear and says, 'Hey!' when you speak to him, don't step on him—he's a soldier, stationed at the Fort.

"Had a wrestling match with one of the most sprightly, this very morning, and took the skin off the poor, tender old devil in several places. Doc made a surpassingly fine seam at one of the places afterward—Doc's pretty good with a needle and thread. The patient is in his bunk now, being rubbed with hot things by one of the rheumatics. I've tried to get the Doc to prescribe a plunge in the river every morning for the barracks, and I've urged the Captain to order it, but it's no use."

"Peculiar treatment for rheumatism," smiled Mackenzie.

"It's the only thing they haven't tried, and I'm inclined to think it would work a change."

There was a brief silence, during which Forsyth studied the young officer attentively, but Ronald was never still very long.

"What are you going to be, if not a soldier?" he asked, curiously. "You're— you're not a missionary, are you?"

"Do I look like one?"

"Can't say—missionaries are deceiving; but I hope not. The Pottawattomies tomahawked the last one and fried the remains. They're not yet ready for the soothing influences of religion."

"I have come to teach my young cousins," said Forsyth, slowly, "and to help my uncle as I can. I graduated from college last year, and went to Detroit to teach, but I—I didn't do very well." His pale face reddened as he made his confession. "Uncle John and Aunt Eleanor have kindly offered me a home with them," he went on. "They're the only relatives I have."

"They are relatives enough," remarked the Ensign. "Mrs. Mackenzie is the kindest woman and the best cook that ever lived, isn't she, Chan?"

The sleeper made no reply, so Ronald strode over to him and shook him roughly. "Wake up!" he bellowed. "Is Mrs. Mackenzie a good cook, or isn't she? Answer!"

The half-breed was frightened for a moment, but quickly realised the situation. "What?" he asked.

The question was repeated, with sundry shakes for emphasis. "Yes," grunted Chandonnais, sheepishly, "she good cook."

"Sit up straight, then, and look your prettiest. You can't sleep all day and all night, too." The restless visitor made a rapid tour around the counters, carefully examining the goods upon the shelves. "Nothing here I can use," he announced, returning to the fire.

"What was that silver thing the Indian had on?" asked Forsyth. "It looked like a coin of some kind."

"That was his precious medal. Captain Wells gave it to him, and he prizes it more than he does the hair of his lordly top piece. When Birdie dies, you'll find that sacred medal nailed to him, and if it doesn't accompany him to the happy hunting-grounds, his ghost will haunt the miserable mortal who has it. Don't mind a plain ghost myself, but a ghost with a tomahawk might be pretty bad."

"I make silver things for the Indians, sometimes," Mackenzie said. "They call me 'Shaw-ne-aw-kee,' meaning 'The Silver Man.'"

A face appeared at the window for an instant, and peered furtively within. It was so silent and so white, in the midst of the swirling snow, that it might have been a phantom of the storm. Then the door opened slowly, creaking ever so little on its hinges, and was softly closed. They felt, rather than heard, a presence in the room.

Forsyth, turning, saw a wisp of a woman, bent and old, in a faded blue calico dress which came scarcely to her ankles. Her shoes were much too large for her, and badly worn. A ragged shawl, of uncertain colour and pattern, was her only protection from the cold.

It slipped off as she came toward the fire, moving noiselessly, and Forsyth saw that her hair was snow white and her face finely traced with wrinkles. Mackenzie looked also.

"Mad Margaret," he whispered to Forsyth, in a swift aside. "Don't say anything."

The half-breed's eyes had a wolfish glitter which no one saw. Forsyth rose, bowed politely, and offered her his chair.

If she saw him, she made no sign. Coming closer to the fire she crouched on her knees before it and stretched her frail, delicate hands toward the grateful warmth. Ronald's flood of high spirits instantly receded.

For a long time they sat there in silence. Mackenzie and the Ensign were looking into the fire, thinking, perhaps, of things a thousand miles away, while Forsyth and Chandonnais narrowly watched the woman.

Unmistakable madness, of the dumb, pathetic kind, was written on her face. Her unseeing eyes were faded blue, her cheeks were sunken, and her chin delicately pointed. Solitude went with her always. She might have been alone, in the primeval forest, before a fire some unknown hand had kindled, among wild beasts of whom she was not afraid. Some eerie influence was upon her, for, after a little, she moved nervously, and peered into the flames, muttering to herself.

"Oh, Lord," groaned Mackenzie, "she's goin' to have one of her spells!"

How often the poor, crazed creature had sought him, when the tempests swept her soul, only he could tell. He leaned forward and took hold of her hand. "Margaret," he said; "Margaret."

The touch and the voice seemed to quiet her, but she still looked searchingly into the flames. Chandonnais rose, reached up to the chimney-shelf, and took down a violin. With the first touch of the bow upon the strings, she left Mackenzie and went to him, kneeling at his feet, with her eyes fixed hungrily upon his face.

Strains of wild music filled the room—music which no man had ever heard before. A tender, half-hushed whisper, the tinkle of a brook, a twilight subtleness of shadow, then a low, crooning note, as if the brook had gone to sleep. Strange sounds of swaying branches came from the violin, with murmurs of a mighty wind, then, of a sudden, there seemed to be dawn. The tinkle of the brook began again, with a bird note here and there, at the beginning of a great crescendo which swept on and on, as the music of the river was woven in. Question, prayer, and mating call, from a thousand silvery throats, rioted through the tapestry of sound, then merged into a deep, passionate tone of infinite sweetness, as if the river had found the sea, or a man's tortured soul had come face to face with its ultimate peace.

"Play," said Mad Margaret, brokenly, "play more."

Once again the bow swept the strings, bringing forth a melody which breathed rest. It was quiet and hushed, like the woods at twilight, or the shore of a sea that knows no storm. Through it ran a haunting cadence, with the rhythm of a lullaby, and Margaret rocked her frail body back and forth, unconsciously keeping time. When it was finished, she sat quite still, but on her face was the rapt look of the seer.

"I see blood," she said, very distinctly. "Much blood, then fire, and afterward peace."

It was the old, old prophecy, which she had made a thousand times. "Much blood," she repeated, shaking her head sadly.

"Where, Peggy?" asked Ronald, suddenly.

"Here," she answered, making a wide circle with her arms.

"What else do you see?" he asked again, looking at her intently.

She drew her hand wearily across her forehead and closed her eyes for an instant, then went to him, and put her hands on his knees.

"I see you," she said, meaningly.

"Where, Peggy?" His voice was low and very gentle, as if he were speaking to a child.

"Here, with the blood. You shall have many sorrows, but never your heart's desire."

"Never my heart's desire?"

"No. Many sorrows, at the time of the blood, but not that."

"What is my heart's desire?"

---

"It has not come, but you will know it soon." She looked at him keenly for an instant, then laughed mockingly, and almost before they knew it, she had darted out into the night like the wild thing that she was.

No one spoke until after Chandonnais had put the violin in its place on the chimney-shelf and clambered up the ladder which led to the loft.

"Who is she, Uncle?"

"Nobody knows," sighed Mackenzie. "She appeared, unexpectedly, the very day we came here. Sometimes months go by without a glimpse of her, then, for a time, she will come every day."

"How does she live?"

Mackenzie shrugged his shoulders. "We give her things," he said, "and so do the Indians and the people at the Fort. Black Partridge says he has seen her catch a gull on the lake shore, strangle it, and eat it raw. At the full of the moon, when her rages come on her, she speaks very good English. At other times, she mutters something no one can understand, or else she does not speak at all. She is harmless, I believe. She is only one of the strange things one finds in a new country."

"How did you come to settle here, Uncle?"

"I hardly know. It's a good place for trading, and the Fort is near by. I like the new places, where a few make their own laws, and I like the prairie. I can breathe here, but the hills choke me."

"Never my heart's desire," mused the Ensign. He was sitting with his elbows on his knees and his chin in his hands, gazing into the fire. He did not know that he had spoken aloud.

"Do any of us ever find it?" asked Forsyth.

"Not often, I guess," answered Mackenzie. "When we do, we are disappointed and begin to seek for something else."

From across the river, muffled by the storm, came the deep, sonorous notes of a bell. "Taps," said Ronald. He hurried into his overcoat, without a word of farewell, and bolted.

Forsyth followed, to close the door after him, and then went to the window to look at the dark, floundering figure silhouetted dimly against the snow.

"Breezy young man," commented Mackenzie.

"Yes," answered Forsyth, after a moment's silence, "I like him."

# CHAPTER II
## NEW ACQUAINTANCES

The next morning was cold and clear. The sun shone brilliantly, revealing unsuspected diamonds set in the snow. Forsyth woke late, wondered sleepily where he was, and then remembered.

His room was at the western end of the house, which faced the south, and from his window he could see the Fort and the Agency on the other side of the river. A savoury suggestion of frying bacon, penetrating the rough log partition, impelled him to dress hurriedly. As he broke the ice in his water pitcher, he wondered whether the Ensign had taken his regular plunge, and shivered at the thought.

When he reached the large room which served as kitchen, dining-room, and parlour, he found the family already assembled. Chandonnais was just leaving the table, and Mrs. Mackenzie sat at the head, pouring coffee from a quaint and battered silver pot which had been her grandmother's.

"Good-morning," she said cheerily, "I thought most likely you were beat out from travelling, and I told John to let you sleep."

She was a large, fair woman, matronly in every line, and her face was delicately pink. Her abundant hair was ashen blonde, escaping in little curls at her temples, and at the second glance one saw that it was rapidly turning grey. She had a wholesome air of cleanliness, and her blue eyes mirrored the kindness in the depths of her motherly heart.

Her brood was gathered around her, and every face had been scrubbed until it shone. The baby sat at her right and pounded the table madly with his pewter spoon, to the evident delight of his father. Maria Indiana was sipping warm milk daintily, like the four-year-old lady that she was, and Ellen and Johnny conducted themselves with more dignity than is common to people of seven and nine.

Forsyth had made friends with the children the evening before, and, of his own accord, had extended the schooling to all but the baby.

"It's going to be a sight of comfort to me," said Mrs. Mackenzie, "to have the young ones out from under foot half the time. The baby don't bother much. I tie him in his chair, give him something to play with, and he's all right."

"Where am I to teach, Aunt Eleanor?"

"In the next room, I guess. There's a fireplace in there, and you can have it all to yourselves. Just wait till the breakfast things are out of the way and I'll see to it."

At this juncture the Ensign appeared, smiling and debonair. "Morning! Am I too late for coffee?"

"You've had some already this morning, haven't you?" asked Mackenzie.

"Well, now, that depends on what coffee really is. Of course they called it that, but it isn't to be mentioned in the same breath with Mrs. Mackenzie's." Robert noted that there was an extra cup on the table, and surmised that the delicate hint was not infrequent.

"Thank you," continued the visitor in a grateful tone; "you've saved my life."

"I wish I had a dollar for every time I've saved your life," laughed Mrs. Mackenzie.

"So do I, for you are a good and beautiful woman, and you deserve a fortune, if anybody ever did."

"Go away, you flatterer. You remind me of a big, motherless chicken."

"Gaunt and chicken-like I may be, but never motherless while you live. A little bread and butter, please, to go with the coffee."

"Wouldn't you like some bacon?" asked Mackenzie, hospitably.

"Well, perhaps—a little. Mrs. Mackenzie cooks it beautifully."

"Ellen," said her mother, "get another plate."

"You're so good to me," murmured the Ensign, drawing his chair closer to his hostess. "Are those doughnuts?"

"They are."

"I remember once, when you gave me a doughnut, just after drill. I can taste it yet."

"Is that so? I'd forgotten it."

"Now that I think of it, you didn't, but you said you would, some time."

She laughed and pushed the plate toward him.

"Ye gods!" he exclaimed, sinking his white teeth into a doughnut, "what cooking! What a woman!"

"I think I'll ask to be excused," said Mackenzie, rising and pushing back his chair.

"Certainly," responded the soldier, with a gesture of elaborate unconcern. "Don't stay on my account, I beg of you. Think of real cream in your coffee!" he sighed, scraping the pitcher with a spoon. "I could drink cream."

"You're not going to," put in Mrs. Mackenzie, pointedly.

"I know it," he answered sadly; "I only wish I were."

When the last scrap of food had disappeared from the table, he stopped eating, but not before.

"That makes a man feel better," he announced, "especially a suffering and dying invalid like me. Come on, Forsyth, I'm going to take you over to the Fort for a bit."

It did not occur to Robert to question the mandates of this lordly being. "All right, wait till I get my coat and hat. I'll be back in a few minutes, Aunt Eleanor, to open school."

"The devil you will," observed Ronald, as they left the house. "What a liar you are!"

The path which led to the gate was well trodden, early morning though it was. "Indian tracks," said the Ensign, pointing to a narrow line on the snow; "you can always tell 'em. They keep their feet in single file—no company front about their walking."

An unpainted fence surrounded the Mackenzie premises, and at the right and left of the gate were four tall Lombardy poplars, two on each side. Brown sparrows chattered and fought in the bare branches, scorning to fly away at their approach. The house had been built on a point of land which projected into the river and turned it sharply from its course. Between the patches of snow the ice glittered in the sun.

"Salubrious spot," commented George, as they struck the frozen surface of the stream. "Don't get too near that hole. It's my bath-tub and it's weak around the edges."

Near the middle of the river was a large, jagged space in the ice and on the snow around it were finger-marks and footprints.

"Rather looked for you out this morning," Ronald continued. "Was disappointed."

Robert shrugged his shoulders, but made no reply.

"That happy architectural combination which we now approach," his guide went on, professionally, "is Fort Dearborn. Intoxicated party drew the plans and other intoxicated parties followed 'em. I could improve it in several places, but I'm obliged to make the best of it. The flag-pole, in the middle of the parade-ground, is seventy-five feet high, though you wouldn't suspect it, on account of the heroic proportions of the other buildings, and it interferes most beautifully with everything.

"Regular fort, though. Officers' quarters, barracks, offices, guard-house, magazine, and other modern inventions. Commanding officer has a palatial residence to himself. The Lieutenant is supposed to live in half of it, but he doesn't. Those warts at the south-east and north-west corners are block-houses, made after a Chinese diagram. The upper story overhangs to give a down range for musketry and keep the enemy from setting fire to the Fort. The double stockade is where the genius comes in, however. See how it slants and balances to corners. Makes the thing look like a quilt pattern. Would wear on the mind of a sensitive person.

"Hello, Charley! Here's where we get in. You see there's a sunken road to the river and there's a subterranean passage also, with a well in it, which insures the water-supply in case of a siege. We've got three pieces of light artillery—six-pounders—and our muskets, bayonets, and pistols. That's the Agency House outside. Your uncle is Government Indian Agent and sutler for the garrison and trader on his own account. This is where the Captain lives."

He pounded merrily at the door, then entered unceremoniously, and Robert followed him, awkwardly, into the room where the Captain and his wife sat at breakfast.

Captain Franklin was a grave, silent man on the sunny side of forty, who never spoke without cause, and his wife was a pretty little woman, with dark, laughing eyes. She brightened visibly when Robert was presented to her, for guests did not often appear at the Fort.

"Coffee?" remarked Ronald, with a rising inflection. "You're a lucky man, Captain, to have such coffee as Mrs. Franklin makes, every blessed morning of your life. I only wish I were as fortunate," he added impersonally.

Robert bit his lips to keep from smiling as the Ensign's wants were promptly supplied. "Won't you have some too, Mr. Forsyth?"

"No, thank you, Mrs. Franklin. I've been to breakfast."

The emphasis on the personal pronoun caused George to look at him meaningly, as he asked if he might have a bit of toast and an apple. While he ate, Mrs. Franklin talked with Forsyth and the Captain listened in silence.

"Are you going to stay?" she inquired.

"Yes, I hope so. I am going to teach my young cousins and help my uncle in any way I can. I graduated from Yale last year and went from there to Detroit, but as soon as I heard that Aunt Eleanor was willing to take me in, I started and got here yesterday, just before the storm."

"Did you have a pleasant journey?"

"Yes, fairly so. I came by way of Fort Wayne, with Indian guides and relays of horses."

"Any news?" asked the Captain.

"No, only the usual symptoms of discontent among the Indians. The officers in Detroit think there may be another outbreak soon."

"I don't—there's no earthly reason for it."

"Indians aren't particular about reasons," put in Ronald. "Come along, Robert, we're going over to the Lieutenant's."

When they entered, Mrs. Howard was clearing away the breakfast dishes, and after the introductions were over, Ronald did not hesitate to express his disappointment.

"Get that starving kid some coffee, Kit," said the Lieutenant, and Ronald gladly accepted the steaming cup, with polite regret at the trouble he was causing and with profuse praise of the beverage itself.

"Sugar?" asked Mrs. Howard.

"No, thank you—just put your dainty finger in for a moment, if you will be so kind. Your hand would sweeten the bitterest cup man is called upon to drink. Seems to me I smell pancakes."

He grinned appreciatively at Forsyth as Mrs. Howard went to the iron griddle that swung in the open fireplace. "Not many," he called to her, "six will do very nicely. I don't want to be a pig."

"You are, though," Forsyth assured him in an undertone.

"Shut up!" he replied concisely.

Acting upon the suggestion, Robert turned his attention to his host, and they talked until the pangs of hunger were somewhat satisfied. The Lieutenant and his wife followed them to the door.

"Tell my mother I'm coming over to see her this afternoon," said Mrs. Howard.

"All right," answered Robert. "Who's 'mother'?" he asked, when they got outside.

"Mrs. Mackenzie, of course. Don't you know your own relations when you see 'em? Mrs. Howard is your aunt's daughter and your uncle's step-daughter, so she's your cousin."

"Cousin-in-law, I guess," said Robert. "My father was Uncle John's half-brother, so we're not very closely related. She's nice, though. I wish she were my cousin."

"Coffee doesn't come up to her mother's," soliloquised George, "but it's pretty good. Hello, Doc!" he shouted, to a man on the opposite side of the parade-ground. "Had your breakfast?"

"Good Heavens!" ejaculated Forsyth, "you aren't going to eat again, are you?"

The Ensign turned upon him a look of reproach. "My rations aren't meant for full-grown men," he explained. "If I couldn't get a bite outside occasionally, I'd dry up and blow away. There's a squaw down in the hollow who cooks a pretty good mess, and you can get a bowl of it for a fist of beads. It isn't overly clean, and it's my private opinion it's yellow dog, stewed, or perhaps I should say, curried, but a starving man can't afford to be particular."

"Take me some time," Forsyth suggested carelessly; "I've never eaten dog."

"All right," was the jovial answer, "we'll go. Come on over and meet the Doc."

Robert was duly presented to Doctor Norton, whom the soldier characterised as "the pill roller of the garrison," and soon seized an opportunity to ask him the exact capacity of the human stomach.

"It varies," answered the Doctor, wrinkling his brows in deep thought. "Some people"——

"We must go," George interrupted. "It's time for school."

They parted on the bank of the river, Robert studiously avoiding an opportunity to shake hands. When he entered the house, his pupils were waiting for him.

The room set aside for educational purposes was just off the living-room and a bright fire was burning on the hearth. He found it difficult to teach three grades at once, and soon arranged alternate study and recitation for each, dismissing Maria Indiana in an hour with the first three letters of the alphabet well learned.

The window, like the others in the house, commanded a view of the river and the Fort, and gave a glimpse of the boundless plains beyond. Soldiers went in and out of the stockade, apparently at pleasure, and one or two of them came across, but he looked in vain for the stalwart young officer whom he was proud to call his friend.

At dinner-time he inquired about the neighbours.

"Neighbours?" repeated Mrs. Mackenzie, laughing; "why, we haven't any, except at the Fort."

"Are you and Uncle John really the only people here?" he asked, seriously.

"No, not that. There are a few houses here. Mr. and Mrs. Burns live in one—they are our nearest neighbours—and away up beyond is Lee's place. They don't have anything to do with us, nor we with them. Two or three men and a boy live there, I believe, but we don't see much of them. They're part French and part Indian. Chandonnais used to live with them, and when we came here, he came to us. I guess that's one reason why they don't like us, for Chan's a good boy."

"And Margaret?"

Mrs. Mackenzie's face changed. "Poor old thing," she said sadly, "no one knows where or how she lives. We are not afraid of her, but the Indians are. They wouldn't touch a crazy person under any circumstances."

"Is there a regular Indian settlement here?"

"Yes, there are wigwams all along the river. They are all Pottawattomies and very friendly. The Chippewa and Winnebago tribes are farther north. John has a gift for dealing with the Indians. He has learned their language and their ways, and they treat him as if he were one of them. Did George show you the Fort this morning?"

"Most of it," smiled Forsyth. "We called on the commissioned officers and that young giant ate a hearty breakfast at each place."

"He is the life of the settlement, and I don't know what we'd do without him. I never saw anybody with such an inexhaustible fund of good spirits. Nothing is so bad that George can't get a joke out of it and make us laugh in spite of our trouble. Did you see Doctor Norton?"

"Yes, but only for a moment."

"He's jolly too, and very good to all of us."

"I forgot to tell you when I first came in," said Robert, "but I met Mrs. Howard and she asked me to tell you that she was coming over to see you this afternoon."

"Bless her heart," said Mrs. Mackenzie, tenderly, "she never forgets her old mother."

"You'll never be old, Aunt Eleanor. I believe you have found the fountain of eternal youth."

"What, another flatterer?" she asked, but the heightened colour in her cheeks showed that she was pleased.

During the afternoon, while Johnny struggled manfully with digits and addition, Robert saw Mrs. Howard coming across the river. She was a fair, tall woman, very blonde, with eyes like her mother's. The Doctor stood at the entrance of the stockade, watching her, with something akin to wistfulness in his attitude.

"Poor soul," thought Robert, "I expect he's lonesome."

The afternoon sun stole into the room, marking out patches of light upon the rag carpet which covered the floor, and touched the rude logs kindly as if to gild, rather than to reveal. In the next room women's voices sounded, indistinct, but pleasant, with here and there a low, musical laugh, and the teacher fell to dreaming.

"How many are two and two, Cousin Rob?" Johnny asked, for the third time.

"Four—don't you remember? You learned that this morning."

"Can I go now? I want to see my sister."

"Yes, run along."

The patter of feet died away in the distance, but Robert still looked out upon the river with a smile upon his face. Presently he saw Mrs. Howard going toward the Fort, with two of the children capering along beside her. Something stirred in the dreamer's pulses, indefinite, but none the less real. What man can place it, or knows it when it comes—that first vague longing for a home of his own?

The minutes went by and the light faded until the blood-red sunset fired the Fort and stained the snowy reaches beyond. A door opened, a kettle sang, and some one came in.

"Asleep, dear?"

"No, Aunt Eleanor." He went to her, put his arm around her, and touched her cheek lightly with his lips. "I was only thinking that my lines have fallen in pleasant places."

# CHAPTER III
# THE SECOND IN COMMAND

"Kit," said the Lieutenant, pacing back and forth moodily, "I wish I were in command."

"I wish so, too, dear," responded Mrs. Howard, dutifully.

"Anybody with half an eye can see what is going to happen here, if there isn't a change."

"What change do you mean, Ralph?"

"Any kind of a change," he snapped angrily. "We've got a figure-head for a Captain and the men haven't the faintest idea of military training. There's no reason for postponing drill on account of bad weather—the men haven't been out for over a week now, just because it's cold. The Captain sits by his fire, studying tactics and making out imaginary reports, while his men are suffering for discipline—and clothes," he added as an afterthought.

"What can Captain Franklin do about their clothes?"

"What can he do? Nothing, it seems; but I could. I'd send a man to President Madison himself, if there was no other way. Look at us! We look like Washington's army at Valley Forge!"

The Lieutenant brushed away an imaginary speck on a very shabby uniform. "I'm sorry I entered the army," he went on. "Look at this post, on the edge of nowhere, with about forty men to defend it. I doubt if we have more than thirty in good fighting trim—the rest are worse than useless. All around us are hordes of hostile savages, ready to attack any or all of us on the slightest provocation, and we cannot make even a display of force! No target practice, for fear of wasting ammunition; no drill, because the Captain is lazy; clothes like beggars—idleness, inaction, sloth! Three six-pounders and thirty men, against thousands of bloodthirsty beasts! Things were different at Fort Wayne!"

"Ralph," said Mrs. Howard, quickly, "please don't say that to me again. I have told you twenty times how sorry I am that I asked you to arrange to be transferred. I tell you once more that we will go wherever and whenever you please, to Fort Wayne, Detroit, or even Fort Mackinac. If there is an army post in the United States where things are run to suit you, please get a transfer to it. You will hear no complaints from me. I wanted to be near my mother—that was all."

"Was that all?" he sneered. "I have thought otherwise. You talk like a fool, Kit. You seem to think it's the simplest thing in the world to get a transfer. Do you expect to see a messenger ride in at the gate, with an order from the War Department, or shall I go over and tell the Captain that we leave for Fort Wayne this evening?"

Mrs. Howard moved her lips as if to speak, then thought better of it and remained silent. He stood at the window for a long time, with his back to her.

"You don't seem very sociable," he said at length, "so I guess I'll go out for a bit, especially as I see your friend coming. I never like to intrude." With this parting fling, he left the house, carefully avoiding Doctor Norton, who was crossing the parade-ground.

From where she sat, Mrs. Howard could see her husband, erect and soldierly, making his way to the offices. During the first two years of their married life, she had been very happy, but since they came to live at Fort Dearborn, he had been subject to occasional outbursts of temper which distressed her greatly.

Her face, always expressive, was white and troubled when she opened the door for the Doctor. He understood—he always did. He was one of the few men who are not dense in their comprehension of womankind.

They talked commonplaces for a little while, then he leaned forward and took her cold hand in his.

"Something has bothered you," he said kindly. "Tell me and let me help you."

"You couldn't help me," she answered sadly; "nobody can."

Doctor Norton was not more than thirty-five, but his hair was prematurely grey, and this, together with his kindly manner, often impelled his patients to make unprofessional confidences. Like many another woman, too, Mrs. Howard was strong in the face of opposition, but weak at the touch of sympathy.

"It's nothing," she said. "Ralph is cross nearly all the time, though I don't believe he means to be. He has been that way ever since—ever since the baby died."

She turned her face away, for the little grave in the hollow pulled piteously at the mother's heartstrings when the world went wrong.

"He has always blamed me for that," she went on. "One of the reasons why I wanted to live here, instead of at Fort Wayne, was that I might have my mother to help me take care of the baby. She knew more than I did; was wiser and more experienced in every way, and I thought the little lad would have a better chance. Instead, as you know, he took cold on the way here and did not get well, so his father has never forgiven me."

The tears came fast and her white lips quivered. "Don't, Katherine," he said. It was the first time he had called her by name, and she noted it, vaguely, in the midst of her suffering.

"Don't, Katherine," he repeated. "All we can do in this world is the thing that seems to us the best. We have no concern with the results, except as a guide for the future, and sometimes, years afterward, we see that what seemed like a bitter loss in reality was gain. Some day you may be glad that you lost your boy."

"Glad? Glad I have lost my only child? Doctor, what are you thinking of!"

"Of you. Whatever troubles you troubles me, also. You know that, don't you?"

For an instant she was frightened, but his calm friendliness reassured her. "Thank you," she returned, "you have always been good to me."

"I shall always try to be. Nothing that comes to you is without meaning for me, and you will always have at least one friend." There was an eloquent silence, then the tension of the moment snapped, and he released her hand.

"I'm silly," she laughed hysterically, wiping her eyes. "Have you any medicine for silliness?"

"If I had, I should keep it for those who need it worse than you do. I wish you would go outdoors more. Walk on the parade-ground and across to your mother's,—those two places are certainly safe,—and when you get tired of that, go over to Mrs. Franklin's. She's a nice little woman and she needs cheering up, too. I have a suspicion, Mrs. Howard, that the temperament which urges a man to be a soldier is very seldom elastic enough to include the domestic hearth."

Katherine's face brightened, for she had not thought of that, and the suggestion that others had the same trouble was not without its dubious consolation.

For an hour or more he talked to her, telling her bits of news from the barracks which he thought would interest her, and offering fragments of philosophy as the occasion permitted.

"You're a tonic," she said lightly, as he rose to go; "the blues are all gone."

"I'm glad of that. Now remember, when anything goes wrong, tell me. Perhaps I can help you—at least I can try."

Half-way across the parade-ground he turned back to smile at her as she stood at the window, and she waved a friendly hand in response. It was at this unlucky moment that the Lieutenant left the offices, having had high words with the Captain about the condition of the garrison and the possibility of a war with England.

She was vaguely uneasy when he went out of his way to meet the Doctor, but, though he spoke to him, he paused for scarcely an instant in his rapid stride. He was pleasant enough when he came into the house, and she thought that all was well.

He made no reference to their earlier conversation, but talked easily and indifferently, with a mild desire to please, as is the way of a man who is ashamed of himself.

"Wouldn't you like to go across the river?" he asked.

"Why, yes," she replied wonderingly, "I don't mind."

"Come on, then."

His dark, handsome face was still pale, and the lines of weakness were distinct around his mouth, but Katherine's heart, leaping to meet its desire, turned newly toward him, as a flower lifts its face to the sun.

"Poor boy," she said affectionately, putting her hand on his arm, "you have lots of things to bother you, don't you?"

"That I do, Kit. I suppose you think I'm a brute sometimes."

"No, indeed," she answered, generously.

"You've been hard to get on with lately," he observed.

"Have I, dear?" She was surprised and conscience-stricken; the more so because the possibility had not occurred to her. "I'm sorry," she said after a little. "I'll try to do better."

"I don't think it's altogether your fault," he rejoined. "I've noticed that you get cranky after Norton has been to the house, and I think he has a bad influence over you." The Lieutenant tried to speak jauntily, and failed.

"So, naturally," he continued, clearing his throat, "I've done as any other man in my position would do. I've told him not to come unless he's asked in his professional capacity, and to make those visits when I'm at home."

"Ralph!" It was the cry of a hurt child, and every vestige of colour fled from Katherine's face. She pressed her hands to her breast and leaned against the stockade at the entrance to the Fort.

"Well?" he asked ironically, "have I broken your heart?"

"To think," she said slowly, "that you could be so discourteous to any one, and especially to a friend who has been so kind to us as Doctor Norton. I'm ashamed of you."

"Your actions, Katherine, only prove that I have taken the right course. If I had any doubt before, I am certain now. You will oblige me by avoiding him as much as possible."

He never called her "Katherine" unless he was very much displeased with her, and they crossed the river without speaking. Howard hummed a popular air to himself, with apparent unconcern.

At Mackenzies', all was bustle and confusion. Indians hurried in and out of the house, talking and gesticulating excitedly. The snow on the path was worn as smooth as ice and Chandonnais was running to the Agency building on the other side of the river.

"What is it?" asked Katherine.

"Dunno," said the Lieutenant, laconically.

When they entered, John Mackenzie was, as he expressed it, "pretty nigh beat out." Robert had dismissed school, and was helping him as best he could, though he was heavily handicapped at the start by his ignorance of values and of the Indian tongue.

The space behind the counters was heaped high with furs. Deer hide and moose leather, grey wolf, red and silver fox, muskrat, beaver and bear skins were stacked waist deep around Forsyth and Mackenzie. Unwonted activity was in the air, and the place was full of odorous Indians.

Black Partridge came in, bringing the skin of a gigantic black bear, and a murmur ran through the room. Members of other tribes fingered it enviously, and the Pottawattomie squaws openly boasted the prowess of their chief.

Chandonnais came in from the Agency, with a huge ham under either arm. He went back, laden with peltries, and when he returned, he was rolling a fresh barrel of flour before him. His face was set in an expression of extreme displeasure, for he was constitutionally opposed to work.

"Can I help?" asked Lieutenant Howard.

"Wish you'd go over to the Agency, Ralph," replied Mackenzie, "and bring over as many blankets as you can carry. Chan will go with you—he's got to bring more bacon."

Mrs. Howard had long since retreated to the living-room. The door was closed, but the tumult of the trading station resounded afar.

"Be careful, Rob," said Mackenzie, "that's a sheep skin dyed with walnut juice. He tried it on you 'cause you're green." Turning to the Indian, the trader spoke volubly, even after the would-be cheat had grabbed his sheep skin and started for the door.

"This jawbreaker talk is tellin' on me," Mackenzie resumed. "This is the first time they've ever come on me all at once this way. Mighty sudden, I take it. It's early, too. Usually they do their tradin' on the Q.T., one and two at a time, weeks before. They say this is the last day of Winter and that to-morrow will be Spring."

Chandonnais and the Lieutenant returned, laden with bacon and blankets. The half-breed wiped the sweat from his swarthy face with a very dirty sleeve, and

Howard made no further offers of assistance. Instead, he went over to Forsyth, and began to talk with him.

"What's going on?" asked Robert, "do you know?"

Ralph shrugged his shoulders. "They haven't taken me into their confidence," he replied, "but I suppose it's the annual pilgrimage."

"Where? What for?"

"Didn't Father John tell you? Every year they go up into Canada to get their presents from the British. Damn the British!" he added, with unnecessary emphasis.

"Oh," said Robert, thoughtfully. "In case of trouble, then, the Indians are on their side."

"Exactly. Quite a scheme, isn't it?"

"It's a devilish scheme!"

"Be careful," warned Mackenzie, "some of 'em understand more English than they let on."

The trading fever rapidly spread to the squaws. Those who were not bringing furs for exchange and carrying provisions back to the camp offered moccasins and baskets for sale. Mackenzie shook his head—he had no use for anything but the skins.

Under cover of the excitement, much petty thieving was going on, and it was necessary to keep close watch of the peltries, lest they be exchanged again. The squaws kept keen eyes on the counters, making off with anything desirable which was left unguarded. Chandonnais took a place at the door, finally, to call a halt upon illegal enterprises.

Without the least knowledge of why he did it, Robert bought a pair of moccasins. They were small, even for a woman's foot, and heavy with beads. The dainty things appealed to him, suddenly and irresistibly, and the price he paid for them brought other squaws, with countless moccasins.

"Uncle John," he shouted above the clamour, "please tell them I don't want any more moccasins!"

A few rapid words from Shaw-ne-aw-kee had the desired effect. "Don't see what you want of those things," he observed; "they won't fit anybody."

"Pretty things," remarked Howard, sauntering up. "Whom are they for?"

"I—I—that is, I don't know," stammered Robert. "I just wanted them."

The Lieutenant laughed. "Oh, I see," he said. "Another case of Cinderella's slipper?"

"Yes, we'll let it go at that," returned Forsyth. He had regained his self-possession, but the colour still bronzed his cheeks.

When every possible exchange had been made, and every Indian had been given a small additional present, the room became quiet again. Black Partridge received a small silver ornament which Mackenzie had made for him during the long winter evenings, with manifestations of delight and gratitude.

"What's he saying, Uncle?" asked Robert.

"He's swearing eternal friendship for me and mine."

"Much good that does," said Howard, nonchalantly. "I'd trust a dead Indian a damn sight sooner 'n a live one."

Black Partridge may have caught the gist of what had been said, but he repeated his expressions of gratitude and his assurances of continued esteem. The room, by contrast, was very silent after he went out.

"Lord!" sighed the trader. "What a day!"

Mrs. Mackenzie's voice sounded clearly in the next room. "Yes, dear," she said, "I'll tell him, and I'll explain it all. Don't you fret one mite about it." Then the door opened and Mrs. Howard came in.

She talked with Forsyth for a few minutes, then turned to her husband. "Shall we go home?" she asked, "or do you want to stay here for supper?"

"Better stay," suggested Mackenzie, hospitably.

"No, we'll go," said Ralph. "Good-bye, everybody."

Neither spoke until they entered their own house again, then Katherine put her hands on his shoulders and looked straight into his eyes. "Ralph," she said, seriously, "can't you trust me?"

"I hope so," he returned, drawing away from her, "and as I've fixed it now, I think I can."

"Ralph!" she cried, "you hurt me!"

"Look here," he exclaimed roughly, "I don't want any more of this. I have trouble enough without your pitching into me all the time. This is my house and you are my wife—please remember that."

"There's no danger of my forgetting it," she answered hotly.

"Come, Kit, do be reasonable. I don't want to quarrel."

She smiled cynically and bit her lips to keep back the retort that struggled for utterance. "Whatever you do," her mother had said to her, "don't quarrel with your husband. It takes two to make a quarrel."

Later, a semblance of peace was restored, but long after the Lieutenant was asleep, Katherine lay, wide-eyed and troubled, with bitterness surging in her heart.

From the window of her room she saw the late moon when it rose from the lake, and soon afterward the clock struck three. Then a ghostly pageant passed the Fort. Black Partridge was ahead—she knew his stately figure in spite of the blanket in which he was enshrouded. Behind him came more Indians than she had ever seen at one time, silently, in single file.

The squaws brought up the rear, laden with baggage. The last one was heavily burdened and was far behind. As she straggled along, the pale moonlight revealed something strange upon her head and Katherine recognised her own discarded summer hat of two seasons past. The implied comparison made her laugh in a way which was not good to hear—but no one heard.

Across the river another watcher was taking note of the departure of the Pottawattomies, for Robert had found it impossible to sleep. Physically, he was too tired to rest, and his mind was unusually active. The dainty moccasins hung on the wall of his room and something obtrusively feminine in their presence was, in a way, disturbing, but not altogether unpleasant.

The young man was somewhat given to analysis and introspection, and had endeavoured, unsuccessfully, to solve the freakish impulse which led him to buy moccasins too small for any woman he knew. Further questioning of self brought out the astounding fact that he would not give moccasins to any woman he had ever met, even though these might fit her.

The Indians passing the Fort were a welcome diversion, and he, too, laughed at the one who followed the procession with more than her share of baggage, but he missed the fine point in the matter of millinery. "She looks like the one I bought them of," he said to himself, "but I won't be sure."

The moon faded and grey dawn came up out of the inland sea. A ribbon of light lay across the Fort and the pulses of the river stirred beneath the ice. The blood came to his heart like the sap mounting in the maples, and he felt a sudden uplift of soul. A bluebird paused over the river for an instant, the crimson of its breast strangely luminous against the sky, then from a distant thicket came the first robin's cheery call, and he knew the Indians were right—that it was Spring.

# CHAPTER IV
# RONALD'S VIEWS OF MARRIAGE

Mrs. Howard was trying to sew, but seemed to lack the necessary energy. The Lieutenant paced the room in his favourite attitude—hands crossed behind his back—and gave her his views upon various topics, from the mistakes of the War Department at Washington to the criminal mismanagement of Captain Franklin. He became so interested in this last subject that he spoke as if addressing a large audience, happily unmindful of the fact that his single listener was preoccupied.

"Upon my word, Kit," he was saying, "there isn't a man in barracks who wouldn't make a better Captain than the one we've got."

"His wife is coming," remarked Katherine, impersonally.

"I don't care if she is. Somebody ought to tell him where he stands in the estimation of the officers and men."

His disapproval of his superior officer was reflected in his cool response to Mrs. Franklin's cheery greeting when she came in with her sewing. "I've got something for you," she said to Katherine; "guess what it is!"

"I couldn't guess—what is it?"

"A letter," she answered brightly, "from Doctor Norton! You aren't jealous, are you?" she asked playfully, turning to the Lieutenant.

He made no reply, but gnawed his mustache nervously. Katherine's face blanched as she took the note and tore it open with trembling hands.

There was neither date, address, nor signature. "I understand," it began, "and everything is all right. I beg of you, do not distress yourself about me, and, if I can ever serve you in any way, command me."

The words danced before her eyes as the Lieutenant approached and held out his hand, silently, for the letter.

"It's nothing that would interest you, dear," she said, tearing it straight across.

"Pardon me, I think it would." He quickly possessed himself of the note and fitted the two parts of the page together, laughing as he did so. Only Katherine noticed that his voice shook.

"If you're through with it, I'll burn it," he said quietly, after what seemed an age. Without waiting for an answer, he threw it into the open fire and hurriedly left the house. Then something dawned on Mrs. Franklin.

"Kit," she cried, "can you ever forgive me?"

"What did you think?" retorted Katherine, fiercely. "Would he have sent a note to me if he had meant it for my husband? Why didn't he come over instead of writing?"

"I don't know," murmured Mrs. Franklin. For the moment she was afraid, and as the inevitable surmise forced itself into her consciousness, she gazed at Katherine, horror-stricken and dumb.

"I know what you're thinking," said Mrs. Howard, with forced calmness. "It's very charitable of you, but I'm glad to be able to tell you that you're mistaken."

"You poor child!" exclaimed the Captain's wife. She slipped a friendly hand into Katherine's cold one and was not surprised when the overwrought nerves sought relief in tears.

Little by little, Katherine made a full explanation. "It's too small and too silly to talk about," she sighed, "but I haven't been well lately and the slightest thing will worry me almost past endurance. I don't know what's the matter with Ralph—he is not at all like himself, and that troubles me, too."

"Funny," observed Mrs. Franklin, irrelevantly.

"What's funny?"

"Men in general and husbands in particular. Wallace isn't inclined to be jealous, so I've never had that to bother me, but he's as stubborn as a mule, and I guess that's just as bad. Anyhow, I'd like to trade his stubbornness for something else. I'd appreciate the change for a little while, no matter what it was."

"I wouldn't mind that," said Katherine, with the ghost of a smile hovering around her white lips. "I think I could get along better with a stubborn man than I can with a savage."

"Be careful what you say about savages," put in the other, lightly; "you know my aunt is a full-blooded Indian."

"I've often wondered about that. How do you suppose it happened?"

"It is rather queer on the face of it, but it's natural enough, when you think it over. You know Captain Wells was stolen by the Indians when he was a child and he was brought up like one of them. Even after his people found him, he refused to go home, until his two sisters came to plead with him. Then he consented to make them a visit, but he didn't stay long, and went back to the Indians at the first opportunity. Their ways were as impossible to him as his were to them. I'm glad he married the chief's daughter, instead of a common squaw. He and Little Turtle are great friends."

There was a long silence, then Katherine reverted to the original topic. "I never thought of Captain Franklin as stubborn," she said.

"Didn't you? Well, I just wish you could talk to him a while after he gets his mind made up. Before that, there's hope, but not afterward; and you might just as well go out and speak to the stockade around the Fort. He's contrary, too. Yesterday, for instance, he told me he thought he'd have drill, as the men hadn't been out for a long time. I asked him if some of them weren't sick, and he said they were, but it wouldn't hurt the others any. Just then your husband came in and suggested drill. 'Haven't thought about it,' says Wallace, turning away, and the Lieutenant talked ten minutes before he discovered nobody was listening to him. After he went away, George came in and asked about drill. 'We won't have it to-day,' said Wallace, and that was the end of it."

"Was he like that before you were married?"

"Yes, only not so bad. I mistook his determined siege for inability to live without me, but I see now that it was principally stubbornness. He made up his mind to get me, and here I am. He gets worse as he grows older—more 'sot' in his ways, as your mother would say. I don't see how anybody can be that way. He explained it to me once, when we were first married, but I couldn't understand it."

"How did he explain it?"

"Well, as nearly as I can remember, he said that he dreaded to have his mind begin making itself up. It's like a runaway horse that you can't stop. He said he might see that he was wrong and he might want to do differently, but something inside of him wouldn't let him. It seems that his mind suddenly crystallises, and then it's over. A crystal can be broken, but it can't be made liquid again."

"Is his mind liquid?" inquired Katherine, choked with laughter.

"No—I wish it was. I'm glad you're amused, but I'm too close to it to see the fun in it. Wasn't your husband ever stubborn?"

"No; I don't think so—at least, I don't remember. I suppose he can't help being jealous any more than the Captain can help being mulish. I guess they're just born so."

"Marked," suggested Mrs. Franklin.

"Yes—marked. I hadn't thought of that. Before we were married, Ralph was jealous of everybody who spoke to me—man, woman, or brute. I couldn't even pet the cat or talk to the dog."

"Matrimonial traits," observed the Captain's wife, sagely, "are the result of pre-nuptial tendencies. If you look carefully into the subject before you're married, you can see about what you're coming to."

"I guess that's right. I needn't have expected marriage to cure Ralph of jealousy, but, like you, I supposed it was love."

"My dear," said Mrs. Franklin, with feeling, "many a woman mistakes the flaws in a man's character for the ravages of the tender passion—before marriage."

"Well, I never!" said a soft voice behind them. "Kitty and Mamie talking scandal!"

Both women jumped.

"How did you get in?" demanded Mrs. Howard.

"Came in," replied Ronald, laconically.

"Don't you know enough to rap?" asked Mrs. Franklin, angrily. Like others who have been christened "Mary," she was irritated beyond measure at that meaningless perversion of her name.

"Did rap," answered George, selecting the most comfortable chair, "but nobody heard me, so I let myself in."

"How dare you call me 'Kitty'?" exclaimed Mrs. Howard.

"Soldiers aren't afraid of anything except the War Department."

"How long have you been here?" they asked simultaneously.

"Don't all speak at once. I've been here a long, long time—so long, in fact, that I'm hungry." He looked past them as he spoke and gazed pensively out of the window.

Mrs. Franklin's cheeks were blazing and her eyes snapped. "You're the very worst man I ever met," she said.

The Ensign sighed heavily. "And yet I've never been accused of mulishness," he remarked, rolling his eyes toward the ceiling, "nor of jealousy," he added. His mouth was twitching, and the women exchanged glances.

"I admit an enormous appetite," he continued. "Wonder if it's the ravages of the tender passion?"

Mrs. Howard brought in a plate of cookies and set it ostentatiously within his reach. "Lovely woman!" apostrophised George. "She feeds me! Radiant vision, will you be mine?"

There was a dead silence.

"Queer, isn't it," observed the guest, between mouthfuls, and apparently to himself, "that women should look so pretty when they're mad?"

"Your wife will be pretty all the time, then," said Mrs. Franklin.

"I trust so. She'll have to have a good start at it, or she won't get me, and with the additional stimulus which living with me will give her, she'll be nearly as lovely as the wives of the other officers at Fort Dearborn. I could give her no higher praise. These cookies are all gone."

"I know it," replied Mrs. Howard. "I gave you all I had left."

"If I might presume," said Ronald, "I'd like the prescription they were made by, to give to my wife, when I get one. I suppose it's more in the making than in the prescription, and though I'll undoubtedly like 'em, my native love of truth will oblige me to tell her that they don't come up to those Kitty—pardon me, Mrs.

32

Howard—used to make for me. I always think of you by your first name," he went on. "I know it's wrong, but I can't help it. You're so good to me. Isn't there one more cooky?"

"No, there isn't."

"Your mother makes surpassing doughnuts. Did she ever teach you how?"

"Oh, yes," responded Mrs. Howard, coolly; "but I don't make them very often. I haven't made any for months."

"I have the plan of 'em all written down, in case you should forget how. I'm saving it for my wife. Can I go and look in the pantry?"

"No, you cannot."

"Why don't you get married, George?" asked Mrs. Franklin, by way of a diversion.

"I've never been asked."

"Didn't you ever ask anybody?"

"Oh, Lord, yes! I've asked every girl I've ever met. Say, do you know that I've got so now that I can propose off-hand, as easily as other fellows can after they've written it out and learned it? If there was a girl here at the Fort who suited me, I'd ask everybody to my wedding inside of two weeks."

"Charming diffidence," murmured Katherine.

"Modest soul," commented Mrs. Franklin. "What kind of a girl would suit you?"

"I like the domestic variety. The faithful kind, you know. One who wouldn't gad all the time. Good cook, and that sort of thing."

"Some Indian girl"—began the Captain's wife.

"I know," interrupted George, pointedly; "that runs in some families, but it never has in ours. Wouldn't mind an Indian aunt, maybe, after I got used to her; but a mother-in-law—Lord!"

Mrs. Franklin was angry for an instant, then she laughed. It was impossible for any one to harbour resentment against Ronald.

"I don't think I could ever love an ordinary girl," that intrepid youth resumed, with a dare-devil light in his eyes. "She'd have to be very superior. Lots of girls get married without any clear idea of what it means. For instance, while I was working day and night, trying to earn board and clothes for a woman, I wouldn't like to have her trot over to her friend's house to discuss my faults. If that's marriage, I won't enlist."

"You haven't any faults," put in the Captain's wife, sweetly. "There would be nothing to discuss."

"True, Mamie, I had forgotten that. Thank you for reminding me of my perfection. But you know what I mean. As soon as I got out of sight of the house, she'd gallop over to her friend's, and her friend would say: 'Good-morning, Mrs. Ronald, you don't look fit this morning. What has that mean thing done to you now?'"

Throwing himself thoroughly into the part, the Ensign got up and proceeded to give an elaborate monologue, in falsetto, punctuated with mincing steps and frequent rearrangement of an imaginary coiffure. Mrs. Howard clasped her hands at her waist and the tears rolled down Mrs. Franklin's cheeks.

"And then she'd say," Ronald went on, "'Just suppose you had to live with a mulish, jealous man who wouldn't give you more than nine dresses and eleven bonnets and four pairs of shoes. Yes, that's just what the horrid thing has done. And this morning, when I asked for money to get a few clothes, so I could look more respectable, he gave me some, but I caught him keeping back fifty-two cents. Now, what do you think of that? Do you suppose he's going to take a lot of men out and get 'em all drunk?'"

The entrance of Captain Franklin put an end to the inspired portrayal of wifely devotion. As Katherine had said, he did not look stubborn. On the contrary, he seemed to be the mildest sort of a man, for he was quiet and unobtrusive in manner. His skin was very white, and the contrast of his jet-black hair and mustache made him look pale.

"Did you tell them the news?" he asked Ronald.

"'Pon my word, Captain, I haven't had time. They've been chattering so ever since I came in that I'm nearly deaf with it. You tell 'em."

"I don't know as you'd call it news," said the Captain; "but we can't afford to ignore any incident out here. A Kickapoo runner has come in from the Illinois River, and he says the pack-trains are about to start from there and from the Kankakee, and that they will be here soon."

"It's an early Spring," remarked Mrs. Franklin.

"I'm glad," said Katherine; "I love to be outdoors, and the Winters in this lonesome little Fort are almost unbearable."

"What?" asked Ronald, "with me here?"

"Drill to-morrow," said the Captain, turning to his subordinate. The Ensign saluted gravely, but made no reply.

The Captain lingered a few moments, listening while the others talked. "Are you going home, Mary?" he asked.

"Yes, after a while. I'll go now if you want me to."

"No; never mind. I've got some things to see to."

"Now that," observed Ronald, as the Captain closed the door, "is what I call a true marriage."

"In what way?" asked Mrs. Franklin.

"This deference to a husband's evident wishes. It might have happened to me. Lonesome George comes into the sewing circle and his glad eyes rest on the wife of his bosom. Talk to the crowd a little while and get everybody to feeling good, even though I'm on the verge of starvation. Then I say: 'Darling, are you going back to our humble little home?' and she says: 'Yes, George, dear, when I get good and ready—bye-bye!'"

Mrs. Franklin was eager to ask Katherine how much of their conversation she supposed he had overheard, but he seemed very comfortable where he was, and at last she folded up her work and went home, the Ensign bidding her an affectionate farewell at the door and extending a generous invitation to "come again."

"There, Kitty," he sighed, "at last we are alone. It has seemed so long!"

Katherine turned upon him a look which would have frozen a lesser man than Ronald. "Please call me Mrs. Howard," she requested, icily.

"I can't."

"Why not?"

"Well, some way, it makes me feel as if you were married, and I can't stand it to be constantly reminded of my loss. 'Mrs. Lieutenant' is better, 'cause I'm a lieutenant, in a way, myself, but it's too long. I suppose I can say 'Mrs. Loot,' if you insist upon formality. I came to you with a message, and that is why I have braved your unjust wrath. Your mother sent me to ask you and your husband to come over to supper. I've seen him and he's willing. She's been making doughnuts all the afternoon, and I think there's a pie or two, so get your bonnet and come along."

"Come along!" repeated Katherine.

"Yes, come along. I'm going, too."

"Does she know it?"

"I think she suspects it. If she doesn't, the pleasure will have the additional charm of a surprise. There's the Lieutenant now. We'll all go together."

They met on the parade-ground and she put her hand on her husband's arm timidly, but he did not draw away from her as she had feared he would, and she became intuitively conscious that he had determined to say nothing about the unlucky note.

The sun shone brightly and the March wind swept the cobwebs from her mental vision. Ralph said very little; but Ronald, who never required the encouragement of an answer, talked unceasingly, and it seemed to Katherine that the world was sunny and full of friends.

# CHAPTER V
# THE FIRST FLOWER OF SPRING

There was a report like a pistol shot from the ice in the river, followed by others at short intervals. "That means for us to get out the boats," said Mackenzie to Chandonnais.

Only one of the boats stored in the trader's barn was worthy of the name. It was a large bateau, capable of accommodating a dozen people and a small amount of baggage. The others were pirogues, or logs trimmed at the ends and hollowed out in the centre. One person might be negatively comfortable, but two crowded the small craft to the danger-point.

A pirogue furnished the ordinary means of communication with the Fort, and two or three were fastened to a sapling on the other side of the stream. There was also a good boat, belonging to the Fort, which would hold five or six people. The bateau was used for carrying freight between the Fort, the Agency House, and Mackenzie's.

The river was a narrow, deep, weedy channel, with a very slight fall, and a large sand-bar stretched across the mouth of it. In Summer, one could stand at the end of the broad piazza in front of the house and see the Indians in their light canoes pass the sand-bar at will, go down into the lake, and return up-stream.

Gradually the river filled with great masses of ice, which moved lazily in a circle at the whim of some concealed current, or drifted gently toward the mouth of the stream. For several days there was no communication with the Fort; then Mackenzie broke the ice-jam at the bar, and by the middle of March a boat could easily cross.

Seemingly by preconcerted arrangement, the pack-trains arrived during the last week of March. Twenty horses came from the Illinois and Kankakee districts, and seventeen from the Rock River, loaded with skins. For a year the Indians in the Mississippi valley had exchanged peltries for provisions, beads, and liquor. Five Canadian *engagés*, with rude camping outfits strapped to their backs, walked in leisurely fashion beside the horses.

The skins were stored in the Agency House, awaiting the schooner from the American Fur Company at Fort Mackinac. The horses were tethered on the plains near the Fort, and business was carried on there, except at meal-time, when eight hungry men and four children taxed Mrs. Mackenzie's strength to the utmost.

Three days later the schooner was sighted, bearing down from the north, and, as it was practically the only event of the year, the settlement went in force to the lake shore to see it come in. A corporal's guard, bitterly complaining, was left at the Fort.

With the wind filling her sails, the ship steered south-west until she reached a point exactly opposite the mouth of the river, then turned swiftly, like a bird, and came toward the cheering crowd on shore. The waves broke in foam upon her keel, and amid the shouts of command and welcome and the clatter of the rigging, came the song of a *voyageur*, in a clear, high tenor, which won a separate recognition.

"More men to feed," sighed Mrs. Mackenzie.

"Never mind, Aunt Eleanor," said Forsyth, "I'm going to help you."

"Me, too! Me, too!" cried the children.

Mrs. Howard and Mrs. Franklin promptly offered their services, and Ronald put an affectionate arm about her waist. "Don't bother, Aunt Eleanor," he said; "you've got me."

Forsyth was surprised at the speech, and still more astonished when the Ensign made it good during the hard days that followed. He tied a big blue apron under his arms, unmindful of its ridiculous flapping about his knees, set his cap on the back of his head, rolled up his sleeves, and announced that he was ready for work. Forsyth helped him split wood, bring water, make fires, and wash dishes until his head swam with weariness; but through it all, Ronald was serene and untroubled, keeping up a cheery whistle and a fusillade of comment and observation which lightened the situation exceedingly.

Mrs. Mackenzie found herself taking orders from the young soldier who was the self-constituted master of the cuisine, and learned to obey without question, even when she was sent to her easy-chair early in the morning and kept there during the greater part of the day.

Mrs. Howard and Mrs. Franklin were unceremoniously put out. "Kitty and Mamie," pleaded the Ensign, in an aggravating falsetto, "will you please run home? Your mother has enough to feed without your trotting in to meals." He accompanied the request with a threatening wave of a spoon filled with pancake batter, which had the desired effect.

"There," he said, "I've finally chased 'em out. I do hate to have women bothering around me, don't you, Rob?"

"I've never been bothered," laughed Forsyth; "at least, not in that way."

Swiftly upon the heels of the schooner came the boats from Milwaukee. The cargoes were landed on the lake shore and taken to the Agency by the pack-horses. All day the patient beasts plodded to and fro, carrying furs to the shore, and provisions, blankets, calicoes, prints, and a thousand other things to the storehouse. The small boats from the ship plied back and forth, landing the cargo and taking back peltries, and the men worked from sunrise to sunset.

An unusual amount of friction developed between the several *engagés* and *voyageurs*, and various disputes were settled on the spot with bare fists. Chandonnais had a rare talent for getting into trouble, and few indeed were the fights in which he did not eventually take a leading part.

"Chan," said Mackenzie, at length, "you ain't paid to fight, but to work; and if there's any more of this I'll send you to one of the other posts." This threat was always effectual, for some reason which the trader did not seek to know.

At last the tired horses finished their task and every skin was in the hold of the schooner. The Agency House was filled to bursting with the materials of trade, and a small but precious horde of gold pieces, representing the balance in his favour, was hidden in Mackenzie's leather belt.

There was a day of rest for everybody except Mrs. Mackenzie and her assistants; then Chandonnais surprised the trader by a demand for his year's wages.

"Why, Chan!" exclaimed Mackenzie, "don't you want me to keep it for you as I've been a-doing?"

The half-breed shook his head sullenly.

"Well, it's yours, and you can do just as you please with it, but I guess you'll be sorry for it later. Mind, now, this is all till next year—you don't get any advance."

Chan agreed, and Mackenzie called Robert to witness the transaction. Five shining ten-dollar gold pieces were counted out into a grimy paw that closed upon them quickly, as if in fear.

"Fifty dollars and found," Mackenzie explained to Robert as Chandonnais went away. "I don't grudge it neither, for he's a good boy when he ain't fighting."

The schooner was lying by for a favouring wind, and the pack-trains were waiting to give the horses a needed rest. Mackenzie had made an equitable division of the stores at the Agency, and each of the *engagés* knew exactly what he was to take back with him, and the approximate value of each article in terms of peltries. During the day liquor flowed freely, and at night there was a barbecue on the lake shore.

A young ox was roasted whole, in front of a huge fire which could be seen for miles around. Forsyth and the Mackenzies, with their four children, and the officers and men from the Fort with their wives and families, sat around on the sand and took part in the celebration. A single sentinel patrolled the Fort, cursing his luck, and a few stray Indians watched the festive scene from afar.

Chandonnais had his violin, and the fine tenor of the *voyageur* was lifted in song—old French *chansons* and garbled melodies of the day. The strings of the fiddle were twanged in delicate accompaniment until the singer struck up Yankee Doodle, which, owing to the French accent and the peculiar distortion of the tune, was taken by the company as a humorous performance.

The men ate hungrily, and at last even Ronald was satisfied. Then a sudden thought struck him, and he went over to speak to Captain Franklin. "Good-bye, everybody," he shouted.

"Where are you going?" asked Forsyth.

"I'm going back to relieve that poor devil at the Fort."

In spite of a chorus of protests, he went, and the lone sentry appeared presently, grinning from ear to ear, to feast and revel while his superior officer kept guard with a bayonet over his shoulder. It was such trifles as this which endeared Ronald to the soldiers. There was not a man in barracks who would not have followed him cheerfully to certain death.

The fire died down and some of the men slept peacefully on the sand, while others yawned openly. Chandonnais improvised a weird melody which was strangely out of keeping. There was something uncanny in the air which accorded ill with the festival, and it seemed only fitting and proper when Mad Margaret materialised from the outer darkness and came into the centre of the group.

A hush came over the company and some of the newcomers, who had heard wild tales of Margaret, were secretly afraid. Chandonnais kept on playing, and she watched him with wide, wondering eyes. For a long time the magic of the strings kept her quiet, then she began to mutter to herself uneasily.

"Margaret," said Mackenzie, gently, "come here."

Chandonnais threw down his violin with a gesture of impatience, beckoned to the singer, and walked away rapidly. The *voyageur* rose lazily, yawned, and followed him with seeming indifference.

Margaret's eyes were shining like the live coals which gleamed in the ashes. She leaned forward and picked up the violin, stroking it and crooning to it as if it were a child.

"Margaret," said Mackenzie again, "come here."

She went to him with a dog-like, unquestioning obedience, and sat down in front of him. Mrs. Mackenzie was next to her husband, with the baby in her lap, and Mrs. Howard sat on her mother's left. The Lieutenant was talking with Forsyth and the Captain, and at a little distance, on Mackenzie's right, sat Doctor Norton.

A sharp cry came from the violin, where Margaret's fingers tightened on the strings. "I see blood," she said,—"much blood, then fire, and afterward peace."

No one spoke, and Margaret mumbled to herself, then pounced upon Katherine. She took her by the shoulders and shook her roughly. "You will have your heart's desire," she cried, "at the time of the blood, but sorrow will come with it!"

Before any one else had time to move, Doctor Norton caught Margaret and pulled her away.

"Oh," she shrieked, shaking her fist in his face, "the Red Death has its fingers at your throat!"

Mackenzie picked up the violin, found the bow in the darkness, and began to play—rudely enough, it is true, but in some semblance of rhythm. Margaret quieted almost immediately, and sat down in front of him, rocking back and forth in time with the faltering tune.

"Aunt Eleanor," said Forsyth, over her shoulder, "don't you think I'd better take the children home?"

"Yes, please, if you will."

She put the sleeping baby into his arms, woke Maria Indiana, and directed Ellen and Johnny to go with "Cousin Rob." The procession moved slowly, for the baby was heavy, and the other children were inclined to linger. Mad Margaret had a terrible fascination for them.

As they passed a grove of cottonwoods, angry voices came from the thicket, in a mongrel French which had but little in common with that Robert had learned at Yale.

"It is abominable," cried Chandonnais. "It is too much!"

"So?" laughed the other, mockingly; "and only last year you told me you would pay the price!"

"A year's wages for a common crucifix!"

"It is no common crucifix. It is of solid silver, and it is from the old mission, where it was blessed by Père Marquette himself."

"How do you know?"

"The good Father told me so. It has been blessed by Père Marquette and by all the holy men who have come after him. It will cure disease and keep from all harm."

"Well," sighed Chandonnais, "I'll take it."

Robert heard the clink of the half-breed's hard-earned gold, and wondered whether he had spent the whole of it for a cross.

The next day the prevailing wind of Summer blew warm and strong from the south-west, and the sails of the schooner filled as if in anticipation. Robert thought of the hardy Romans in the Æneid, when "the breezes called their sails," as once again the people gathered on the shore.

Letters and messages to friends at Fort Mackinac, together with many trifling gifts, were pressed upon the crew. A long line of foam lay upon the turquoise water when out in the sunlit distance the ship turned to the north, and hands were waved in farewell long after the others had ceased to see. The Mackenzies were glad it was over, even though a long year was to pass without communication with the outside world, but others were sorry. Chandonnais was non-committal and hummed to himself the song of the *voyageur*.

The pack-trains were loaded, the patient horses bending under a heavier burden than they had brought; the boats started to Milwaukee after all of the *engagés* had been given another round of liquor, and a pack-train followed them north on land. The others, silhouetted against the setting sun, went west over the unbroken prairie; the drowsy tinkle of the bells died away in a silvery murmur, and peace lay on Fort Dearborn.

At the end of the week there was a diversion which was entirely unexpected— as most real diversions contrive to be. Mrs. Mackenzie was in the garden, planting flower seeds, when soft footsteps sounded on the bare earth beside her, and a sweet voice said, "How do you do, Aunt Eleanor?"

"Why, Beatrice!" exclaimed Mrs. Mackenzie, kissing her warmly. "Where did you come from?"

"From Fort Wayne, with Captain Wells—he's across the river. I rowed over by myself. I was so afraid you'd see me coming and wouldn't be surprised."

"My dear! I'm so glad!"

"Maybe you won't be, when I tell you. I've come to live with you, Aunt Eleanor."

"That makes me happier still," said Mrs. Mackenzie, in her stately way. "You are welcome."

"Thank you, Aunty; but I haven't come to be a burden to you, and I trust I never shall be. If I'm ever a trouble, I want you to tell me so and send me away. In the first place, I have fought most terribly with my aunt and uncle at Fort Wayne. They don't know I've come."

"Why, my dear! How could you?"

"Oh, they know it now," said Beatrice, laconically, with her head on one side. "If they don't, the suspense will do them good. Anyhow, they know I'm not there, and that's enough. You know I have a little income of my own, Aunty, so I'm not dependent upon any one, and I'm going to pay my board. If you won't let me," she continued, warningly, seeing disapproval on Mrs. Mackenzie's kindly face, "I'm going back with Captain Wells to-morrow, so now!"

41

"I'll let you do anything you want to, dear, if you'll only stay with me. I have needed a grown daughter ever since Katherine was married."

"Then it's all arranged, and I'll stay with you for ever. I know I never could fight with you."

"Here comes your uncle."

The trader beamed with delight when Beatrice cast herself upon him and kissed him twice. "I've come to live with you," she said, "and I've just fixed it with Aunt Eleanor. Captain Wells is over at the Fort with the soldiers. We brought ten with us—it was quite an army, and the Captain kept up military discipline all along the trail, with me for First Lieutenant. They're going to stay at the Fort, and I'm going to stay here." She pirouetted around him in high spirits.

"You're welcome, Bee; but how did it happen?"

"I fought," explained Beatrice, carelessly. "They told me what I should do and what I shouldn't. Nobody ever says 'must' to me. If you ever want me to do anything, you'll have to say 'please.' Would you mind going over to the Fort after my things, Uncle? I've got a big box with all my worldly goods inside of it."

Mackenzie went, for men always did as Beatrice suggested.

"Come in, dear," said her aunt. "You can have the east room, so you'll get the morning sun."

"How sweet you are, Aunt Eleanor," murmured the girl, with her arm thrown around the other's shoulders, for she was even taller than Mrs. Mackenzie. Her face had the deep, creamy tint which sometimes goes with violet eyes and brown hair with auburn lights in it. Beneath a short nose, tilted ever so slightly, was the most bewitching mouth in the world—small and perfect in shape, dangerously curved, and full of a daring coquetry. When she smiled, one saw that her teeth were small and white and absolutely even, but soon forgot that minor detail. At first glance, no one would have called her pretty; she was like something beautiful which must be studied before it is appreciated.

The arrival of the visitor had effectually broken up the school. "Tuzzin Bee! Tuzzin Bee!" crowed Maria Indiana, delightedly.

"You darling," cried Beatrice, catching the child in her arms; "have you remembered me a whole year?"

Robert was introduced as "a cousin on the other side of the house," and he bent gravely over the girl's hand.

"Are we truly cousins?" she asked.

There was a confused silence, then Robert found his tongue. "I trust we are," he said, with the air of a gentleman of the old school, "for you are the first flower of Spring."

The door burst open and Ronald entered. "What do you think," he shouted; "we've got troops! Captain Wells has brought ten soldiers to the Fort!"

"Miss Manning," said Mrs. Mackenzie, "let me present Ensign George Ronald, of Fort Dearborn."

Beatrice bowed, but he stared at her for an instant, then brought his heels together and raised his hand to his forehead in military salute. There was an awkward instant, then the deep crimson dyed the Ensign's face. He turned—and bolted.

From the window Beatrice saw him, in a pirogue, pulling back to the Fort as if his life depended upon it, then she laughed—a deep, sweet, vibrant laugh, that thrilled Robert to the very depths of his soul.

# CHAPTER VI
## COUSINS

"Aunty," said Beatrice, at breakfast the next morning, "do you think I scared him to death?"

"What do you mean, dear?"

"Why, that young man—yesterday. Mr. Ronald is his name, isn't it?"

Mrs. Mackenzie laughed at the memory of the Ensign's scarlet face. "I think he'll get over it," she said; "don't you, Rob?"

"I certainly do. He's the last man in the world to be afraid of a woman."

"Oh, yes, he'll recover," put in Mackenzie, significantly.

"I think it's lovely here," observed Beatrice, irrelevantly, "and I know I'm going to like it."

"We're going to try very hard to make you happy," said Forsyth, with evident sincerity.

"I've wanted to live with Aunt Eleanor ever since last Spring, when they all came to Fort Wayne. Otherwise, I wouldn't have fought. That is, perhaps I wouldn't."

Rising from the table, she went out on the piazza, and Robert instinctively followed her. If the long journey on horseback had tired her, she showed no sign of it, for she might have been a part of the morning as she stood there, smiling, with the sunlight on her wind-blown hair.

The heavy brown coil, with auburn lights and black shadows in it, had a strange fascination for Forsyth. He liked the way her hair grew around her forehead and temples, and the little curl that escaped at her neck. She was looking away from him, and he thought her unaware of his scrutiny till she said quietly: "Well, how do you like your new cousin? Do you think I will do?"

"Yes," he stammered, dimly grateful for the impulse that kept her face still turned away; "that is, very much."

"How am I going to get my horse over here," she demanded suddenly.

"What horse?" asked Robert, stupidly.

"The one I rode from Fort Wayne, of course. Did I understand you to say you had been to college?"

"Yes; I graduated."

"Really?" Beatrice turned upon him a dazzling smile. "I never should have thought it," she added pleasantly.

"Where is your horse?" he asked, crimsoning.

"You don't see it anywhere, do you?"

"N—no."

"Then, obviously, it's at the Fort, isn't it?"

"I—I suppose so."

"Well, then, we're making progress. Now, how do I get it over here?"

"Swim," said Robert, helplessly, at his wit's end.

Beatrice stamped her small foot upon the piazza. "Uncle John," she called, "come here! How is Queen coming across the river?" she asked, when he appeared.

"Well, now, Bee, I don't know. There's no bridge and no way to go around. She'll either have to come in a boat or swim."

Robert flashed a grateful glance at him, but said nothing.

"She won't get into a boat," said Beatrice, with a puzzled little frown on her face. "We swam a river together once, but she didn't like it, and we both got wet."

"Go down near the bar and come across," suggested Forsyth, having partially recovered his self-possession. "It can't be very deep there."

"No; but the sand is soft. Better leave her at the Fort, Bee, and you can go over there when you want her. It's safer," he added. "The Indians might get her out of my barn, but she'll be all right in the garrison stables."

"That settles it," replied Beatrice. "Here comes Captain Wells."

An erect, soldierly figure came up the path with the characteristic walk of the Indian. His eyes were small and dark, and his face was bronzed like the people among whom he had lived; but when he smiled at Beatrice and bowed with mock humility, all traces of the savage were instantly effaced. He wore the rough garb of the plainsman, and the only suggestion of vanity was in the black ribbon that tied his queue.

"Mackenzie," he said, "I warn you. You have a tyrannical commander-in-chief."

Beatrice pouted prettily. "I'm sorry for Uncle John," she said; "but it's too late to help him now. I've come for keeps."

All the time he was speaking, Captain Wells's piercing glance was fixed upon Forsyth, to whom he had just been introduced, but of whom he had heard at the Fort, and the young man grew vaguely uncomfortable.

"Your pardon, sir," said Captain Wells. "I fear the manners of the prairie seem strange to a gentleman of culture. My only excuse is that your face interests me."

"Come on over to the Fort, Cousin Rob," suggested Beatrice, with ready tact, "and I'll introduce you to Queen. They don't want us here, anyhow."

Together they climbed into the pirogue in which Captain Wells had crossed the river, and with some difficulty reached the opposite shore. Ronald was standing at the entrance, talking with the sentinel, and when he saw them coming he went toward the barracks with more haste than dignity. Forsyth laughed, but Beatrice held her head high, and a faint flush stole into her cheeks.

"Where are the stables, Cousin Rob?"

"This way."

Robert's involuntary gasp of admiration at the sight of Queen instantly placed him high in his fair cousin's favour. "Isn't she a beauty?" she asked.

The little black mare whinnied joyously at the approach of her young mistress, prancing and curvetting prettily in spite of her halter.

"Poor dear," said Beatrice, "you aren't used to being tied, are you?"

She led the horse out on the parade-ground and exclaimed with pleasure at the satin smoothness of the glossy coat. The grooms had done their work well and stood around, grinning broadly, while she praised them. The mare might have hailed from the blue grass country, so perfect were her lines. She was built for speed as well as beauty, and the small black hoofs pawed the ground impatiently, as she rubbed her velvet nose against her owner's cheek by way of a caress.

"There isn't any sugar, Queen," laughed the girl, "and I just came to say good-morning."

"We'll have some rides on the prairie together," said Robert. "My horse isn't much, compared with yours, but he used to get along pretty well on the roads back East."

"Aren't there any roads here?"

"I haven't discovered any, but the prairie isn't bad."

"Come on out now," said Beatrice, "and I'll show you what she can do."

As they passed the barracks, Robert was dimly aware of Ronald's scrutiny from some safe point of observation; but Beatrice chattered merrily until they reached the open space beyond the Fort.

A convenient stump stood near by and she led the mare to it. "Now then, Beauty," she said. In an instant she was mounted on Queen's bare back, and there ensued an exhibition of horsemanship that would have put a cavalryman to shame. Some of the soldiers came out to see the mare change her gait at a word from her rider, and turn readily with neither bit nor bridle. The pins dropped, one by one, from the girl's hair, and when she turned out on the open plain for a final gallop, it streamed out behind her as Atalanta's may have done when she made her last race.

Beatrice was riding like the wind. She went straight on until she was scarcely a speck upon the horizon, then circled back gradually. Queen was on her mettle, and no dame of high degree ever held her head more proudly than the little black mare with the tossing mane. With a last turn she came toward the Fort straight as an arrow, and stopped so suddenly at the word that she was thrown back upon her haunches.

The girl slipped to the ground, laughing and flushed. "Oh!" she cried, "that was glorious, wasn't it, Queen?"

"I'm proud of my cousin," was all Forsyth said; but there was a volume of meaning in the tone.

A groom led the horse away to be rubbed down, and Beatrice began a fruitless search for the lost hairpins, in which Robert refused to join her. "Don't put it up," he pleaded, "you look so much prettier with it down."

"I can't, anyway," she said. "I haven't a single pin."

The heavy mass of brown and auburn hung far below her waist, rippling ever so slightly, and ending in a curl. A pink flush was on her face and her eyes were dancing. "Come," she continued, "they're talking about me over there, and I know it."

She had hit upon the truth, for the Mackenzies were having an animated conference with Captain Wells. "I never suspected there was any trouble," he was saying, "and she didn't mention it. She was waiting for us a piece up the trail, and two men with her were carrying her box. She said she was coming, so the soldiers took her things and she rode with me.

"As she told you, they probably know it now, but I'll see them the first thing when I go back and explain. They'll be glad to know she's safe. She's as skittish a filly as I've ever laid eyes on—she won't wear a bit, nor stand; and that little black devil that she rides is made out of the same kind of timber. The two of them will have the settlement by the ears inside of a month—you wait and see."

Beatrice appeared at this juncture and pointed a rosy finger at Captain Wells. "Perjurer!" she laughed. "You've been taking my character away from me!"

"I never tell anything but the truth, Miss," returned the Captain, awkwardly. "Are you going back with me this afternoon?"

"I told you once," she answered, "that I was going to live with Aunt Eleanor. I'm never going to Fort Wayne again!"

"Do you want me to take a letter or a message to your people?"

"No!" cried Beatrice, with her eyes blazing. "If you dare to mention me to them, or say I sent any kind of a message, I'll—I'll haunt you!"

The Captain went out, murmuring confused apologies; and Robert, feeling himself in the way, went to his room. The moccasins hanging on the wall gave him a vivid moment of self-knowledge. The dainty, arched foot he had seen for the first time when Beatrice stamped on the piazza, might easily have been the one for which the moccasins were made. He stroked the pretty things caressingly, with a soft light in his eyes.

"I knew she was coming," he said to himself; "but how did I know?"

In the afternoon, Mackenzie and the officers rode a little way on the Fort Wayne trail with Captain Wells, who was charged with many letters and messages for friends there, and Beatrice watched the start from the window of the living-room.

"Who's that, Aunt Eleanor, riding beside Uncle John?"

"Captain Franklin, in command of the Fort."

"And who's the mean-looking one, twisting his mustache?"

"Lieutenant Howard, dear—Katherine's husband."

"Oh!" said Beatrice, quickly. "Aren't they happy together?"

There was a long silence. "Not very happy, I'm afraid," sighed Mrs. Mackenzie.

"I'm sorry," said the girl, with genuine sympathy. "Do you think I could help in any way?"

"I don't know, Bee—I wish you could. You will be company for Katherine, and perhaps you can make it easier for her, in some ways, if you try."

"Poor Cousin Kit! Of course I'll try! Look, Aunty," she said, abruptly pointing to a belated rider who was galloping to overtake the others. He had his cap in his hand, and his yellow hair was blowing in the wind. "That's the big boy I scared. Is he married?"

"No," replied Mrs. Mackenzie. Her lips did not move, but her eyes smiled.

"He's handsome," said Beatrice, dispassionately. "I've lived at all the posts— Fort Wayne, Detroit, and Fort Mackinac, and he's the best-looking soldier I've seen. I'd like to paint his picture, if he'd let me."

"I'll ask him, dear; I think he'll let you."

"Aunt Eleanor!" cried Beatrice, reproachfully.

"Why not?"

"Oh—because. Where are those soldiers going, Aunty?"

Mrs. Mackenzie looked out of the window and saw half a dozen men in the boat belonging to the Fort, headed up-stream.

"They're going fishing, I guess. I'll have to go away a little while this afternoon, Bee. Mrs. Burns is sick and she needs me—you won't mind, will you? I'll leave the table all set, and I'll surely be back before dark. Are you afraid to be left alone?"

"No. I'm not afraid of anything; but where is Cousin Rob?"

"He's teaching the children. They don't seem to get much time, someway, in the morning, so they begin right after dinner and study till supper time. I'm so glad to have Robert here—he's doing wonders with them."

"He seems nice," said Beatrice, "and I like him. Can't I go with you, Aunt Eleanor?"

"No, dear—somebody has to stay with the baby. He's asleep, though, and I don't think he'll trouble you."

"I'll take care of him, Aunty. Don't fret about us."

Nevertheless, the house seemed very lonely to Beatrice after Mrs. Mackenzie went away, and she roamed about restlessly. For a time she amused herself by examining the articles on the depleted shelves behind the counters, but the interest soon vanished. She could find nothing to read except a soiled and ragged copy of a paper three months old, which she had already seen at Fort Wayne. The murmur of voices from a distant room, reached her ears with sudden and attractive significance, and her face brightened.

"I don't know as I should do it," she said to herself, but she went to the door and tapped softly.

Robert opened it, in surprise, and Beatrice stepped into the room. "I've come to visit the school," she said.

"Goody!" cried Johnny.

She seated herself on the window ledge and smiled radiantly at the embarrassed teacher. Discipline had been difficult from the beginning, and the guest made matters worse.

"Now, then, Johnny," Forsyth said, "what were we studying?"

"Eight times three."

"Yes, and how many are eight times three?"

"Twenty——"

"Twenty-one," said Beatrice.

"Twenty-one," repeated Johnny, readily, with the air of one who has accomplished a difficult feat.

Robert frowned and bit his lips. "Eight times three are twenty-four, Johnny. Write it ten times on your slate—that will help you to remember."

"What a gift for teaching," murmured Beatrice. Robert flushed, but did not speak, and there was no sound in the room but the pencil scratching on the slate.

"Cousin Rob?"

"Yes, Johnny. What is it?"

"Why, Cousin Bee just said eight times three were twenty-one. Did she tell a lie, or didn't she know?"

"Never mind, Johnny; just attend to your lesson."

"Mamma says it's wicked to tell lies," observed Ellen, virtuously, sucking her slate pencil.

Beatrice was enjoying herself hugely. She flashed a wicked glance at Forsyth as she said, "I'm so glad I came!"

"Go on with your work, Ellen. I want you to write that sentence five times without a mistake. Maria Indiana, bring me your primer. Begin here."

"Tan't. Baby's fordot."

"Oh, no, you haven't. We learned this yesterday, don't you remember? Now, then,—'I see,'—what's the rest of it?"

"I see a tat."

"Where?" asked Beatrice, lightly, and Maria Indiana gazed at her, sadly bewildered.

"Where is the cat?" she asked again. "I don't see any."

"Here, Baby," said Robert; "look at the picture."

"I don't like a picture cat," said Beatrice, with a tempting smile, as she held out her arms to the child.

"Tuzzin Bee!" crowed the baby, running to her, "me loves oo!"

"I've got this done now," said Johnny. "Eight times three are twenty-four."

"That's a mistake," put in Beatrice. "Didn't I tell you it was twenty-one?"

"Cousin Rob," asked Ellen, in deep trouble, "if Cousin Bee has told a lie, will she go to hell?"

"No," sobbed the baby; "me doesn't want Tuzzin Bee to go to hell!"

Robert's face was pale, and there was a dangerous look in the set lines of his mouth. He went to Beatrice, took her by the shoulders, and gently, but firmly, put her out of the room, then locked the door.

"Well, I never!" she said to herself.

Beatrice was not given to self-analysis, but she could not keep from wondering why she felt so queer. She knew she had no right to be angry, and yet she was furious. She was certain that she would have done the same thing if she had been in his place, and much earlier at that; but the fact did not lessen the enormity of his crime.

"He dared to touch me!" she whispered, with her face hidden.

The long afternoon faded into dusk, and then Mackenzie came home. "Where's mother?" he asked.

"She went to see Mrs. Burns. She said she was sick."

"Have you been lonesome, Bee?"

The girl bit her lips. "Not very," she answered grimly.

School was dismissed and the children trooped into the living-room. Robert spoke pleasantly to his uncle, but took no notice of Beatrice.

"Uncle John," she said at length, "what do you think of a person who takes a lady by the shoulders and puts her out of a room?"

"If you had been a lady," retorted Robert, "I wouldn't have put you out."

"Don't quarrel," said Mackenzie. "Life is too short to fuss." He took Chan's violin from the chimney-shelf in the next room, and began to play a lively tune. Ellen and Johnny pranced around the tea-table, and Maria Indiana, with faltering steps, endeavoured to imitate them.

Beatrice laughed, and Robert's heart softened, though he had been very angry with her only a little while before. He was about to beg her pardon for his seeming harshness, when the door burst open and Mrs. Mackenzie rushed in, breathless and white with fear.

"The Indians!" she cried. "The Indians!"

"Where?" shouted Mackenzie, springing to his feet.

"Up at Lee's! Killing and scalping!"

# CHAPTER VII
# THE ALARM

With rare presence of mind, Beatrice blew out the candles, and they made their way to the river in the darkness. The mist was rising from the bare earth and the air was heavy with dew. There was no outward sign of danger; but the grey shadows were portentous of evil, and in the very stillness was a nameless fear.

Mrs. Mackenzie had the baby in her arms. "Smother him if he cries," said the trader, in a low tone, but, fortunately, the child kept quiet. Maria Indiana began to wail and her father shook her roughly. "Keep still!" he whispered warningly.

Beatrice took charge of the other children, who did as they were told without a murmur of complaint. The bateau lay at its moorings and they got into it with as little noise as possible. Mackenzie and Robert were at the oars.

The stream was narrow, yet the minutes passed like hours, and the sound of the oars seemed carried far into the night. "Careful, now," whispered Mackenzie. Robert took the little girl in his arms and they ran up the esplanade to the Fort.

Dim shapes of horror seemed hovering around them as they strained their ears to catch the savage cry which had blazed the red trail of torture from Jamestown to the Lakes. Soldiers ran to meet them, picked up the two older children, and hurried with them into the Fort. As they entered the stockade, the heavy gate crashed into place.

"Thank God," breathed Mackenzie, "we are safe!"

On the parade-ground was a scene of confusion. Men ran to and fro, carrying ammunition and pails of water to the blockhouses and points marked on the stockade. Pine knots, thrust between the bars, blazed fitfully, throwing a lurid light here and there and making the darkness deeper by contrast.

From the windows and open doors of the officers' quarters came stray gleams of light. White-faced men and women ran in and out of the shadows, hoarse cries of command were heard, and it seemed like some vivid dream.

Beatrice ran to the stables, and Queen whinnied when she felt the girl's soft hand upon her. "Hush," she said, "we came together, Beauty, and we'll stay together—while we're here," she added, with a little choke in her voice.

Over by the barracks a man and a boy were talking to Captain Franklin, while a little group of people listened. Beatrice, with Queen's halter in her hand, went near enough to hear.

"I knew something was wrong," the man was saying. "A dozen of 'em came in all painted up, but Frenchy and White seemed to think it was all right and went on talking to them. I says to the kid here, 'They ain't Pottawattomies, and we'd better get away if we can. Do as you see me do.'

"So we went out to the canoes, and two of the red devils followed us to ask where we were going. I told 'em we were going over to feed the cattle and we'd be back soon to get supper. When we got across we pulled some hay and pretended to get the cattle together, but as soon as we got behind a stack, we ran for the Fort. Two shots were fired after we left, and God only knows what they're doing up there now. There must be thousands of them in the woods."

"Where's Chan?" asked Mrs. Mackenzie.

"Haven't seen him since noon," replied her husband. "He'll have to look out for himself."

"Where are the soldiers who went fishing?" asked Beatrice.

"They haven't come back," answered the Captain; "but they're armed."

"That won't do any good," said Lieutenant Howard. Two of the soldiers standing by ran to the blockhouses without waiting for an order. The deep-throated guns thundered a warning, and confused echoes came back, but there was no other answer.

Preparations for fight went on. The men in the blockhouses were ordered to stay there, and others were assigned to the same posts. Still others were stationed at the magazine and at regular intervals along the stockade. The gates were heavily guarded, and Captain Franklin ordered the women and children to the officers' quarters, but only Mrs. Mackenzie obeyed.

"I'll stay here," said Mrs. Franklin, in open defiance.

"Wait till we are attacked," cried Katherine.

"Queen and I will stay together," said Beatrice, proudly.

Ronald was rapidly loading the army pistols and distributing them among the women. Beatrice was standing with her arm thrown over the mare's neck when he came to her, and the fitful light of the pine knots shone full upon her face and her glorious hair. Her eyes were bright and she breathed rapidly, but no one could have said she was afraid.

For a moment they stood there, looking into each other's eyes. "When the first Indian leaps the stockade, put it to your temple and fire," said Ronald, almost in a whisper.

Beatrice took the heavy pistol from him with a steady hand. "Give me another cartridge," she said.

"What for?"

"For Queen. I won't have her hurt, and she goes first."

The Ensign obeyed, with another long look at the girl. "You're a thoroughbred," he said. For a breathless instant they faced each other, then Ronald clicked his heels together, saluted, and turned away.

Something stirred painfully in the girl's heart. As in a dream, she saw Mrs. Mackenzie and the children going into Lieutenant Howard's, watched Forsyth and the trader as they loaded their muskets, and heard Katherine's terrible laugh when she put the cold muzzle of the pistol to her temple to see how it would feel.

Then Franklin and Ronald passed her. "I won't give an order," the Captain was saying; "it's a job for volunteers."

"May I have them?" asked the Ensign.

"Yes—six. We can spare no more."

A moment later a clear voice sounded above the clamour, "Attention!"

There was the rush of hurrying feet, an instant's wondering silence, then Ronald spoke. "Boys," he said, "Mrs. Burns has a baby a day old, and there is no one with her but her husband. I'm going after them—who's going with me?"

The soldiers, to a man, rallied around him. "I!" came from every throat. "I'm going!"

"Six only," he said. He quickly selected his men, they snatched up their guns, and, with a warning "hush!" from him, they went to the bateau in which the Mackenzies had crossed.

"Steady!" came Ronald's low voice, then the oars murmured in the water and the heavy gate rumbled into place once more.

Forsyth, stunned by the whirl of events, was leaning on his musket, staring vacantly into space. Across the parade-ground his face appeared to Beatrice in the last flicker of a burnt-out knot. All her pent-up anger returned to her, and, still smarting under the memory of his affront, she left her horse and went over to him.

"Why didn't you go with him?" she demanded.

"Who—where?"

"Ensign Ronald!"

"I—I don't know," he stammered.

He had told the unvarnished truth, but she interpreted it in her own way. "I'll tell you why you didn't go," she said, with measured distinctness. Then her eyes flashed and her breast heaved.

"Coward!" she blazed.

Robert started as if he had been struck, but before he could speak, she had left him and gone back to Queen.

Her lip curled as she saw him standing there, leaning on his musket, with his head bowed. His habit of self-analysis asserted itself, and he began to wonder whether she had been right. The blood that had left his heart came back in tides of pain, and the word burned itself upon his consciousness. "Coward," he said to himself, "coward! She called me a coward!"

Yet he knew that what she had said did not matter so much as the possibility that she had spoken truly—that his self-respect meant more than any woman's praise or blame. His reason told him that; but her scornful, accusing face flitted before him and he had an impulse to get away—it did not matter where. Still dazed, he went to the blockhouse at the north-west corner of the stockade and joined the men there.

On the parade-ground Doctor Norton was making grewsome preparations. A stretcher was placed near each blockhouse, and others at regular intervals. Bottles were ranged in rows upon the ground, and piles of bandages showed whitely under the flare of the torches.

He looked up, to find Katherine at his side. "Let me help you," she said.

"No; there's nothing you can do just now, but I'm afraid we'll have our hands full later if—Go and scrape some lint," he broke off abruptly, "and make some coffee. Get the other women to help you."

Here the Lieutenant passed them, without seeming to see them, and she followed him with a guilty feeling in her heart.

When she entered her own house, she found her mother there, scraping lint and making bandages, while a pot of strong coffee was already steaming on the hearth and piles of cut bread were stacked upon the table.

"This is all we can do, dear," said Mrs. Mackenzie.

"Let me help you, mother—I'll get some more old linen."

Mrs. Franklin came in with her arms full of white cloth, which she tore into strips and wound tightly, ready for immediate use. They worked by the light of a single candle, and the three loaded pistols lay on the table in front of them.

"If we sleep to-night," said the Captain's wife at length, without pausing in her task, "I'll take Miss Manning and Mrs. Burns, when the boys come back."

"Mother and the children can stay here," said Katherine; "but I haven't room for any more."

"That's all right," answered Mrs. Mackenzie. "The men can go to the barracks."

More than an hour passed, but nothing was heard from the rescue party, and the fear of danger deepened. The Lieutenant came in, endeavouring to conceal his nervousness.

55

"That's good," he said, indicating the piles of lint and bandages. Then he drank a cup of strong, black coffee, and paced back and forth uneasily.

"Where are the boys?" asked Katherine. "Isn't it time for them to come back?"

"No, I don't think so; we could hardly expect them yet."

"Couldn't some of the others go after them?"

"Heavens, no! We haven't fifty men here, and we need every one. Chan is missing, seven have gone after Mrs. Burns, and six are on a fishing trip—that's fourteen out of our small force. In their place we have Father John, Forsyth, and the man and boy from Lee's. The Indians are probably gathering in the woods and making ready to attack us. God!" he said, under his breath, "why can't we have troops!"

Katherine warned him with a glance which almost imperceptibly indicated Mrs. Franklin, who was hard at work, seemingly absorbed in her task. "Where's Wallace?" she asked, without looking up.

"Walking around the parade-ground. He's safe," he added bitterly; "don't worry about him."

Mrs. Mackenzie and Katherine both frowned at the emphasis on the last word. "Don't worry about me, either," he continued; "I'm going now."

Katherine went to the door with him. "Can I do anything more, dear?" she asked.

"No," he said roughly, "unless you want to mind your own business for a while!" He laughed harshly, pushed her from him, and went out.

"Ralph isn't well," she sighed, going back to the table; "and I'm afraid something has happened outside, too. I wonder where the boys are?"

The whole garrison was asking the same question secretly; but no man would openly admit that there was ground for anxiety. Beatrice had tied Queen to the flag-pole, and was besieging the Doctor with inquiries.

"Tell me," she pleaded, for the third time, "haven't they been gone long enough to get back?"

"Yes," he answered finally; "they have. They should have been here long ago."

"I knew it!" she exclaimed. "I'm going to the blockhouse to see if they aren't coming!"

She called to those above her, but no one heard, so she went up the ladder. "Where are they?" she cried, bursting in upon the startled group.

Even as she spoke there was a faint "halloo" from the west. "They're coming," shouted Robert, but his voice was lost, for the sentinel at the gate had heard also.

The parade-ground filled with people, and Beatrice had turned to descend the ladder, when Robert caught her by the arm.

"Beatrice!" he gasped. "Let me know the worst—do you despise me?"

"Yes," she answered, coolly. "Please let go of me, and never dare to touch me again."

The gate was lifted and seven men came in, carrying the mattress on which lay Mrs. Burns and her baby. Mrs. Franklin led the way to her hospitable door, where Mrs. Mackenzie and Katherine were already waiting to do what they could in the way of making the mother and child comfortable.

It was Mrs. Mackenzie who first noticed that Ronald was not with them. "Where's George?" she asked, in a low tone.

"He's gone up the river, ma'am," answered one of the soldiers. "We begged him not to, but he would go, and he wouldn't let a one of us go with him. He thought he heard a noise, so he went up-stream to see what it was."

Mr. Burns had seen no Indians, but, like the others, thought they were gathering in the woods. He was far away from the house at the time the man had shouted the warning; but he had heard the two shots at Lee's and the guns from the Fort.

"Captain," said Lieutenant Howard, "I'll be one of a party to go and find Ronald. He's probably up at Lee's."

"You won't," growled the Captain, biting his mustache. "Just because the young fool chooses to risk his life for nothing, I won't expose five or six men to danger. We have none to spare."

"How did he go?" asked the Doctor of Mr. Burns.

"He took my boat. He'll pull back down-stream quick enough if anything is wrong."

"No he won't," returned the Doctor, warmly; "you don't know the lad."

Robert walked back and forth on the parade-ground, sorely troubled on his own account, and deeply concerned for the safety of his friend. Mackenzie shared his anxiety, but quickly vetoed the suggestion that they two follow him.

"'T ain't no manner of use, Rob," he said, kindly. "We're under military orders, and you heard what the Captain said. Besides, that dare-devil boy ain't afraid of anything, and I guess he'll come out with a whole skin—he always has."

"Were you thinking of going after him, Cousin Rob?" asked Beatrice, sweetly.

He started at the sound of her voice, then looked full in her face with no sign of recognition. Beatrice met his eyes squarely until he turned on his heel and walked away, followed by a peal of light, mocking laughter that cut into his heart like a knife.

"What's the matter between you and Rob?" asked the trader, curiously.

"Nothing," answered the girl, shrugging her shoulders; "but I was amused a little while ago because he was so frightened—he was scared almost to death."

Mackenzie's eyes glittered as he peered at her keenly from under his bushy brows. "Don't say that again, my girl," he said, huskily, "for fear doesn't run in the Forsyth blood. His grandfather was killed at Lexington."

"A boat is coming," shouted a man from the blockhouse. Shortly afterward, the fishing party came in, tired but triumphant, with a long string of river fish. They had seen no Indians, and had not met Ronald.

"Did you hear the gun?" asked the Captain.

"Yes, sir," replied one of the soldiers. "We were up on the North Branch and thought it was a warning, so we laid low for a while. Then, as we didn't hear anything more, we came on down as quietly as we could."

"Everything all right at Lee's?" asked Lieutenant Howard.

"As far as we saw, sir."

Still there was uneasiness regarding the Ensign. Katherine was pale, Mrs. Franklin was crying, and Beatrice had her small hands clenched tightly together. Suddenly they all knew how much they should miss him if——

Then there was a familiar whistle outside, the sentinel opened the gate, and Ronald came in with a big black and white dog in his arms.

"I thought I heard him howling," he said, in answer to the torrent of questions, "so I went on up to Lee's to get him. The devils have been there all right,—the guns must have frightened them away.

"Yes," he continued in a low tone, in answer to a whispered question from Howard; "White and Frenchy. White was shot and stabbed in the breast and poor Frenchy was scalped—the whole top of his head lifted off. The dog was guarding the body."

"What's that?" asked Mrs. Franklin, from the edge of the group where all the women were standing together. "Speak louder—we can't hear."

The deep-toned bell tolled taps, and there was a general movement toward quarters. "I was just talking about the dog," shouted Ronald to the women.

"He fought me at first," he continued, addressing the Lieutenant and the Doctor; "but I soon won his heart. Poor old boy," he said, stroking the dog, "he didn't want to be made into a stew, did he?"

"We must go up to-morrow," said the Lieutenant.

"What are you going to call him?" asked the Doctor.

"Major, I guess—we haven't a major here."

Lieutenant Howard's white teeth showed in a sarcastic smile. "You might call him 'Captain,'" he said, twisting his mustache, "for the same good reason."

# CHAPTER VIII
# THOROUGHBREDS

The guard was doubled that night and the small force was ready for instant action. Sentinels patrolled the river bank and stood at the gates; while in the blockhouses the cannon were trained through the port-holes, and men kept vigilant watch.

At three o'clock the terrified bleating of the sheep aroused every one but the children. A sentinel fired his musket and retreated to the Fort, then a heavy gun rumbled ominously.

Once again the parade-ground filled with people. "What is it? What is it?" they cried.

"Indians," Captain Franklin explained. "They went after the horses, but didn't find them, so they stabbed the sheep and turned them loose. The sentry saw some of them in the pasture, and fired, then ran to the Fort. A tomahawk just missed him—it grazed his head and struck a waggon wheel. The cannon must have frightened them away."

So it proved, for the next morning a trail of blood led from the pasture toward the woods. The sheep lay dead on the plains around the Fort, but search parties found nothing, though they scoured the woods thoroughly for miles around.

Chandonnais appeared at the usual time for work, but refused to say where he had been. When he was asked unpleasant questions, he always pretended that he did not understand, and from this position neither man nor woman could swerve him a hair's breadth.

Lieutenant Howard, with four men, went up the river to Lee's and buried the two victims of the night before. "It wasn't good to look at," he said to Ronald, when he returned.

"I know," answered the Ensign; "I found out that much last night. I didn't dare strike a light, but I felt——" He turned his face away and swallowed hard. "Don't tell the women," he concluded.

"I won't," said Howard, "and I've made the boys promise not to talk. There's no use of making things worse than they are."

Major sat at Ronald's feet, listening intelligently, and thumping the ground vigorously with his bushy tail. "Poor old boy," said his new master, affectionately; "it was pretty bad, wasn't it? He's a nice dog, isn't he, Howard?"

"Washing would help him."

"He's going to have his Spring bath the first warm day. How do you suppose dogs know whom they belong to? Major knows he's mine, and nobody could get him away from me."

Beatrice came out of Captain Franklin's and took a careful survey of the Fort. It was a gloomy place at best, but the disorder of the night made it worse.

"Good-morning," said the Lieutenant, as he passed her on his way home.

"Good-morning," returned the girl, including Ronald in the salutation. Then she whistled to the dog, but he paid no attention to the call other than to lean heavily against his master.

"He's mine," laughed Ronald, meeting her, "and you can't have him. How do you like living in the Fort?"

"I don't like it," she answered disdainfully. "It's about as cheerful as a tomb. I'm glad we're going home."

Ronald lifted his brows inquiringly. "Who's going home?"

"Why, all of us—Uncle John, Aunt Eleanor, the children, and—and Cousin Rob."

"Oh, no, you're not! You're going to stay here."

"Who said so?"

"I say so," replied George, mischievously.

"Can't I go out of the Fort?"

"No."

"We'll see," said Beatrice, tossing her head.

She ran to the gate, but he was there before her and effectually barred the way.

"Let me pass," she said icily.

"I'm sorry, Miss Manning, but you can't go without permission from the Captain. You are under military orders, and no soldier or citizen is to leave the Fort without a guard. After sunset no one but the sentries can pass the gates."

"For how long?" demanded Beatrice.

"Till the Captain orders otherwise."

"And I'm to stay here, then, without a hat, or even a clean handkerchief, until His Majesty sees fit to let me go to my own home in broad daylight!"

The colour flamed in her cheeks, and her eyes snapped dangerously. The Ensign was enjoying the situation hugely, and thought Beatrice was the prettiest girl he had ever seen. In fact, he was on the point of saying so, but, fortunately, thought better of it.

"You can go if I go with you," he suggested.

"Then I'll stay here," announced Beatrice, with unconcealed scorn. She walked away from him with her head high, and went straight to Captain Franklin.

"Gone to see if I lied to her," laughed Ronald to himself. "She's a mettlesome damsel—devilish mettlesome."

"That is my order," said the Captain, in answer to her question, "and it must be obeyed."

"Can't I go home at all?"

"Certainly, for a few minutes at a time. Ask Ensign Ronald to go with you this afternoon."

The Captain turned away, and Beatrice gazed at his retreating figure with fire in her eyes. "Fool!" she said aloud, stamping her foot; "I won't ask him. I'll stay here till I die before I'll ask him!"

Captain Franklin's house immediately became offensive to her, and she knew Robert was at Katherine's, teaching the children. The parade-ground was odious, because Ronald was walking briskly around it for exercise. Her uncle passed her with the coolest kind of a nod, remembering what she had said about Robert the night before,and she began to wish she had never left Fort Wayne.

Only the stables remained, and she went there to see the friend who never failed her. Queen pranced in her stall and tapped with her dainty hoofs impatiently.

"I can't take you out, Beauty," she said sadly, "because they won't let us leave the Fort."

Queen put her nose into the girl's neck and was immediately slapped. "You're not allowed to do that," said Beatrice, sternly, turning away. Queen whinnied and Beatrice understood that the offender was very sorry and very lonely, and would never do it again, so she went back.

"I'll take you around the Fort if you'll be good," she said. Her saddle was hanging there, but she preferred to ride without it, so she replaced the halter with a bridle and went out, mounted, hoping Ronald was not there.

But he was still walking around the parade-ground, with Major in his wake. Queen pricked up her ears but went on, obediently, at the slow pace which was better than nothing. Ronald smiled to himself as Beatrice crossed and turned so that if he kept on he would appear to be following her.

Twice, three times the procession went round the square, with the dog bringing up the rear, before a bright idea struck the Ensign. By slow-degrees he slackened his pace, and as they passed Lieutenant Howard's for the fifth time, Mrs. Mackenzie came out on the piazza.

"What's the matter, Bee?" she called; "can't you catch him?"

In half a minute Queen was in her stall, much surprised, and not a little displeased at the sudden termination of her exercise. "You wretch," whispered Beatrice, as she dismounted; "whatever possessed you to follow him?"

The coast was clear when she left the stables, but she went to Mrs. Howard's in a bad humour. She was not upon good terms with any one, and would have have started back to Fort Wayne that afternoon if it had been possible. She smiled grimly as she realised that, by her own act, she had forever cut herself off from her friends there. "I'll have to fight it out here," she said to herself; "I seem destined to fight."

Mrs. Franklin went to Mrs. Howard's to invite Beatrice to dinner, and was much disappointed when she refused. "Thank you," Beatrice said, trying hard to be pleasant; "but I'll stay with Aunty and Cousin Kit this time. I haven't a doubt you'll get tired of me, though, before His High Mightiness lets me go home."

She could have bitten her tongue out for the unlucky speech, but, to her relief, the Captain's wife misunderstood. "I saw you at the gate this morning," she laughed, "arguing with George. It's no use—he always has his own way."

"What a narrow escape!" she exclaimed, as Mrs. Franklin went out. "Aunt Eleanor, this is one of my bad days."

"You mustn't say any day is bad, dear," replied Mrs. Mackenzie, "because each one is what we make it. We begin afresh every morning with the day in our own hands. I'm sorry this has happened; but I'm very glad we had the Fort to come to, and I am sure you can find something pleasant here if you only look for it."

Nine people crowded around Mrs. Howard's table at dinner time, but Mackenzie and Robert barely spoke to Beatrice. The tribal instinct was strong in the trader, and Robert was of his blood. Katherine perceived that something was wrong and did her best to produce harmony, in which she was ably seconded by her husband. The Lieutenant was in a very pleasant frame of mind.

"Cousin Bee," said Ellen, "are you coming to visit the school this afternoon?" Beatrice was talking with Katherine and did not seem to hear.

"Tuzzin Bee," screamed Maria Indiana, "is oo tummin?"

"No, dear," answered Beatrice, quickly.

"Why not?" asked Mrs. Mackenzie, innocently; "it might amuse you, Bee."

"I doubt it," said the girl. "I'm going to help Kit."

"Cousin Rob put her out," explained Johnny, "because she told a lie."

Above everything else on earth, Beatrice hated to wash dishes, but she plunged into the work with a will after dinner, as a penance, and in spite of Mrs. Howard's protests.

"It's so good of you to help me," sighed Katherine, as the last dish was put away; "for mother is tired out, and I have a headache. None of us slept much last night, I fancy."

"I know I didn't, but I seldom sleep in the daytime. I wish you and Aunt Eleanor would go and lie down. I can take care of myself."

"All right," answered Katherine, "if you don't mind."

Beatrice sat by the window a little while after the house became quiet, then went over to Mrs. Franklin's, but there was no response to her rap. "Everybody's asleep, I guess," she said to herself.

She went to the gate and looked out longingly into the bright Spring sunshine. The sentinel passed her with his musket over his shoulder, and went on around the Fort. She heard his measured steps die away in the distance, and wondered, mechanically, how long it took him to make the round.

It seemed a long time before she heard him coming. A pirogue was tied to a sapling on the river bank and the oars lay near it. Across the stream the lonely house was beckoning to her to come. She slipped out of the gate and leaned up against the stockade outside. Then the sentry passed again.

"Against orders, Miss," he said.

"What?" asked Beatrice.

"Standin' outside."

"Oh," she said, returning to the gate. "Can I stand here?"

"Yes'm, if you don't go no further. Orders is to stay inside."

"All right." She smiled brilliantly, then inquired, in a tone of polite interest, "Are you all alone here?"

"Yes'm. My mate's at mess."

"Too bad. It's lonely for you, isn't it?"

"Yes'm, but I'm used to it."

He went on, and she watched him till he turned the first corner. A backward glance assured her that the parade-ground was deserted, so she edged out of the gate again, and, under cover of the stockade, ran to the pirogue, snatched up the oars, and started across.

The blood beat hard in her pulses, but she was not afraid, and the rare delight of disobeying military orders set her head awhirl. She expected to see the esplanade fill with soldiers, shouting to her to come back, but nothing happened. She reached the other bank safely, tied the pirogue, and ran into the house. From the window of the living-room she saw the sentry pass once more. His head was bowed and he did not notice that a boat was gone.

Then Ronald came out of the Fort alone and took another boat. She shrank back to the farthest corner of the room, and her heart stood still until she saw him turn up-stream. "There," she said to herself, "he's disobeying orders, too, for he's gone without a guard. If he can do it, there's no reason why I shouldn't."

Unconsciously, Beatrice had sustained a high nervous strain for too long a period. The quarrel with her aunt and uncle at Fort Wayne had been an affair of no small moment at the time, and the preparation for the journey and the long horseback ride had told upon her strength. The excitement of her arrival, new scenes and new faces, and the fright of the night before had taxed her still further, and her trouble with Robert had hurt her more deeply than she knew. She had reached the fine dividing line between a let-down and a break.

The indescribable loneliness of the house was depressing. The bare walls seemed to whisper back and forth, and the table, still set for supper, had a ghastly look about it. The rooms were not merely alone, but untenanted. Cold ashes lay upon the hearths, the dust had settled upon the chairs, and the sunlight outside only served to heighten the gloom.

In the schoolroom the books were piled neatly upon the table, and the slates were clean—ready for the next day's task. She experienced an unwonted twinge of conscience as she entered, unrebuked, and remembered how exasperating she had been.

At the Fort she had thought of many things she needed, but now her errand seemed purposeless, and the pleasures of disobedience began to pall. She went into her room, gathered up some of her toilet articles, and stood there, listlessly, watching the sentinel as he passed again without missing the boat.

"They're fine soldiers," she said to herself. "They know lots."

Then her heart gave a great leap, for there was a soft step at the back door. Some one entered very quietly, and she became as cold and immovable as if she had been made of stone. The catlike tread moved slowly into the living-room, and she trembled like an aspen. She tried to raise the window, thinking that she could scream if she could not get out, but her hands shook so that it was useless. Meanwhile the intruder came nearer, with the same stealthy steps. No one had crossed the river and the sentinel was not in sight.

Some one opened the door of the schoolroom and closed it with the least possible noise. Then the hushed steps came nearer still, but the window would not move. Her door was open, but she knew the flimsy lock would not hold, even if she could manage to shut it. An instant—now—she tried to shut her eyes, but could not—horror upon horror came upon her—then Ronald entered her room.

For a blind instant the earth whirled beneath her, then the flood-gates opened and Beatrice wept. He did as any other man in his place would have done and put a protecting arm around her, but, though sorely tempted, manfully refrained from kissing her.

"I'm so sorry I frightened you," he said, with bitter self-reproach. "Don't, Beatrice—Miss Manning,—please don't cry any more!"

As soon as she was conscious of her position, she drew away from him, still sobbing. It was not only her fright, but the natural result of the high tension at which she had lived for more than a week. He left her and rummaged around until he found a bottle of brandy, then he brought her a glass of water liberally strengthened with it.

"Here," he said, "drink this."

She obeyed, and in a few minutes began to recover her self-possession. "How did you get here?" she asked.

"I went up the river a little way, landed on this side, and walked down to the back door. You didn't suppose I'd let you come over here alone, did you?"

"Did you see me when I came?"

"Certainly. I expected you to do just what you did, and I kept my eye on you. I knew you were in the house, because I saw the boat outside, but I didn't mean to frighten you. I just thought I'd look around until we met."

"You—you—walked so softly," she said, with quivering lips.

"Did I? That's the first time I've ever been accused of that. It must have been your imagination."

"Perhaps," she answered, with a long sigh.

"If you have everything you want, we'll go back now."

Scarcely conscious of what she did, she stooped to pick up the things that had fallen to the floor. They seemed utterly useless for all time, but she felt the necessity of action. As they turned to leave the room, he took her cold hands in his and looked down into her wet eyes.

"Promise me," he said, "that you will never again disobey a military order."

She hesitated, and he repeated it.

"How do you know I'd keep a promise?" she asked, to gain time.

"Because you're a thoroughbred."

Something in his eyes subdued her. "I promise," she said, almost in a whisper.

"All right. Now, we'll not say anything about this to any one—do you understand?"

She was still trembling when he helped her into the pirogue, and neither spoke while they were crossing. When they entered the gate, Captain Franklin met them.

"Did she ask you to take her over?" he inquired of Ronald.

The Ensign's eyes met his squarely. "Yes, sir."

"Did you go together? I thought I saw you going alone."

"We went together. She was waiting for me outside."

"Very well. I will have no disobedience of my orders—remember that, both of you."

"Don't faint," George whispered, warningly, as the Captain walked away. "It's all right now, but that's the first time I ever lied—in my official capacity."

Beatrice put a small, icy hand into his own. "Thank you," she said quietly; "you're a thoroughbred, too."

# CHAPTER IX
# ON THE FORT WAYNE TRAIL

As silently as they had gone, the Indians returned. No one but the sentinels saw the ghostly procession when it passed the Fort from the southward, in the grey mists of dawn. Black Partridge was still at the head, the others following him in single file.

The deserted wigwams in the hollow were as they had left them, and inside of an hour they had taken up the thread of existence at the point where the annual pilgrimage had broken it off. Some exchanges of gifts were made among them; but, in the main, each one was satisfied with what he had received.

Early in the morning the chief went to the trading station, and, finding it deserted, went immediately to the Fort in search of his friend Shaw-nee-aw-kee. They had a long conversation on the parade-ground, and soldiers and civilians gathered around them, listening impatiently until the interpreter was ready to speak.

"I understand it now," said Mackenzie to the Captain. "He says that while they were up in Canada, the Chippewas and Ottawas sent speeches among them, saying the northern tribes had heard that the Pottawattomies and Winnebagoes were not upon good terms with the white people and that they desired them to be friendly. His own people only laughed, but the Winnebagoes determined to show their independence in a refusal to obey the commands of other tribes. So a dozen braves came here to take some white scalps, that they might flaunt them in the faces of the others. He says a large force was waiting in the woods, and that they would doubtless have killed every one outside of the Fort, even if they did not make an attack upon the Fort itself, but that the guns of the White Father frightened them away."

Here the chief began to talk again, with many gestures.

"He says," continued Mackenzie, "that we need not now be afraid, since he and his people have returned to protect us. He is sorry that his friends have suffered during his absence, and after this a part of the tribe will always remain here, while the others go after their gifts."

"We can go home, then," said Mrs. Mackenzie.

"Isn't he splendid!" exclaimed Beatrice. "I'd like to paint his picture. Do you think he'd let me, Uncle John?"

It took a great deal of explanation to make Black Partridge understand, but he finally consented, on condition that the picture would be given to him. "He's afraid the white squaw will make a charm," said Mackenzie.

"All right," laughed Beatrice. "I can make several sketches, and he can have one of the pictures. He needn't know I make more than one."

By night the Mackenzies were in their own home again, and, as the weeks passed, the fear was forgotten by all save Beatrice. She could not enter her own room without a vivid remembrance of her fright, coupled with the consciousness that she had cried like a baby, and that the Ensign had put his arm around her unrebuked. She hated herself for her weakness and blamed herself bitterly for her foolishness, because, if she had only stopped to think, she would have known the difference in sound between a moccasin and an army boot.

Still, at night, she would sometimes start from troubled dreams with the same deadly fear upon her and tremble long after she knew she was awake and safe. Behind it all was something she did not care to think of, but memory gave her no peace.

Pictures, clear and distinct, intruded upon her mental vision against her will. She saw Robert leaning on his musket, the only man in the Fort who was not up and doing when danger seemed imminent, and shuddered at the look on his face when she called him a coward. In his eyes there had been something of the same reproach with which a dog regards the well-loved master who has unjustly struck him. "Lexington!" she said to herself over and over again; "his fathers fought there, and I called their son a coward!"

Swiftly upon the memory came the sound of his voice when he had cried, "Beatrice, do you despise me?" and the sight of his strained, eager face, as he waited for her to speak. The knowledge of her answer made her shrink from herself with bitterness and shame. The obvious course of apology lay open to her, but her pride refused to humble itself that far. Time and time again she had determined to make partial atonement in that way, but her stubborn lips would not move to shape the word "forgive."

Robert seemed to have forgotten, and each day he made himself dearer to the Mackenzies. Between the trader and his college-bred nephew there slowly grew one of those rare friendships possible only to men. Mackenzie had not spent his life upon the frontier without learning to understand his fellow-man, and to read, though perhaps roughly, the inner meaning of outward semblances. In Robert he saw the blood of the Forsyths undefiled—the martial spirit was there, educated, refined, and tempered until it was akin to polished steel. From his mother the boy had received broad charity and a great gentleness, as well as the adamantine pride which is at once the strength and terror of a woman's heart.

Mrs. Mackenzie had quickly learned to love him, and with her he took the place of a grown son. He helped her in countless little ways, and often sat with his arm thrown over her shoulders while she sewed upon the rough garments her husband wore, and talked to him as she worked. The children idolised him.

From all this Beatrice felt herself an outcast, though there was no visible evidence that she was not one of them. The trader laughed and joked with her as he always had done, and her aunt regarded her with tender affection. Maria Indiana and the baby adored her, and the other children openly admired her, in spite of a lingering belief that she had broken one of the Ten Commandments. Still, she was not satisfied, for every day she remembered, with a pang of self-reproach, and Robert stood aloof. He never failed to be courteous and considerate, yet between them was a cold, impenetrable distance which never softened in the slightest degree.

Beatrice and Ronald were great friends. His unnatural shyness had worn off, but he did not treat her with the easy familiarity the other women at the post had learned to expect from him. He was quite capable of teasing Mrs. Howard and Mrs. Franklin to the limit of their endurance; but Mrs. Mackenzie and Beatrice were included in the manifestations of deep respect.

Mr. and Mrs. Burns decided to leave the post and go to Fort Wayne, where they had relatives, as soon as Mrs. Burns was able to travel. The man and boy who had escaped from the Indians at Lee's determined to go with them. The farm was too far away from the Fort to be altogether safe, and a kind of disembodied horror had hung about the place since the killing of the two men and the savage mutilation of their bodies.

Black Partridge and a few of the Pottawattomies volunteered to accompany them to Fort Wayne whenever they might be ready to start. For a time it was thought best to take one of the waggons at the Fort; but Spring was at hand, and there would doubtless be streams which a waggon could not successfully ford.

Ronald assisted Mr. Burns in selecting and packing the few things they were to take with them, and their household effects were distributed among the Indians who were to compose the guard. The four white people were to ride horseback and the Indians were to follow on foot, riding the horses back when the others had safely reached Fort Wayne.

"Miss Manning," said Ronald one afternoon, "we are having trouble in finding a horse suitable for Mrs. Burns. Would you be willing to lend her yours?"

"No, I wouldn't," snapped Beatrice.

"The horse will be brought back safely," pleaded the Ensign.

"No, she won't, because she isn't going."

Ronald's face changed and he left her without another word.

"I don't care," said Beatrice to herself; "she couldn't ride Queen anyway. Queen wouldn't let her—nobody has ever ridden her but me." Later, it occurred to her that she might have explained more fully to Ronald, but she put the thought from her as unworthy of a proud spirit. She knew that he had put her down as selfish, but repeatedly told herself that she did not care.

The day was set for their departure, and they were to start at sunrise. The night before, Beatrice found it impossible to sleep, and, long before daylight, she got up and dressed. Because there was nothing to do in the house and she was afraid of waking the others, she went out on the piazza.

Across the river there were signs of life, and she got into a pirogue with the laudable desire to say good-bye to Mrs. Burns. When she reached the Fort, Mrs. Franklin and Katherine were already up and assisting Mrs. Burns in her preparations for the journey; but the Captain and Lieutenant Howard were not there.

Suddenly it occurred to Beatrice that she might take Queen and ride a little way along the trail. She had been over the ground before and was not afraid to come back alone. Without saying anything of her intention, she appeared on the parade-ground, mounted, and met a chorus of protests.

"It isn't safe for you to go alone," said Mrs. Franklin.

"Please don't, Bee," added Katherine.

"Really, Miss Manning," observed Doctor Norton, "it is not best for you to go."

"I'm not afraid," replied the girl, with a toss of her head.

The party she had determined to escort, individually and collectively, offered feeble objections, which were immediately waved aside. "I'm going," said Beatrice, "because I want to, and because it would break Queen's heart if we went back now."

"What's all this fuss about?" inquired Ronald, sauntering up, and rubbing his eyes.

The women explained all at once, in incoherent sentences; but Beatrice did not appear to hear any part of the conversation until he ended it by saying, "She can go if she wants to, because I'm going along."

Beatrice bit her lip. "You are not," she said, in a tone of command.

"Yes, I am," he laughed; "and, moreover, you are never to ride out of the gate of the Fort unless an officer goes with you."

She turned and looked at him scornfully, and Ronald, still laughing, saluted. "A military order, Miss Manning."

It was scarcely light when they started, with Beatrice leading the way. Queen's eager feet fairly flew, and the girl's pulses caught the exultant sense of life. The others fell far behind, and Beatrice doubled and crossed on the trail wherever it was possible.

They had gone about six miles from the Fort when she reined in and waited for the others to come up, then made her adieux.

"Why do you say good-bye?" asked Ronald.

"Why, because I'm going back now."

"Oh, are you coming back? I thought you were going to Fort Wayne."

She made no reply, but watched the four riders as they turned a little away from the lake and went south-west over the prairie. A pack horse, Black Partridge, and four other Indians were following them.

"What made you think I was going to Fort Wayne?" she asked.

"Nothing, only you had such a good start. Besides, you live there, don't you?"

"No," she said slowly, "I live here. I fought at Fort Wayne."

"Indeed!" remarked Ronald, with polite interest. "Indians or soldiers?"

The pink flush upon her face deepened. "Shall we go back, now?"

"As you please, Miss Manning."

She went ahead, leaving him to follow or not as he chose.

"I wish Major was here," he called to her.

"Why?" she asked, over her shoulder.

"Because it's the same kind of a procession we had around the parade-ground, and I enjoyed that so much."

Beatrice apparently had not heard, for she went on at the same leisurely pace. At her right, touched here and there with silver, the lake lay like a sheet of dusky pearl. Far in the east was spread the glowing tapestry of dawn, and the rising wind stirred the girl's hair faintly as she looked across the water, with the sunrise reflected on her face.

Ronald saw her pure, proud profile, touched to exceeding beauty by the magic light of morning, and an unconscious, childish wistfulness in the lines of her mouth. A lump came into his throat and he swallowed hard. The morning was in his blood, and he had a quick sense of uplifting, as if his heart had suddenly found its wings.

Then Beatrice turned still more toward him. "It's beautiful, isn't it?" she asked, softly.

All of her harshness seemed to have fallen from her; she was radiant and exquisitely womanly in this new mood, and the boy's soul knelt in worship.

"Why wouldn't you let me come alone?"

"Because I didn't want you frightened," he answered.

71

The dimple at the corner of her mouth was barely manifest as she said, demurely, "You should have stayed, then; for you are the one who frightened me."

"I'm sorry," he said. "I told you that before."

"Yes, I know." She sighed, and added, "It was awful, though, and I shall never forget it."

"Neither shall I."

He was beside her now, for the trail had widened, and he put his hand upon the small white one that held Queen's bridle.

"That day," he said huskily, "you put your hand in mine,—when we met the Captain,—a little, cold hand."

She nodded, but did not take her hand away. "I was dreadfully frightened then, and you saved me."

His blood leaped in his veins. "That's nothing—I'd do more than that for you, any time. I had my reward before I had earned it."

The girl's violet eyes opened wide. "I don't understand."

"Have you forgotten that I had my arm around you, just for a minute? I have dreamed of it ever since—dear."

For an instant she saw him as if he had been a young Greek god, strangely met in the fields of Arcady; then the glamour passed and he was only an awkward soldier in a shabby uniform. She cut Queen with her riding-whip and went furiously ahead, but a boyish, troubled face was close beside her.

"Have I offended you?"

Beatrice smiled with calm superiority. "You shouldn't say such things," she replied; "you're far too young."

"Huh!" he retorted, with spirit, "I'm twenty-five!"

"Twenty-five?" she repeated incredulously; "I don't believe it. Why, I'm twenty myself, and I never thought you were more than eighteen."

She laughed wickedly as she saw him squirm. Through long experience she had found that shaft one of the most effective in her repertory, which was not by any means limited. More than once it had quenched an incipient declaration as effectually as if it had been a shower of cold water.

They rode in silence till they reached the Fort. "Shall I take you across?" he asked.

"No, thank you; I can go by myself, if there is no military order against it; but you may take Queen to the stables, if you like."

She dismounted, taking no note of his proffered assistance, and went to the river without another word. He watched her until she landed, then turned away, leading Queen. "A rose, a little rose," he said to himself; "but, oh, the thorns!"

When Beatrice arrived, she found the family in a state of high excitement. Mackenzie was just preparing to go over to the Fort and ask that a search party be sent out to look for her. He had surmised that she had returned to Fort Wayne until he found that none of her things were missing, and he received her explanation in stolid silence.

"Why didn't you tell us, Bee?" asked Mrs. Mackenzie. "You gave us all a fright."

"Dear Aunt Eleanor," she cooed, rubbing her soft cheek against Mrs. Mackenzie's, "I'm so sorry. I didn't know I was going till I got ready to start,—I never know,—and I did not dream that any one would care."

Robert had been conducting a private search on his own account, and a tell-tale relief crossed his face when he came in and found her at the breakfast table.

"Were you worried about me, Cousin Rob?"

The deep, vibrant contralto voice thrilled him, but he told his lie well. "No," he answered, carelessly, "of course not. Why should I be?"

The new mood of softness lasted all day. Beatrice did not stop to analyse, but she was dimly conscious that something strange had happened to her. At twilight she went out on the piazza, humming happily to herself, and Robert smiled at her as she came toward the open window of his room.

He had an old sword in his hand and was rubbing the thin blade with a handkerchief. "What are you doing?" she asked, curiously.

"Just cleaning this."

"Is it yours?"

"Yes, it is now; but it was my grandfather's." He straightened instinctively, as if in answer to some far-away bugle, and looked at her without seeming to see. "He fought at Lexington."

His voice betrayed his pride of blood, and his nostrils dilated with a quick, inward breath. His hands moved lovingly along the keen blade—and then Beatrice humbled herself.

"Cousin Rob," she began, impulsively, "I want to tell you something. I'm sorry and ashamed for——"

Scarlet signals were flaming in her cheeks, and he interrupted her. "Say no more about it," he said generously; "we were all unaccountably excited, and at such times we say and do things that otherwise we would not. Forget about it."

"I'll be glad to," she answered earnestly; but in her heart of hearts she knew she was not forgiven.

# CHAPTER X
# A GLEAM AFAR

As warm weather approached, the children grew restless under so much schooling, and Robert made Saturday a holiday. In order to help his uncle more efficiently, he was trying to learn the Indian tongue, but found it far more difficult than Greek and Latin, and made many ludicrous mistakes. Mackenzie was very patient with him, and Black Partridge made occasional comments and suggestions, being deeply flattered by the college man's desire to learn from him.

The trader had told him of the great school in the East, where Forsyth had learned everything that was written down in books, and yet could not talk with the Indians, or make a fire by rubbing sticks together; and the implied superiority of the chief had its own subtle gratification.

The women at the Fort were very fond of Beatrice, and she made daily visits there, but time began to hang heavily upon her hands. Without knowing why, she was restless and unhappy, and, after the manner of her sex, attributed it to some hidden illness of the body rather than the mind.

"I feel as if I simply must go somewhere or do something," she said to Doctor Norton, in a vain effort to explain her unrest.

He examined her pulse and tongue, then laughed at her. "You're all right," he said; "there's nothing on earth the matter with you."

"There is, too," she contradicted. "I don't feel right and I need medicine."

"Quinine?"

She made a wry face. "No, I don't need that."

"Sulphur and molasses?"

Beatrice turned up her nose in high disdain. "Is that all you can think of?"

"No," replied the Doctor, "I have other remedies, but I want to give you something that would please you. If you feel that you need medicine, my entire stock is at your service. I ask only for the right to supervise your selection, as we don't want you poisoned."

They were sitting on the piazza, and the girl's laugh reached the schoolroom and set the teacher's heart to throbbing. He could steel himself against her smiles and her playful pouting, but when she laughed, he was lost.

"I don't think you'd care much," observed Beatrice, "whether I was poisoned or not, just so you didn't have to give up any of your precious medicines. You're selfish—that's all."

"What more can I do, Miss Manning? I've offered you all my worldly goods. Which bottle do you want?"

"Thank you, I've decided not to rob you. I'll die, if I have to, without medical aid."

"Some people prefer it," murmured Norton.

"How did you happen to come here?" she asked abruptly.

He started slightly, remembering the face that led him, like a star, from one frontier post to another, but he merely said: "An army surgeon has no choice. We go where we are sent by the powers that be."

"I'd hate to be sent anywhere."

"I believe you," replied the Doctor, smiling; "and if you were told you couldn't go anywhere that place would immediately become desirable."

"Wonderful insight," commented Beatrice. "Or perhaps some one has told you?"

"No, I don't always have to be told. I can see some things, you know."

"That's what Katherine told me. She said you could see through anything or anybody, especially a woman. Your glance goes right through us and ties in a bow-knot behind. I can feel the strings dangling from my shoulders now."

Robert came to the door, followed by the children, who were eager to get outdoors for the short recess they had every day. Beatrice had a little insight of her own, and had noted the change in Norton's face when Katherine was mentioned, and the quick, inquiring look in Robert's eyes as he greeted them both.

"Forsyth," said the Doctor, "I'm going now, and I turn this refractory patient over to you. She needs to get outdoors and walk till she drops—it's the only cure for impudence. Will you see that she does it?"

"Certainly, if she will go with me."

"I'll go," put in Beatrice, "if I have to take medicine."

They watched the Doctor until he started across the river. "Perhaps," said Robert, "you'd rather some one else would go with you. If so, it can be easily arranged."

"Now, Cousin Rob," said the girl, coaxingly, "don't be horrid to me. You're the only cousin I have, except Katherine and the infants; and as long as I'm here you'd better make the best of me."

His heart suddenly contracted. "Are you going away?"

"I can't," she laughed. "I have nowhere to go."

Robert smiled curiously. "When do you want to go, and where?"

"Saturday morning," she replied; "to the woods, after flowers."

"Very well," he said, quietly, turning away.

To one of them the days passed slowly, but on Saturday, when Beatrice expressed surprise at the rapid flight of time, Forsyth unhesitatingly chimed in. She looked at him narrowly when she thought he did not know it, and put him down as a self-absorbed prig.

She was at odds with herself when they started, but it was one of those rare mornings which May sets like a jewel upon the rosary of the year. They walked north along the lake shore, and, since silence seemed to suit her, he wisely said nothing.

Gradually peace crept into her heart, and as they approached the woods they turned to the west, where white blossoms were set on thorny boughs and budded maples were crimson with new leaves.

"You were good to bring me here," she said gratefully; "it seems like an enchanted way."

"I am glad to give you pleasure," he replied conventionally.

The ground was still hidden under the brown leaves of October, that rustled gently with a passing breeze or echoed the fairy tread of the Little People of the Forest, playing hide-and-seek in the wake of Spring. As Beatrice walked ahead of him, it seemed to Forsyth that she belonged to the woods, as truly as did the nymphs and dryads of old.

Buttercups scattered garish gold around them, and beyond, among the trees, the wild geranium rose on its slender stalk, making a phantom bit of colour against the background of dead leaves. Between the mossy stumps budded mandrakes were huddled closely together, afraid to bloom till others had led the way. Beatrice looked around her and drew a long breath, then gently stroked a satin bud upon a bare stalk of hickory.

"Why don't you pick something?" asked Robert, with a laugh. "That's what we came for, isn't it?"

"No, I can't pick things. I feel as if I were hurting them. Suppose you lived here in this lovely place and a giant came along and broke you off at the waist to take your head home with him—how do you suppose you'd feel?"

"I don't think I'd feel anything after the break. Besides, that's not a fair hypothesis. There is no real analogy."

"Hy-poth-e-sis," repeated Beatrice, looking at him, mischievously; "did I pronounce it right?"

"Of course—why?"

"Because," she answered, with her eyes dancing, "it's a nice word and I'd like to learn it. I want to say it to Doctor Norton. Some of his words are as long at that, but they're not nearly so complicated, and I yearn to excel in his own specialty."

76

The girl's mock reverence for his learning irritated him unspeakably, and he closed his lips in a thin, tight line.

"Cousin Rob," she said, putting her hand on his arm, and with bewildering kindness in her tone, "can't you take me just as I am?"

The temptation to take her, just as she was, into his arms, made him draw back a step or two. "I always make a point of that," he said, clearing his throat.

Then a vista opened before them, which might have been a field of Paradise. Across the plain, where the dead goldenrod of Autumn still lingered, there were white blossoms on invisible branches, set against the turquoise sky, as still as stars of frost. It was as though a cloud of white butterflies had paused for an instant, with every dusty wing longing for flight.

Great white triliums bloomed in clusters farther on, with here and there a red one, lonely as a lost child. Far to the right was a little hollow filled with wild phlox, shading from white to deepest lavender, and breathing the haunting fragrance which no one ever forgets.

"Let's go to the lake," she said.

Tall bluffs rose on either side where they turned eastward, with triliums and dog-tooth violets within easy reach, and a robin's cheery chirp was answered by another far away. Slanting sunbeams came like arrows of light into the shadow of the woods, and at the shore line was an expanse of sand which shone like silver under the white light of noon.

"Why do you stand there?" asked Beatrice. "Why don't you sit down?"

"I was just looking at something."

"What?"

"Come here—perhaps you can see."

She strained her eyes in the direction he indicated, but unsuccessfully. "I don't see anything," she said; "what is it like?"

"I don't know. It's something shiny, but it isn't a bird, because it doesn't move."

"Birds aren't shiny, anyway," objected Beatrice. "Let's eat our lunch."

"I'm willing, for it's getting heavy, and I'd rather carry it inside."

Beatrice laughed until the tears rolled down her cheeks. "That's the first time I ever heard you say anything funny," she said, wiping her eyes. "Mr. Ronald is always saying funny things."

A dubious smile crossed Robert's face, and there was a long silence. "I wish you'd show me that shiny thing again, Cousin Rob," she said at length; "I'm interested in it."

"You didn't seem to be."

"That's because I was hungry," she explained. "I feel better now, and by the time we've finished our lunch I'll be absorbingly interested in it."

Robert stood on the sand, in the same place as before, and saw the silvery gleam again. Then she took his place and saw it, too. "Why," she said, "isn't it queer? Do you think it's the sun on a birch?"

"No, it's too high, and birches don't often grow on the very edge of the shore."

"That isn't the edge."

"Well, it's near it. The light just hangs in the air. There doesn't seem to be anything behind it. I've often seen stray gleams in the woods and tried to find them, but I never found anything. It's a daylight will-o'-the-wisp."

"Let's follow this one," suggested Beatrice.

They walked along the hard sand, close to the water, stopping every few steps to find the gleam. Sometimes it was only a thread of light, detached and unrelated to anything around it, then in other places it was a white glare, like the reflection thrown from a mirror.

Often they lost it, but found it again a little farther on. Beatrice was tired but determined, and kept on for what seemed miles. Then they stopped several times without finding it. "Let's go up into the woods," she said; "perhaps we'll see it again from there."

They climbed the steep bluff of sand, with the aid of bushes and cotton wood saplings, and for an instant caught the light again, then it vanished. The girl was pale, and Robert feared they had come too far.

"We'll go back," he said, "as soon as you rest for a little while. Why didn't you tell me you were tired?"

"Because I'm not," she retorted. "I'm willing to rest a little while, but I'm going to find it."

They sat down under the spreading branches of an elm for a few minutes, then, in spite of his expostulations, Beatrice started north again. "We can walk till midnight," he pleaded, "without finding it, and it's foolish, anyway."

"No, it isn't; see there!"

In the air, between the bluff and the lake, hung a shimmering thread of light which seemed close by, and all at once he became as eager as she. They walked rapidly for a few moments, then Beatrice stopped.

"Why," she said, in a high key, "it's a house!"

"Be careful," warned Robert, "we'd better go back."

"I'm not going back till I see. I've come too far!"

A little farther on, they came to it. Set far back into the bluff, so that only the face of it was visible, was a little one-roomed cabin, built of logs. The door was open, but the place was empty, as Beatrice discovered. "Come in," she said hospitably.

"We'd better go back," said Forsyth, warningly. "Come!"

"I will, in just a minute."

She took a long look about the room, then came out. From the top of the cabin, which projected only a foot or so from the bluff, and suspended from a whittled branch not quite weather-worn, hung a silver cross, fully eight inches high, with a wondrously moulded figure of the Christ stretched upon it.

Robert's eyes followed hers, and for a few minutes neither spoke. "That's what we saw," she murmured, in a low tone; "that's the light that led us here—the sun upon the cross!"

"Come," said Robert, firmly, taking her by the arm.

Reluctantly she let him lead her away, and they turned south, keeping close to the lake shore, but out of the sand.

"Who lives there?" she asked.

"Why, I don't know—how should I?"

"It was neat inside, and there was blue clay and chips in the cracks, just as there is at home. There was a fireplace, too, but I didn't see any chimney."

"There was a chimney, though, of some dark-coloured stone. It looked like a stump on the bluff. I noticed it while you were inside."

"There's no dark-coloured stone around here."

"Then it must have been limestone darkened with mud. I didn't get near enough to see."

"Somebody lives there," said Beatrice. "There was a narrow bed, with a blue-and-white patchwork quilt upon it, and two chairs made out of barrels, and a little table and shelves,—do you think Indians live there?"

"It's possible. Some of them may be more civilised than the rest and prefer to live in a house—in the Winter, at least," he added, remembering the panes of glass in the front of the house, either side of the door.

"It's queer that a cross like that should be there."

"Stolen," he suggested promptly, "from some Catholic church in the wilderness."

"I'll tell you what," she said, after a long silence; "let's say nothing about it to any one—just keep it a secret for the present. What do you say?"

"I'm willing." The idea of a secret with his pretty cousin was far from unpleasant to Robert.

"Because, if the others knew, some of the soldiers would go there—Mr. Ronald would be the first one. Besides, I've noticed that if you really want to find out about anything, you always can, though it takes time. I'd rather we'd find out by ourselves, wouldn't you?"

Robert thought he would.

"I think," she continued, "that some of the Indians live there, as you said, and that the cross was stolen and hung over the door for an ornament. Perhaps Black Partridge lives there—he seems to know more than the rest."

"Yes; that's possible. Anyhow, we'll find out without asking anybody,—is that it?"

"That's a bargain. Whoever lives there doesn't want to be bothered, for you can't see the house at all except from the shore; and in Summer, when the canoes are passing, it must be pretty well hidden by the saplings and the undergrowth on the ledge in front of it. There's just one place there where anybody can get down—a steep little path, worn smooth."

"You saw a great deal in a few minutes, didn't you?" asked Robert, admiringly.

"Of course," she answered, with a toss of her head. "A woman can see more in one minute than a man can see in sixty—didn't you know that?"

"I didn't, but I do now."

Silver-winged gulls glistened in the sun for a moment, then plunged into the cool softness below. A rabbit track wound a leisurely way across the sand and disappeared at the bluff. Down a ravine came a tiny stream, murmuring sleepily all along its way to the lake.

Beatrice sighed and her eyes drooped. "Take me home," she said.

The blue of the water grew deeper, then changed to grey. The white clouds turned to rose and gold, touched with royal purple, and the wings of the gulls no longer shone. A bluejay with slow-beating wings sank to his nest in a lofty maple, and, somewhere, a robin chirped mournfully, as if he, too, were tired.

At last they came to the edge of the woods and saw the house, with the four tall poplars at the gate, the shimmering gold of sunset upon the river, and the Fort beyond. The exquisite peace of the woods had been like that of another sphere. There was a twittering of little birds in swaying nests, a sudden chill, a shadow, and a mist. The fairy patter was hurried and hushed, the rustling leaves were quiet, and she leaned wearily upon his arm.

"Tired?" he asked tenderly.

"Yes," she answered, smiling back at him, "but happy. Thank you for a perfect day."

# CHAPTER XI
# A JUNE DAY

On a warm morning in June, Beatrice took her despised sewing under an unwilling arm and went over to Mrs. Howard's. Mrs. Franklin was there also, and they all sat on the porch, under the impression that it was cooler there than indoors.

"I wish you girls would show me how this goes," pleaded Beatrice. She was making herself a gown of pink calico, and encountering new difficulties at every turn.

"Where's your pattern," asked Katherine.

"I haven't any map," returned Beatrice; "I lost it. I sawed this out by an old one."

"It looks as if it had been sawed," laughed Mrs. Franklin. "Why didn't you ask Mrs. Mackenzie to help you cut it?"

"Because I didn't want Aunt Eleanor to be ashamed of me."

"She doesn't mind us," put in Katherine.

"Stop teasing," commanded Beatrice, "and show me how to put the thing together. Which piece goes where?"

Mrs. Franklin took the skirt and Katherine went to work at the waist, pinning and basting firmly, so that there could be no mistake in the result. Beatrice leaned lazily against the side of the house and watched them admiringly, praising their skill now and then in accents suspiciously soft.

"She's been taking lessons from George," remarked Mrs. Franklin. "That's the way he gets things done."

"Speaking of angels——" said Katherine.

Ronald crossed the parade-ground and joined the group. "What's that thing?" he asked, contemptuously indicating the pink calico.

"It's clothes," replied Beatrice, with spirit; "don't you wish you were going to have new ones?"

The Ensign's answering laugh had a hollow sound to it, for the shabby clothing at Fort Dearborn was a sore spot with both officers and men, even though new and proper raiment was said to be on the way.

"You might make me some," he suggested, "and I'll promise to encourage you while you do it."

"No, thank you," she returned loftily; "you'd be in the way."

"I expect I'm in the way now," he observed, making himself more comfortable against the pillar of the porch. "When needles fly, women's tongues fly faster; when women sew, they rip their husbands to pieces."

A faint flush came into Mrs. Franklin's face as she bent over her work.

"I'll wager, now," continued Ronald, "that when you saw me coming, you had to change the subject. Mrs. Franklin was explaining the vagaries of the Captain, Mrs. Howard was telling what she was obliged to put up with, and Miss Manning was talking about me."

The implication sharpened the edge of the girl's tongue. "You ought to be very glad you're not married," she said sweetly; "and it goes without saying that you never will be. Nobody on earth would have you!"

"Don't quarrel, children," put in Katherine, hastily. "Here comes Ralph."

The Lieutenant sat down opposite Ronald and wiped his forehead. "Lord!" he exclaimed, "isn't it hot!"

"Get a little closer to Miss Manning," advised the Ensign. "She's in an icy mood this morning."

Beatrice and Howard smiled at each other understandingly. "Be careful what you say," warned Mrs. Franklin; "they've decided that they're cousins."

"Yes," replied the Lieutenant, "we've got it all settled. We're step-cousins-in-law once removed. Want to go for a ride, Ronald? Forsyth and I are going a little way down the trail."

"Which trail?"

"Fort Wayne, of course."

"Yes, I'll go," said the Ensign, rising; "it can't be any hotter on horseback than it is here."

When the three men rode off, Beatrice pouted. "Why didn't they ask me to go?"

"I guess they're going swimming," returned Mrs. Franklin, "for Mr. Forsyth had some towels."

"Here's your waist," said Katherine; "did you shrink the goods?"

"Did I what?"

"Shrink it. Wash it, you know."

"Indeed I didn't. Why should I wash it when it's new?"

"Here's your skirt," said Mrs. Franklin. "You'd better make a narrow hem and run atuck or two above it so you can let it down. I'm going home now, because Wallace is all alone. Good-bye."

Beatrice went to work gingerly, and Mrs. Howard watched her for a few moments, then took pity. "I'll help you," she said, "I have nothing else to do."

The work progressed rapidly, and they went into the house frequently to fit the gown. "I can wear it to-night, I believe," said the girl, delightedly. "I didn't know sewing was so easy!"

"Don't be too hopeful—there's lots to do yet."

Noon came on apace and the heat increased. Shimmering waves hung over the parade-ground and vibrated visibly. There was not a tree within the enclosure of the Fort, and the flag hung limply from the staff, stirring only when the hot wind from the south-west swept over the sandy plains.

Doctor Norton came out, looked around the deserted Fort, and crossed to Lieutenant Howard's.

"Where are you going?" asked Beatrice, indicating an Indian basket he was carrying.

"I'm going to the woods—primarily, to find a cool place, and, secondarily, to gather roots and simples. Some of my medicines have given out and I'm going to make a new supply if I can find the proper plants."

Katherine was sewing busily and took no part in the conversation, but there was a scarlet signal on either cheek.

"If you get enough of anything," said Beatrice, "the poor souls under your care can have some of it, can't they?"

"Certainly."

"What do you expect to get around here?"

"Oh, lots of things. Wild ginger, for instance—would you like some of that?"

"Don't care for it," she answered conclusively.

"Would you like a concoction of May apples?"

"I believe I would—it sounds well."

"My dear girl," said Norton, seriously, "the root of the mandrake is such a deadly poison that the Indians give it to their enemies."

"I must remember that," murmured the girl. "I may need it for mine."

The Doctor laughed, then turned to Mrs. Howard. "Are you well?" he asked anxiously.

Katherine's eyes met his. "Yes," she answered, but her voice was scarcely audible. There was an uneasy moment for both of them, then he went away.

Beatrice took up her sewing again and saw that Katherine's hands were trembling. "He's an abrupt person," she said; "don't you think so?"

"Yes," answered the other, in a low tone.

"He's lovable in a way, though, don't you think so? I wonder why he has never married?"

Katherine started and her lips moved, but there was no sound. Beatrice looked into her face for an illuminating instant—then she knew.

"Katherine!" she cried, in horror.

Mrs. Howard dropped her work and fled into the house, trying to lock the door, but the girl was too quick for her.

"Katherine, dear!" cried Beatrice, with her arms around the trembling woman, "don't be afraid of me! You poor child, don't you know a friend when you see one?"

"Friend?" repeated Katherine, in a rush of unwilling tears; "I have none!"

"Yes you have, dear; now listen to me. I'm your friend, and there's nothing in the world that could make me anything else. Tell me, and let me help you!"

The words brought back the memory of another day, when the winter snows lay deep upon the ground, and a man's voice, dangerously tender, said the same thing.

"There's nothing wrong, Bee—don't, oh, don't think that of me!"

"I couldn't, dear—no one could!"

The curtains were drawn and the house was dark and comparatively cool. Within that soothing shadow, Katherine gathered courage to face the girl, and, little by little, hint at the tempest raging in her soul.

It was the old, common story of a proud woman with a hungry heart, denied love and sympathy where she had a right to expect it, and tempted unwillingly, but tempted none the less.

"Men are beasts!" exclaimed Beatrice, angrily.

"Don't say that, Bee! Ralph has a great deal to bother him, but I can't help wishing he were different. If he were only as he used to be! If I knew, or even thought he loved me—if he would try to understand me—if he wouldn't always misjudge me—but now——"

"You're brave enough to fight it out and win, Kit—I know you are!"

"I hope so; but what hurts me most is the fear that he—that he knows—that I—that I care—and pities me!"

"Who? Ralph?"

"No—the—the——"

"I understand," said Beatrice, quickly; "you mustn't let him know. Besides, you don't really care. Women often mistake loneliness for something else—don't you think so?"

"Perhaps. Oh, if he would only go away, where I would never see him again—if he only would—sometime, in the long years, things would come right between Ralph and me!"

"You'll have to wait, Kit. Life is made up of waiting, for women, and it's the hardest thing for us to do. Oh, I know," continued Beatrice, with a harsh laugh; "I fought something out myself once, but I won. It was hard, but I did it, and I'd do it again—I wouldn't be coward enough to run away. When things hurt you, you don't have to let anybody know. You can shut your lips tight, and if you bite your tongue hard it keeps back the tears. I always pretend I'm a rock, with the waves beating against me. Let it hurt inside, if it wants to—you don't have to let anybody see!"

The girl's fine courage insensibly strengthened the woman. "I'm so glad you know," she sighed.

"I'm glad, too. I'm going now, Kit, and I wish you'd lie down a little while. Don't forget I'm your friend, and I'll always help you when I can, and anyhow, I'll always try."

It was characteristic of Beatrice that she went home without any demonstrative farewell. She had been gentle, sympathetic, and genuinely sorry for her cousin, but there was an inner hardness somewhere which the other felt.

Overwrought by emotion, Katherine slept for hours, and when she awoke a cool breeze had risen from the lake and was moving her white curtains to and fro. Dull sorrow was gnawing at her heart, but the stab was gone.

She dressed and went out, without any particular object in view. The loneliness of the house depressed her, and she felt that she must get away from it; yet she did not wish to talk to any one.

As she went toward the gate the Captain's wife met her. "Where are you going?" she asked.

"To—to the little lad," faltered Katherine.

"Oh," said the other, quickly, turning away as if she had been hurt. For a moment the childless woman envied the other her grave.

Half a mile from the Fort, in a hollow near the river, was a little mound, marked only by a rude slab of limestone and the willow that grew above it. At the sight of it her eyes filled.

"Oh, Baby," she sobbed, pressing her face against the cold turf above him, "I wish I was down there beside you, as still and as dreamless as you! You don't know what it means—you never would have known! Oh, I'd rather be a stone than a woman with a heart!"

"Katherine!" cried a man's voice beside her; "Katherine!" Norton's arm lifted her from the grave and held her close. "Dear heart," he said, "is the world unkind?"

She drew away from him, but he still held her cold hand in his. "My heart aches for you, Katherine—can't you tell me?"

"You never lost a child," she whispered, clutching at the straw.

"That is true, but I have lost far more. I——" He stopped and bit his lips upon the words that struggled for utterance. "Come away," he said, gently.

---

He led her to the bank of the stream, where they sat down under a tree. She leaned against it, unconscious that he still held her hand.

There was a long silence, in which she regained, in some measure, her self-control. "I can't think what's wrong with me," she sighed. "I've cried more in the last six months than in all my life before. I'm not the crying kind—naturally, that is."

"Don't think about that, for nature knows a great deal more than we do. Cry all you want to, and thank God you have no grief beyond the reach of tears."

"Beyond—tears?"

"Yes; there is another kind, which I am glad you do not know. It cuts and burns and stings till it is the very refinement of torture, and there is no veil of mist to blind the eyes."

She looked at him curiously. "You——?"

"Yes," he answered, with his head bowed; "that is the kind of grief I know the best."

"I—I'm sorry," she said, stirred to pity.

"Why should you be sorry for me?" he asked, with a rare smile. "There are countless joys in the world, but the griefs are few and old. The humblest of us can find new happiness, but there has been no increase of sorrow since the world was first made. There is a fixed and unvariable quantity of it, and we take turns bearing it—that's all. Nothing comes to any of us that some one before us has not met like a soldier, bravely and well."

"You are strong, but I have no strength."

"There are different kinds of strength, Katherine, and of these the one most to be prized is what we call endurance, for lack of a better word. One can always bear a little more, for we live only one day at a time, and to-morrow may bring us new gifts of which we do not dream."

Lengthening shadows lay on the river and the sun hung low in the west, but they talked on. She forgot everything but the peace of the moment, which came to her sore heart like a benediction. Without knowing it, she was very near to happiness then.

The Doctor's voice was soothing, as if he were talking to a child, and she did not dream that he was fighting the exquisite danger of her nearness with all the power at his command. At last she leaned forward with her eyes shining, and put her hand on his. "Thank you," she said, softly, "for helping me!"

The man's blood leaped in his veins, and he sprang to his feet. He walked back and forth on the bank of the river for some time before he dared trust himself to speak.

"Your happiness is very near to me," he said, trying hard to keep his voice even, "you must always remember that. And for me, it is enough to be near you, even if——"

She stretched out her hands and he lifted her to her feet. "I must go," she said.

"Yes, you must go, and go alone. I will stay here until you have had time to get back."

The deference to circumstances jarred upon her and she did not answer. Her hat was lying by the child's grave, and as he picked it up for her, she said: "Why, there are violets all around. I never saw those before."

"Didn't you?" he asked diffidently; "I thought you came often."

"No," she said, in a low voice, "not very often. Who put them there?"

He lowered his eyes at her question, and then she understood. "Did you plant flowers on my baby's grave?" she cried.

There was a tense moment before he dared to look at her. "Yes," he answered, slowly, "because——"

They were standing face to face, with the little grave between them, and the woman's heart quivered with a strange and terrible joy. There was no need of words, for, all at once, she knew why, during the four years of her marriage, he had followed her from one post to another. She saw a new meaning in his sympathy when the little lad died and her husband blamed her so bitterly; moreover, she knew that her battle was with herself, not him, for the unyielding edge of Honour lay between them, and, even if she would, he would not let her cross.

For his part he, too, was uplifted, because without words she understood, and answered with love in her eyes. Undisguised and unashamed, her heart leaped toward him, but he stood with his hands clenched so tightly that the nails cut deep into the flesh.

Neither had heard nor seen, but she felt an alien presence, and turned. Not six feet away from them stood Lieutenant Howard, with his face ashen grey. He had an armful of flowers—purple flags and yellow lilies from the marsh and clover from the fields.

When he knew that she saw him, he came to the grave, stooped, and put the flowers upon it. The Doctor stepped back, but Howard took no note of him whatever. "It is a strange place for a tryst," he said, with forced calmness. "Katherine, will you come home?"

They went all the way to the Fort without speaking, and when they reached their own house, he stood aside for her to enter, then followed her in and locked the door.

Trembling with weakness, he sat down and drew her toward him. "Katherine, have you anything to say to me?"

Strangely enough, she was not afraid, and the terrible joy was still surging in her heart.

"Only this, Ralph—that you have wronged me and misjudged me; but you know this—that I never told you a lie in my life. As long as I bear your name I will bear it rightly; while I call myself your wife, you may know that I am faithful to you and to myself. That is all I have to say, but for your sake and my own—and for the little lad's sake—be just a little kind to me!"

Her voice broke at the last words, but he rushed past her and went out. From the window of her room she saw him pacing back and forth on the plains beyond the Fort, fighting his battle with himself. She knew she had hurt him past all healing and pitied him subconsciously; the dominant knowledge warred with her instincts.

When he came in to supper, his face was still pale, but his voice was even and controlled. He ate but little, and they talked commonplaces until afterward.

"Katherine," he said, "I remove the embargo; you may have—him—or any of your other friends at the house as often as you please. I will not force my wife to make clandestine appointments outside!" He laughed harshly and went out, but, though she waited for him till long past midnight, he did not return.

For her there was no rest. Pity, shame, fear, pride, and ecstasy struggled for mastery in her soul. The sound of moving waters murmured through the night with insistent repetition as the waves came to the shore. In the dark hours before dawn she saw a man, indistinctly, walking on the prairie, with his hands clasped behind him and his head bowed.

At first she thought it was Ralph, but, straining her eyes through the darkness, she saw that it was the other, and her heart beat hard with pain.

"Dear God," she murmured brokenly, "oh, give him peace, and help me to be true!"

# CHAPTER XII
# IN THE NORTH WOODS

"Come on, Doc," said Ronald.

"Where?" asked Norton, lazily.

"Across the river, of course; don't you see the mob over there?"

The large yard in front of the Mackenzie house was fairly well filled with people when they arrived. Mr. and Mrs. Mackenzie, Forsyth, Chandonnais, Lieutenant and Mrs. Howard, and Mrs. Franklin were standing behind Beatrice, who was painting in water colours. Black Partridge, in all the glory of his feather head-dress and his most gorgeous blanket, was posing for his picture. The chief endeavoured to preserve the appearance of calm, but in reality he was greatly excited.

Doctor Norton and the Lieutenant exchanged cool salutations, and Katherine was scarcely more cordial. All three of them had decided to ignore past events, but there was an element of difficulty in the situation, none the less.

"How do you suppose Birdie can wear a blanket in July?" asked Ronald. "I should think he'd be roasted to a turn."

"It's his best blanket," explained Beatrice, selecting another brush, "and he wants it in his picture."

"I'd rather my clothes would be painted separately on a day like this," murmured Ronald.

"I didn't know you had more than one suit," remarked the artist, with a flourish of her brush; "you can't properly say 'clothes.'"

"Well, 'clo', then," retorted the Ensign, "if it suits you better; but some day you'll see me in a brand-new uniform."

"It's what I'm living for," answered Beatrice. "Somebody get me some more water."

A dozen hands were outstretched, but it was Forsyth who secured the cup, and he was rewarded with a radiant smile when he returned.

"Ain't that smart, now!" exclaimed the trader, delightedly, as the unmistakable features of Black Partridge appeared upon the paper. Chandonnais was grinning broadly, and even Ronald and the Lieutenant condescended to praise.

"To think that we've had a real artist here for months and never knew it!" exclaimed Mrs. Franklin. "Why didn't you let us know about it before?"

"Because," answered the girl, "as an old lady at Fort Mackinac would have said, I didn't 'feel to paint.'"

Mrs. Mackenzie was restraining the children with difficulty, for each and every one of them yearned to take a brush and assist in the delicate task. At last she took the baby and went into the house, leaving Maria Indiana to Katherine, and the two older children to their father and Forsyth.

"There," said Beatrice, with a critical squint at her work; "it's almost done."

Against a background of delicate green, the Indian, in his scarlet blanket, stood boldly and properly pictured. The colouring was very good and she had caught the spirit of the pose.

"Let me show it to him," suggested Robert.

She was wiping her brushes and did not see the expression of dismay on the chief's face when he beheld his counterfeit presentment, but she saw him snatch the picture out of Robert's hand and heard his indistinct mutterings when he fled like a deer.

"Well, what do you think of that!" she gasped. "What was he saying, Uncle John?"

"I didn't catch it, Bee—did you, Rob?"

Forsyth had made a little progress in the language, but had understood only a word or two. "It was something about the 'Great Spirit,' I think, but I didn't get the connection."

"That's gone, anyhow," said the Doctor. "You meant it for him, didn't you?"

"Why, yes, eventually; but it wasn't done."

"It was done enough for him, evidently," observed Ronald; "he seems to prefer his pictures a little rare. Are you ready to make mine now?"

"Indeed, I'm not going to paint you. I'm going in to help Aunt Eleanor."

Mrs. Howard followed her. The Doctor offered to row Mrs. Franklin across the river, Chan disappeared, and the Lieutenant went over to the Agency House with Mackenzie. Ronald looked at Forsyth and laughed.

"Everybody's moving," he said. "Let's go over and get Major and go swimming."

"You go after Major," suggested Robert, "and I'll get some towels of Aunt Eleanor. We'll go up north."

Ronald embarked in a pirogue and Forsyth went into the house. "I don't see where it's gone to," Mrs. Mackenzie was saying. "Are you sure you haven't it, Katherine?"

"What have you lost, Aunt Eleanor?" he asked.

"Why, my blue-and-white patchwork quilt—a white one with blue stars in it. It was washed and put away clean last Fall, and now it's gone."

90

Beatrice was looking at him in a way that puzzled him. "I'm sure I haven't seen it," he hastened to say. "Am I suspected?"

"Of course not," returned Mrs. Mackenzie; "but it's a strange thing to happen right here in the house. I wish you'd go up to the loft and see if it's on Chan's bed—he may have taken it by mistake."

Forsyth climbed the ladder to the empty loft, but no quilt was to be seen. The rude shakedown on which the half-breed slept had only blankets for covering. He looked around curiously, for he had never been in the loft before, but he did not envy Chan his quarters. There was only one window in the desolate place, and that scarcely deserved the name, for it was merely a small aperture in the front of the house. The floor was comparatively clean, but there was a pile of rubbish in one corner, which he promptly investigated. He had hardly expected to find the quilt, but he was surprised when he discovered a ham, a side of bacon, and a large piece of dark blue calico hidden under the nondescript heap.

"I expect he gets hungry in the night," thought Robert, remembering Chan's ferocious appetite.

"No quilt there, Aunt Eleanor," he said, when he went down. "May I have some towels?"

"The Indians must have taken it," she sighed, "but I don't know when nor how."

Beatrice was in a brown study, but Robert, even though he was gifted with rather more than the average man's discernment, did not know what she was thinking about. Remembering the conversation he had overheard the night of the barbecue, he had thought it likely that the cross over the door of the house in the woods had been stolen from the half-breed by an Indian, or else, after the manner of others somewhat higher in the social scale, Chan had taken unto himself an Indian wife.

Except as it concerned Beatrice, the matter did not interest him, and he forbore to tell her what he knew, lest the "secret" between them should come to an end. Her curiosity about the mysterious cabin had increased rather than diminished; but Robert had refused to go with her when she wanted to investigate it again, and she did not quite dare to go alone.

Ronald was waiting for him outside, and the dog trotted along beside them in high spirits, lavishing moist caresses upon his master, and punctuating his expressions of affection with exuberant barks.

"Down, Major, down!" commanded Ronald, "or I'll throw you into the lake."

The shadowy coolness of the woods was invigorating, and they walked on, heedless of the distance. "When we find a deep place," said Forsyth, "we'll dive into it from the bluff."

"No we won't," returned Ronald, conclusively. "I knew a fool once who broke his neck in just that way. No loss to the world particularly, but unpleasant. They'd miss us mightily at the Fort."

When Robert saw that they were approaching the neighbourhood of the cabin, he said that he was tired.

"So 'm I," answered the other. "Let's sit down and get cooled off before we go in."

Major was far ahead, ranging back and forth eagerly in pursuit of some small animal that had escaped him. "Something has happened," continued Ronald; "guess!"

"Couldn't guess—what is it?"

"That's right," laughed the Ensign, slapping his knee; "nobody could guess. We've actually got our new uniforms!"

"You don't say so! Where are they?"

"At Fort Wayne."

"Oh, you haven't got them, then?"

"No, but we've almost got 'em. Some of the boys are going this week sometime, as soon as the Captain can make up his mind to send 'em. I wish I could go, too, but they'll need nearly all the horses—fifty-eight new uniforms, you know. I've thought seriously of borrowing Miss Manning's horse and taking the trip—I need a change."

"She wouldn't let you have it."

"I hadn't intended to ask her," explained Ronald. "Lord, but she'd be mad! I'd give a pretty penny to see her when she found out I'd done it! I'd really rather see her good and mad than to take the trip, but I can't do both. If I have one pleasure, you'll have the other."

"I'd rather not, thank you—I'd much prefer to be out of the way of the storm. I hope you won't do it."

"Well, I'm not going to," said the Ensign; "at least, I don't think I am. I'm more or less subject to impulses, however."

A shrill feminine scream brought both men to their feet. "What was that?" cried Forsyth.

Major came toward them from the north, on a dead run, with his tail between his legs and panting for breath. "What's the matter, old boy?" shouted Ronald. The dog took shelter behind his master, trembling violently.

"He isn't hurt," said the Ensign, after looking him over carefully, "he's just scared. Do you think we'd better go up and see what's wrong?"

"No," answered Forsyth; "everything is quiet now. Major probably got into trouble with a squaw. It was a woman's scream."

"Maybe so," assented Ronald, sitting down again. "Anyhow, it was none of the women at the Fort, and I'm in favour of letting the Indians fight their own battles."

The dog, still frightened, insisted on lying uncomfortably close to his master. "Move over a bit, Major," he suggested; "you're too warm to sit by."

"He's all right," laughed Forsyth, as the dog refused to move; "let him alone."

"Do you know," said Ronald, after a silence, "that scream sounded like Mad Margaret's voice. Don't you think so?"

"Perhaps, now that you speak of it; but I haven't seen her for a long time."

"Neither have I, and I don't want to. Do you remember the night you came?"

Forsyth nodded.

"I can't get that out of my head—the way she looked at me when she told me I should never have my heart's desire. Someway, it sticks."

"You're not superstitious, are you?"

"Not exactly, but it was rather uncanny, if you remember,—at least it would have seemed so if she had said it to you."

"That's true," admitted Robert.

"I'm not afraid of anything in this world," resumed the Ensign; "but I don't want to tackle the next before I get to it—if there is any next."

"What do you think about the next world, anyway?"

"Well," answered Ronald, seriously, "I don't think much about it, and that's a fact. Nobody knows any more about it than anybody else, and I don't see why one man's opinion isn't as good as another's. Personally, I have always felt that if I was decent and honest and minded my own business, I'd get my share of anything good that night be coming after I got through here. Actions, to my mind, are a good deal more important than beliefs."

"That's so, too, but I've learned to keep pretty still about those things, for I've been accused more than once of too much liberality."

"The chaplain at West Point was a nice old fellow, and he used to tell us that if we were good soldiers and abided by the army regulations, we wouldn't get into trouble after we died. I've always remembered it and I've marched by it ever since."

"Let's go in now," suggested the other, after a long silence.

"All right—come on, Major!"

The sun was shining brightly on the water, and the dog barked joyously as they plunged in. "Keep him here," said Ronald, "I'm going on out." Robert watched him enviously as he swam north-east with a long, free stroke, until he was almost out of sight. The dog was eager to be after him, and, having no collar, was not easily controlled. When he came back, aglow with life, it seemed to the other that he had the clean-limbed beauty of a young Greek god.

"You go now," shouted Ronald, "and I'll amuse the pup."

Forsyth swam straight out, with an exultant sense of power in breasting the waves, and his pulses thrilled with something so vital, keen, and elemental that it seemed as if he could go on forever. When he turned back, he saw the gleam of light far to the northward, where the sun shone on the cross, and thought of Beatrice, happily, and of the day in the woods. He was well in toward shore when his muscles suddenly lost their strength—as if he had forgotten how to swim. He called once, but faintly, then unutterable darkness surrounded him.

When he came to his senses he was lying on the sand, and Ronald was rolling him over and over and pounding him vigorously. A whine sounded indistinct and far, as if it were leagues away, even while the dog was licking his face.

"My God, man," said the Ensign, with white lips, "I'd almost given you up!"

The voice beat painfully upon his ears and his senses were confused, but he tried to sit up. "What was the matter?" he gasped.

"Cramps, I guess—that's the usual thing. We'd better have let Major drown and gone out together. I had a nice time getting both of you back to shore."

Ronald continued his violent treatment until the other protested. "Don't hit me again," he said faintly, "I'm all right!"

"Pile into your clothes, then, or you'll take cold."

He obeyed, but slowly, for he was thoroughly exhausted and movement was difficult. Ronald was dressed long before he was, and insisted upon helping him.

"There, now you're fixed," he said, at length; "and if you're good for it, we'll go back to the bank and sit down a bit. There's no hurry about going home."

Forsyth was faint when they reached the tall tree they had started from, and was more than willing to rest. His speech was still thick, but he stammered his thanks.

"You owe it to Major," explained Ronald, diffidently, "for I never would have seen you. He started out, all of a sudden, and I went after him. Of course I wondered what had happened when I didn't see you, but I thought you were swimming under water. He found you, though. Good old boy," he added, patting the dog.

"I'm much obliged to both of you," said Robert weakly. "I've been in the water more or less all my life, and nothing like that ever happened to me before."

"Hope it won't again—the first time came mighty near being the last."

Forsyth had more strength than he appeared to have, but the shock was severe. "There's no hurry," said George, "and we won't go back till you're ready for a long walk. Say, how did you feel?"

"Why, I don't know exactly. I was all right, and I was thinking what a glorious swim I was having and how fine the water was, when all at once I couldn't move, and everything was black. I think I called you, though."

"Didn't hear you, but I guess the dog did. Queer, isn't it, that it should come just after we had been talking about death and the hereafter and so on?"

"Perhaps it was a warning."

"You're superstitious, now," returned Ronald; "but there's no getting out of it—when we get near the jumping-off place it makes us feel devilish queer. I was nearly crazy when I got you to shore and found you were dead—the thing came so quick, why, it was like a stroke of lightning."

"If that's death, though, it's nothing to be afraid of. Everything was black and soft, and there was no hurt to it—just a stop."

"Do you know," said the Ensign, "I've never seen very many dead people, and I've never seen anybody who had been killed in an accident—suddenly, you know. Those fellows up at Lee's were the nearest to it, but I didn't see them." His face whitened and his hands clenched instinctively. "God!" he breathed, between his set teeth, "I hope I'll be spared a death like that, at the hands of the red devils. I want to die like a soldier—in battle!"

"Come," said Forsyth, smiling, "we're getting serious—let's go back."

"Do you feel all right?"

"Yes; I'm a little shaky, but I guess I'm good for it. Don't say anything about it at the Fort, nor anywhere else—the women would make a great row."

"As you say—it's your business, you know."

In spite of Forsyth's valiant efforts, his progress was slow. "I'm as weak as a woman," he complained, when he was forced to stop and rest for the fourth time.

"You'll make it all right," said the other, cheerily; "take your time. And say, when we get back, come on over to the Fort and get a good stiff drink of whisky—that will set you on your pegs as quickly as anything."

When they came to the river Forsyth sat down and waited until Ronald went down to Mackenzie's, got a pirogue, and came up after him. "Didn't see anybody," said Ronald, in answer to a question, "and it's just as well. You're pretty white around the gills yet."

"Steady," he continued, as the boat grazed the shore, "and in ten minutes you'll be a new man."

Mrs. Franklin and Mrs. Howard were playing battledore on the parade-ground, while Beatrice and the Lieutenant watched them from the piazza. Captain Franklin, Mackenzie, and a couple of Indians were standing in front of the Captain's quarters, and Ronald yearned to join the group and see what was going on. He gave Robert his flask, bade him take it slowly, and rushed out.

The Indians were just leaving, and Captain Franklin had started back to the house, when one of them turned back and said something.

"What did he say?" he asked of Mackenzie.

"Nothing," replied the trader, with the dull colour bronzing his face; "they ain't our folks, you know."

"I insist upon knowing," said Franklin, peremptorily.

Mackenzie came nearer and lowered his voice to a whisper. "He said something about the women over there,"—indicating Mrs. Franklin and Mrs. Howard. "He said 'the white chief's wives are amusing themselves very much. It will not be long before they are hoeing in our corn-fields.'"

"Humph!" snorted the Captain.

"Oh!" laughed Ronald, "I must tell 'em!"

"Shut up," said the Captain; "you will do no such thing!"

"All right," returned the younger officer, good humouredly, "they're not my wives!"

# CHAPTER XIII
# GIFTS

"Cousin Rob," said Beatrice, the next morning, "I think you're dreadfully stupid."

"Why?"

"Because—yesterday, you know."

"You're indefinite."

"Why, when Aunt Eleanor was telling about the quilt that was stolen—a white quilt, with blue stars—you didn't know where it was."

"Did you?"

"Of course I did—it's in the little house in the woods."

"I wasn't in the house, Bee—you told me about it, but I didn't see it."

"Well, anyhow, you should have known," she concluded, with truly feminine inconsistency.

"Perhaps," smiled Robert; "but I'd rather not know, and then there'd be an excuse for your telling me."

A faint colour came into the girl's cheeks. "I had an awful dream about you last night," she said, in a low tone; "I dreamed you were drowned in the lake."

Robert started, but managed to control his voice. "I'm not drowned," he answered, with apparent lightness; but he was wondering whether Ronald had broken his promise. Still, no one had crossed the river, from either side, since the accident—he was sure of that.

"Be careful, won't you?" Beatrice pleaded earnestly.

"Certainly—but would you care?"

All the rosy tints faded from her face and the mist came into her eyes. Her "yes" was scarcely audible, but it moved the man strangely. "I'd do anything to please you, my dear—cousin," he said tenderly.

"Quarrelling?" asked Mackenzie, from the doorway.

"Not this time," laughed the girl.

"I've got something to tell you, Bee. Black Partridge was here early this morning, long before you were up, and apologised for running off with the picture—that is, as nearly as an Indian ever apologises. From what he said, I infer that he thinks the Great Spirit dwells in you, but he is willing for you to finish it. The medicine-man of the tribe told him good would come from it, rather than evil, so he left it here to be completed."

"All right," she answered; "I'll go to work at it now and try to get it done before he changes his mind again."

Robert brought the picture and her paints, and they sat down together on the piazza while she added the finishing touches. "Couldn't we make a frame for it?" asked Robert.

"What could we make it of?"

"He'd prefer beads, wouldn't he?"

"Yes, I suppose so," she said, with a puzzled little frown; "but I don't know how to make a bead frame."

"I should think a plain wooden frame might be whittled out, smeared with pitch or rosin, and the beads stuck on while it was hot."

"You're a genius, Cousin Rob. Get the beads off uncle and make it while I'm finishing the picture."

Mackenzie willingly placed his stock at their service, and, after taking careful measurements, Forsyth found a piece of soft pine and made a narrow, flat frame. Beatrice finished her work in time to help set the beads in the rosin, and Mackenzie and his wife came out to admire the result.

The picture was framed to their satisfaction when Black Partridge, somewhat shamefaced, appeared at the trading station. He took it with every evidence of delight and made a long speech to Mackenzie, of which Robert understood only a little.

"What does he say?" asked Beatrice, impatiently.

"He says he is very thankful and very grateful and much pleased, and that as long as he lives neither of you shall ever want for a friend. He says while the sun rises and sets and the stars move in their courses, Black Partridge will be the faithful friend of the paleface and her lover."

Robert was much embarrassed, but Beatrice only laughed. "Tell him he is very welcome," she said, "and that when we need a friend we will not hesitate to call upon Black Partridge."

The speech was duly repeated, with additional assurances which Mackenzie knew would please the chief, and the visit was ended with much ceremony.

Ronald was coming across the river, and Beatrice lingered upon the piazza until he opened the gate, when she gathered up her paints and went into the house without a word of greeting. There was a shade of annoyance in the Ensign's salutation, but he made no allusion to the girl.

"Come on out for a bit," suggested Robert; "I want to talk to you."

They went north along the river bank in silence until they were out of sight of the house, then Robert turned suddenly and faced him.

"Say," he said, "did you tell any one about my—about yesterday, you know?"

"No," answered Ronald, meeting his eyes squarely; "why?"

"Oh—nothing. Are you sure you didn't say anything that would lead any one to suspect?"

"'Nary peep, unless I talked in my sleep. When I found out that you'd drained my flask of everything but the smell, I went to Doc after a new supply, and when he asked me what had become of it I told him you'd taken to drink, but that was all. Now, I'll ask you a few questions. Why doesn't Miss Manning want me to come over?"

"Why, I don't know," replied Forsyth, wonderingly; "doesn't she?"

"Doesn't look like it," grumbled the other. "Didn't you see her gallop into the house the minute I opened the gate?"

"I didn't notice."

"You would, if she'd done it to you." Ronald was plainly in a bad humour. "What's more, if I speak to her, she never answers me decently. A girl never treated me like that before," he fumed; "just wait till I get my new uniform!"

"When is it coming?" asked Forsyth, glad of the chance to change the subject.

"Dunno—the boys are going to start early in the morning, but there's no telling when they'll get back."

"Are you going?"

"Indeed, and I am not. How can I go when there's no horse for me?"

"I thought you were going to—to borrow," stammered the other.

"Hardly!" The Ensign stopped and wiped his forehead with his sleeve. "Suffering Moses!" he said, "wouldn't she be mad!"

"Yes, I think she would, but I don't see why. She lets you lead Queen, doesn't she?"

"Oh, Lord, yes! I'm allowed to lead the beast twenty times around the Fort every day for exercise—she said we both needed it, and she didn't want to ride while it was so hot,—but she particularly impressed it upon me that under no circumstances was I to mount. A groom—a stable boy,—that's what she thinks I am! I believe I'll tell her to lead her own nag!"

"I wouldn't," returned Forsyth.

"Why not?" demanded the other. "What do you know about women?"

"Not very much," admitted Robert, laughing; "but we're all at sea there, I fancy."

Gradually Ronald's temper improved, and in a short time he was his sunny self again. Peace dwelt in the woods along the river, and where the young officer stretched himself full length under an overhanging willow, the quiet coolness of the unsunned spaces put an end, insensibly, to his irritation.

"Say," he said, "did you ever write poetry?"

Forsyth smiled, remembering certain callow attempts in his college days. "Yes, I called it that."

"Then you're the very man for me," announced George, "for I'm going to write a poem!"

"What about?"

"Oh—er—anything. Poems don't have to be about anything, do they? It's to go with a present—a birthday present, you know."

"To a girl?"

Ronald laughed long and loud. "No," he cried; "of course not! It's a little tribute ofaffection for the Captain! Lord, but you're green!"

"How can I help you with it if I don't know the circumstances?" demanded Forsyth. "What is the present?"

"The present isn't much—the poem is the main part of it. It's an Indian basket that Mrs. B. P. made for me in return for two fists of beads." Ronald took off his cap, felt around carefully inside of it, and at length produced a slip of paper, much worn. "I've got some of it," he said, "and I thought if I kept it on my head it might stimulate thought, but it hasn't."

"Let's hear it."

The poet cleared his throat and read proudly:

"Lovely lady, take this basket;
'Tis your willing slave who asks it."

Robert bit his lips, but managed to turn a serious face toward Ronald. "Is that all you've got?"

"That's all, so far. I thought myself into a headache about it, but I couldn't write any more. What shall I put in next?"

"I don't want to seem critical," observed Forsyth; "but you've got a false rhyme there."

"What's a 'false rhyme'?"

"'Basket' and asks it'—'ask it' would be all right."

"It doesn't fit. We'll leave that just as it is—nobody but you would notice it, and you're not getting the present."

"What do you want to say next?"

"Well, I don't know, exactly," replied Ronald, confidentially. "Of course, I want it to be personal in a way, with a delicate reminder of my affection at the end of it."

"You've got a 'delicate reminder,' as you call it, in the second line."

"Never mind that; go to work."

"Lovely lady, take this basket;
'T is your willing slave who asks it,"

repeated Robert, thoughtfully. "It was made by an Indian maiden—how would that do?"

"That's all right, only it was a squaw."

"It was made by an Indian squaw, then," continued Robert. "What rhymes with squaw?"

"Dunno."

"Paw," said Forsyth.

"It was made by an Indian squaw
With a dark and greasy paw."

"Shut up!" said Ronald. "She'd throw it out of the window if she thought it wasn't clean. Call her a maiden if you like."

"It was made by an Indian maiden—there isn't any rhyme for 'maiden.'"

"Laden," suggested George, after long and painful thought.

"That's good, if we can work it in."

"It was made by an Indian maiden—
With my love it now goes laden.

"How's that?"

"Fine!" beamed Ronald. "Say, I didn't know you were a poet!"

"Neither did I," replied Forsyth, modestly.

"Lovely lady, take this basket:
'Tis your willing slave who asks it.
It was made by an Indian maiden—
With my love it now goes laden."

"That's simply magnificent!" said Ronald. "We ought to write another verse, hadn't we?"

"As you say."

"If we can do another one as good as that, it'll be a masterpiece. My name ought to come in at the end, hadn't it?"

"Nothing rhymes with 'Ronald,' does it?"

"I didn't mean that—I meant my front name."

"Oh," said Forsyth. He was wondering how the girl in Fort Wayne would like the poem, and longed to ask questions about her, but felt that it would be improper.

"'Forge' is the only thing I can think of for a rhyme," said the Ensign, at length; "that wouldn't do, would it?"

"My heart is burning like a forge,
All because I love you—George."

"How's that?"

Ronald's delight knew no bounds. "The very thing!" he shouted. "Now, all we have to do is to put two lines above it and it will be done. That's the end of the verse, you know."

"Might put her name in," suggested Robert, not without guile.

Ronald appeared to consider it carefully. "No," he said, "that wouldn't do. One name is enough to have in it. Something ought to go in about her looks, don't you think so—eyes, or mouth, or skin?"

"'Skin,'" repeated Robert, laughing; "girls never have 'skin.' They call it their 'complexion.'"

"Thought you didn't know anything about women," George said, looking at him narrowly.

"Oh, come now, I can't help knowing that—any fool knows that!"

"Except me," put in the Ensign, pointedly. "However, I'll let the insult pass for the sake of the poem. Put in something about her mouth, can't you?"

The vision of Beatrice's scarlet, parted lips, with their dangerous curves, came before Robert.

"Reddest roses of the South
Are not sweeter than your mouth,"
he suggested.

"Man," said Ronald, soberly, "you're a genius. Write it down quick before it gets away. Now I'll read the whole thing:

"Lovely lady, take this basket;
'T is your willing slave who asks it.
It was made by an Indian maiden—
With my love it now goes laden.

"Reddest roses of the South
Are not sweeter than your mouth;
My heart is burning like a forge,
All because I love you—George.

"Sounds like Shakespeare, doesn't it?"

"I wouldn't say that," answered Forsyth, with proper modesty.

"Got any good paper to write it on?"

"Only a little, but you're welcome to it."

"All right, let's go back and get it. Say, do you think she'll be pleased?"

"She can't help being pleased," Robert assured him.

"I'm ever so much obliged," said Ronald diffidently. "I never could have done it so well alone."

When they reached Mackenzie's, Beatrice came out on the piazza as Robert went in after the paper, and she was evidently inclined to conversation.

"Where have you been?" she asked sweetly.

"Oh, just up-stream a little ways," replied Ronald, carelessly.

"Have you had Queen out this morning?"

"Yes, I rode her half-way to Fort Wayne and back. She got pretty well used up, but it did her good."

"How dare you!" flamed Beatrice, stamping her foot.

Ronald laughed and leaned easily against the side of the house while she stormed at him. Even Robert's appearance did not have any effect upon her wrath.

"Say, Rob," said the Ensign, when she paused to take breath, "your cousin here doesn't seem to know a joke when she sees it. She thinks I'd ride that old gun-carriage she keeps in the garrison stables. Calm her down a bit, will you? Bye-bye!"

The fire died out of the girl's eyes and her lips quivered. Her breast was heaving, but she kept herself in check till Ronald slammed the gate, then her shoulders shook with sobs.

"Bee!" cried Robert. "Don't, dear!"

Instinctively he put his arm around her, and she leaned against his shoulder, sobbing helplessly, her self-control quite gone. Ronald was untying a pirogue at the landing, when he looked back and saw the inspiring tableau.

"Good Lord!" he said, under his breath, as Robert, with his arm still around her, led Beatrice into the house.

Later in the week, as Robert was on his way to breakfast, he met Maria Indiana in the long, narrow passage back of the living-rooms. "What have you there, baby?" he asked.

Maria Indiana held out a small Indian basket of wonderful workmanship, filled with berries, fresh and fragrant, with the dew still on them. Tucked in at one side was a note, written upon his own stationery, as he could not help seeing. "It's for Tuzzin Bee!" lisped the child. "Misser George said nobody mus' see!"

The little feet pattered down the passage, but Robert stood still for a moment, as if he had turned to stone. Then wild unrest possessed him and stabs of pain pierced his consciousness. "Fool that I was!" he said to himself, bitterly; "blind, cursed fool!"

All at once he knew that he loved Beatrice with every fibre of his being—that she held his heart in the hollow of her hand, to crush or hurt as she pleased. He was shaken like an aspen in a storm—this, then, was why her flower-like face had haunted his dreams.

Swiftly upon the knowledge came a great uplifting, such as Love brings to the man whose life has been clean. It was a proud heart yielding only to the keeper of its keys—the absolute surrender of a kingdom to its queen.

Beatrice was late to breakfast, as usual; and Robert, acutely self-conscious, could not meet her eyes. She brought the basket with her and offered the berries as her contribution to the morning meal. Between gasps of laughter she read the poem, thereby causing mixed emotions in Forsyth. "Did you ever hear anything so ridiculous?" she asked, wiping the tears of mirth from her eyes.

Robert wished that the giver might see the rare pleasure his gift had brought to the recipient, but swiftly reproached himself for the ungenerous thought.

"It was nice of him to remember your birthday, Bee," said Mrs. Mackenzie, who was always ready to defend Ronald.

"How did he know it was my birthday?" demanded Beatrice.

"I told him," replied Mrs. Mackenzie. "He asked me, long ago, to find out when it was and to let him know."

"Clever of him," commented Beatrice, somewhat mollified. "Why didn't you get something for my birthday, Cousin Rob?" she asked, with a winning smile.

"Perhaps I did," he answered; "the day is still young."

He had already decided what to give her, and knew that his offering would not suffer by comparison with Ronald's, even though no poem went with it; but when he went to his room to look in his box for the moccasins he had bought so long ago, he was astonished to find that they were gone.

He ransacked the room thoroughly, but without success. He could not even remember when he had seen them last, though he knew he had taken them down from the wall of his room and put them away. Still, he was not greatly concerned, for he was sure that he could go to the Indian camp and find another pair.

After school he started off on a long, lonely tramp, and returned at sunset, empty handed and exasperated. Beatrice had on her pink calico gown, and was sitting demurely upon the piazza—alone. She seemed like a rose to her lover, and he was about to tell her so, but she forestalled him.

"Where's my birthday present?" she asked, sweetly; "I've been looking for it all day!"

Then he told her about the moccasins he had for her, though he failed to mention the fact that he had bought them for her long before she came to Fort Dearborn. "When I went after them this morning," he said, "I discovered that they had been stolen. I've been out now to see if I couldn't get another pair, but I couldn't even find a squaw who was willing to make them. You don't know how sorry I am!"

"Never mind," she said soothingly, "it's no matter. Of course, I'd love to have the moccasins, but it's the thought, rather than the gift, and I'd rather know that you found out from Aunt Eleanor when my birthday was, and tried to give me pleasure, than to have the pleasure itself."

The colour mounted to Robert's temples, but he could not speak. He felt that his silence was a lie, and a cowardly one at that, but he was helpless before the girl's smile.

"What's that?" asked Beatrice, suddenly, pointing across the river.

There was a stir at the Fort. Men ran in and out, evidently under stress of great excitement, then a tall and stately being, resplendent in a new uniform, came out and turned a handspring on the esplanade.

"What's up?" shouted Robert.

Ronald turned another handspring and threw his cap high in the air before he condescended to answer. "Bully!" he roared; "we're going to fight! War is declared against England!"

# CHAPTER XIV
# HEART'S DESIRE

Those who had complained of Captain Franklin's lax methods were silent now. The fortifications were strengthened at every possible point and pickets were stationed in the woods, at points on the lake shore, along the Fort Wayne trail, and at various places on the prairie. There was no target practice for fear of a scarcity of ammunition; but the women were taught to handle the pistols, muskets, and even the cannon in the blockhouses.

Mackenzie, Forsyth, and Chandonnais divided the night watch at the trading station. At the first sound of a warning gun, the women and children were to be taken to the Fort. As before, Beatrice was to go to Captain Franklin's, Mrs. Mackenzie and the children to Lieutenant Howard's, and the men to barracks.

"I guess I'll move over anyway," said Beatrice. "I wouldn't care to make the trip in the night. I'll sleep at the Captain's and eat wherever I happen to be."

Mrs. Franklin was not told of the plan until Beatrice and Robert appeared at her door with the enterprising young woman's possessions, but she made her guest very welcome.

"Why didn't you tell me you were coming?" she asked.

"What would be the use of telling you?" inquired Beatrice. "You'd be obliged to say you wanted me, so I just came."

The Captain's wife was genuinely glad, for of late she had been very lonely. Franklin was always more or less absorbed in his own affairs, and the feeling between Lieutenant Howard and his superior officer did not tend to promote friendly relations between the women. There had been no open break, but each felt that there might be one at any time.

Ronald was in high spirits. Since he had given Beatrice the basket she had treated him more kindly, and he led Queen twenty times around the Fort every day for exercise, without a murmur of complaint. Beatrice stood at the gate and kept count; while, across the river, Forsyth sat on the piazza and envied the Ensign, even during his monotonous daily round.

Among the officers at the Fort the declaration of war had not been altogether unexpected, for vague rumours of England's arrogance upon the high seas had reached the western limits of civilisation, but the situation was covered only by general orders from the War Department.

For once, Lieutenant Howard agreed with the Captain, in that there seemed to be no great possibility of a British attack. However valiantly defended, the Fort could not be held long in the face of a vigorous assault from the enemy, since the fighting force numbered less than sixty men, but England would have nothing to gain from that quarter. Other points were far more important than Fort Dearborn, but the garrison was ready to fight, nevertheless.

Ronald was more sanguine, and lived in hourly hope of hearing the signal of the enemy's approach. He sharpened the edge of his sword to the keen thinness of a knife blade, and slept with one hand upon his pistol. Doctor Norton, too, was making elaborate preparations in the way of lint and bandages, and Ronald helped him make stretchers enough to last during a lifetime of war.

But the days passed peacefully, and there were no signs of fighting. The Indians were particularly lawless, but confined their violence to their own people, though they had lost, in a great measure, their wholesome fear of the soldiers at the Fort.

"The devils are insolent because they think there's going to be trouble, and in the general confusion it will escape notice," remarked Ronald, as he sat in the shade of Lieutenant Howard's piazza. "I'm in favour of stringing up a few of 'em by way of example to the rest."

"Yes," replied Howard, twisting his mustache, "and in a few minutes we'd have the entire Pottawattomie tribe upon us. You don't seem to understand that they knew war had been declared long before we did, and that even now, in all probability, they are in league with the enemy. No people on earth are too low down for England to ally herself with when she wants territory."

"True," answered Ronald; "but I'm not afraid of England. She's had one good lesson, and we'll give her another any time she wants it."

"We've got enough on our hands right here," sighed the Lieutenant, "without any more foreign wars. We've got to have it out with the Indians yet, and fight our way step by step. The trail of blood began at Plymouth and will end—God knows where. England is more or less civilised, but she isn't above setting the Indians upon us to serve her own ends."

"What are you talking about?" asked Beatrice, coming across from Captain Franklin's.

"Yes, do tell us," said Katherine, from the doorway.

"Affairs of state," answered the Lieutenant, easily.

"Any British in sight?" inquired Beatrice.

"Not yet," replied Ronald; "but the entire army is likely to drop on us at any minute."

"What would you do?" she asked curiously.

"Do?" repeated Ronald, striding up and down in front of the house; "we'd call in the pickets, bar the gates, man the guns, and send the women and children into the Captain's cellar."

"Could Queen go, too?"

"Can Queen go down a ladder?"

"She never has," answered Beatrice; "but she could if she wanted to—I'm sure of it."

"If that's the case," said Lieutenant Howard, "we'd better offer her to the British officers as a trick horse and buy off the attack."

"If they come in the daytime," continued Beatrice, ignoring the suggestion, "I will go out to meet them all by myself. I'll put on my pink dress and my best apron, and carry a white flag in one hand and the United States flag in the other. When the British captain comes running up to me to see what I want, I'll say: 'Captain, you are late, and to be late to dinner is a sin. We have been looking for you for some time, but we will forgive you if you will come now. The invitation includes the ladies of your party and all the officers.' They never could shoot after that."

Katherine joined in the laugh that followed, but her heart was uneasy, none the less. Like Ronald, she was continually expecting an attack and knew there could be but one result. She believed that the Indians and the British would make common cause against them, when the time came to strike.

"I'll tell you what," said Ronald, "some of us ought to go out and drag in Mad Margaret. If we stood her up on the stockade, there isn't an Indian in the tribe who would dare to aim an arrow or throw a tomahawk toward the Fort."

"I've never seen her," said Beatrice, thoughtfully.

"I hope you never will," answered Ronald, quickly. "She's crazy, of course; but she has an uncanny way about her that a sensitive person would consider disturbing. She pranced into the Fort on a Winter afternoon two years ago and prophesied a flood, followed by a terribly hot Summer, and no crops. When the Spring rains came, the river spread on all sides, and, sure enough, there were no crops that year."

"Was it hot, too?"

"Oh, Lord! Was it hot? If hell is any hotter I don't care to go to it."

"You talk as if that was your final destination," observed Katherine.

"That's as it may be," returned the Ensign. "I've often been invited to go, and several times I've been told that it was a fitting place of residence for such as I."

"I didn't know about that," said the Lieutenant, thoughtfully, referring to the fulfilment of the prophecy.

"You weren't here," explained Ronald. "It was before you came—in 1810, I think."

"Cousin Rob told me about her," said Beatrice. "He said she came to Uncle John's the same day he did, and he's seen her once or twice since. She always says that she sees much blood, then fire, and afterward peace."

"Yes," growled the Ensign; "she's for ever harping on blood. She stuck her claws into me that night, I remember—told me I should never have my heart's desire."

"What is your heart's desire?" asked Beatrice, lightly.

The Summer faded and another day came back. Once again he sat before the roaring fire at the trading station, with Forsyth, Mackenzie, and Chandonnais grouped around him, while phantoms of snow drifted by and sleet beat against the window panes. Then the door seemed to open softly and Mad Margaret made her way into the circle. Chandonnais' wild music sounded again in his ears, then he felt the thin, claw-like hands upon him and heard the high, tremulous voice saying, "You shall never have your heart's desire"; and, in answer to his question, "It has not come, but you will know it soon."

The blood beat in his ears, but he heard Beatrice say, once more, "What is your heart's desire?"

A flash of inward light revealed it—the girl who stood before him, with the sunlight on her hair, and her scarlet lips parted; strong and self-reliant, yet wholly womanly.

Ronald cleared his throat. "You shouldn't ask me such questions," he said, trying to speak lightly, "when all these people are around."

"We'd better go, Kit," remarked the Lieutenant; "we seem to be in the way."

"Anything to please," murmured Mrs. Howard, as they went into the house.

Ronald was looking at Beatrice, with all his soul in his eyes. "I—I must go," she stammered. "Aunt Eleanor will want me."

"Don't—dear!" The boyishness was all gone, and it was the voice of a man in pain. The deep crimson flamed into her face and dyed the whiteness of her neck just below the turn of her cheek. She did not dare to look at him, but fled ignominiously.

He did not follow her, but she heard him laugh—a hollow, mirthless laugh, with a catch in it that sounded like a sob. She never knew how she crossed the river, but she was surprised to find Forsyth waiting for her. As he helped her out of the pirogue, he said; "I was just going after you—we feared we had lost you."

"I'm not lost," she said shortly, "and I don't want people running around after me!"

The shadow that crossed his face haunted her, even while he sat opposite her at dinner and laughed and joked with her as usual. When Mrs. Mackenzie took the baby away for his afternoon nap, with Maria Indiana wailing sleepily at her skirts, Beatrice went to her own room, fearing to be alone with Robert. She was strangely restless, and something seemed to hang over her like an indefinite, threatening fate.

Outside was the drowsy hum of midsummer, where the fairy folk of the fields rubbed their wings together in the grass and the sun transformed the river to a sheet of shining silver. Ronald came out, took the good boat which belonged to the Fort, and pulled down-stream with long, steady strokes. The river was low, but he passed the bar with little difficulty and went on out into the lake.

Beatrice heard Robert singing happily to himself, but she could not stay any longer where she was. She gathered up her sewing and climbed out of the window, ungracefully but effectively, and went back to the Fort.

Katherine saw her coming and smiled. That morning, with quick intuition, she had read the secret in Ronald's heart, and suddenly knew how much she cared for the boy who teased and tormented, but never failed her if she needed him. In her own mind, she had written down Beatrice as an unsparing coquette, and determined to take up the cudgels in behalf of her victim.

The girl sewed nervously, breaking her thread frequently, but she kept at it until Katherine said, very gently, "Bee, George cares for you."

"I know!" snapped Beatrice. Her thread broke again, and her hands trembled so she could scarcely knot it.

"And Robert, too," said Katherine, presently.

"I know!"

"Well, dear, what are you going to do about it?"

"Cousin Kit," said the girl, angrily, "if you're going to lecture me, I'm going back home." She folded up her work, but Mrs. Howard put a restraining hand upon her arm.

"Don't, Bee. You know we talked about my trouble together—why can't we talk about yours?"

"I haven't any trouble!" Beatrice's face was flushed, but her voice was softer, and she seemed willing to stay.

"What are you going to do about it?" asked Katherine, once more.

"What can I do about it?" cried Beatrice, in a high key—"why, that's simple, I'm sure! I can go to Mr. Ronald and say, 'Please, Mr. Ronald, don't ask me to marry you, because I'm going to marry Cousin Rob. He doesn't know it yet; in fact, he hasn't even asked me, but I'm going to do it just the same.' Or, I might go to Cousin Rob and say, 'My dear Mr. Forsyth, I hope you won't ask me to marry you, because I'm going to marry Mr. Ronald, who hasn't asked me as yet. In fact," she continued, with her temper rising, "I've about concluded that I won't marry anybody!"

"Bee, dear, I'm only trying to help you—please don't be cross to me. Which one do you care for?"

"Neither!" cried Beatrice, in a passion. "I don't care for anybody, and I'm never going to be married. I'd be happy, wouldn't I? Tied up—chained like a dog—take what my master gave me—slave—drudge—bear whatever burden he saw fit to put upon me—eat my heart out in loneliness—cry all day and all night for my lost freedom. Marry? Not I!"

"Marriage means all those things, as you say," said Katherine, after a silence; "but the bitterest part of it is that, when you find your mate, you have to go. The call is insistent—there is no other way. It means child-bearing and child loss—it means a thousand kinds of pain that you never knew before,—loneliness, doubt, sacrifice, misunderstanding,—and always the fear of change. Before, you think of it as a permanent bond of happiness; later, you see that it is a yoke, borne unequally. You marry to keep love, but sometimes that is the surest way to lose it.

"They say," continued Katherine, with her face white, "that after the first few years the storm and stress dies out into indifference, and that happiness and content are again possible. But oh," she breathed, "those few years! If man and woman must go through the world together, shoulder to shoulder, meeting the same troubles, the same difficulties and dangers, why, oh, why, didn't God make us of the same clay! We are different in a thousand ways; we act in opposite directions, from differing and incomprehensible motives—our point of view is instinctively different, and yet we are chained. Sex against sex it has been since the world began—sex against sex it shall be to the bitter end!"

"Katherine!" sobbed Beatrice, "I know! That is what I am afraid of! All the time I keep tight hold of myself to keep from caring, because I dare not surrender. If I yield, I am lost. If I loved a man, he could take me between his two hands and crush me—so; I should be so wholly his!"

"Yes," said the other, bitterly, "and many times he will crush you, just to see if he can—just to see that he has not lost his command of you. Power is what he must have—power over your mind and body, your heart and your soul—for every little unthinking action of yours, you are held responsible before the bar of his justice. His justice," she repeated, scornfully, "when he does not know what the word means. You have a little corner of his life; you give him all of yours in return. We are bound like slaves that never can be free—God made it so—and we obey!"

There was a tense silence, then a step was heard upon the piazza, and Katherine opened the door to her husband. Beatrice managed to wipe her wet eyes upon her sewing before he saw that she was there.

"Well," said the Lieutenant, easily, sinking into a chair, "what have you girls been doing?"

"Oh, we've just been talking," answered Katherine, diffidently.

"Talking, talking,—always talking," he continued. "What would women do if they couldn't talk?"

"They'd burst," remarked Beatrice, concisely.

"I guess that's right," laughed the Lieutenant; "but you needn't fear it will happen to you."

"You're mean to me," said Beatrice, gathering up her work, "so I'm going home."

"Don't be in a hurry," put in Katherine.

"I haven't been—you don't want me to live here, do you?"

"We should be charmed," replied the Lieutenant, gallantly.

"I'll consider it," she said shortly. "Good-bye!"

"Tempestuous sort of a girl," commented Howard, as Beatrice disappeared. "She'd play the devil with a man, wouldn't she?"

"That's exactly what she's doing."

"Which man?" asked Howard, curiously.

"Messrs. Ronald and Forsyth," answered Katherine, laughing. "How blind and stupid you are!"

The Lieutenant's disposition had undergone outward improvement of late. By common consent he and Katherine had started afresh, making no reference to past disagreements, and he had wisely ceased to question her motives or her actions. He let her understand that she might do as she pleased in all things, and, naturally, she was not willing to take undue advantage of her tacit freedom. Still, the old happiness and confidence were gone.

Forsyth had the second watch that night and was sitting on the piazza, listening for the warning guns of the pickets on the lookout for the enemy, when Ronald came across the river.

"Thought you were here," he said, "so I came over, as I couldn't sleep."

"I'm glad you did," returned Robert. "It gets pretty lonely out here about three o'clock in the morning."

"Are you sleepy?"

"Not a bit."

"Who comes on next, and when?"

"Chan's watch begins at three—it isn't far from that now."

112

"Call him up, then, and let's go out awhile. I can't sit still."

"All right."

When the half-breed, muttering sleepily, was finally stationed on the piazza, with instructions to listen for the guns, they walked out to the river.

"Which way?" asked Robert.

"Either—I don't care."

The moon was shining brightly and the earth was exquisitely still. The Fort, transfigured by its mantle of silver sheen, might have been some moss-grown feudal castle, with a gleaming river at its gate. Ronald walked rapidly, and his breath came in quick, short jerks.

"What's gone wrong with you?" asked Forsyth, kindly.

"I don't know how to put it," said the soldier, after a long silence, "for I never was good at words; but,—well, you like Beatrice pretty well, don't you?"

"Yes, don't you?"

"She's my heart's desire," said Ronald, thickly.

They were in the forest now, where the tall trees stood like the pillars of a cathedral, and the moonlight, softened by the overhanging branches, fell full upon Robert's face, white to the lips with pain.

"Old man," said Ronald, huskily, "one of us is going to get hurt."

"Yes," returned Forsyth, dully, "I suppose so—we can't both have her."

"Perhaps neither of us can, but—well, whatever happens—say, it isn't going to interfere with our friendship, is it?"

"No!" cried Forsyth; "a thousand times, no!"

Ronald wrung the other's hand in a fierce grasp and choked down a lump in his throat. "She's too good for me," he muttered; "I know that as well as anybody, but, on my soul, I can't give her up!"

"She's for the man she loves," said Forsyth, "and for no other. She wouldn't marry a king if she didn't love him."

"Well," sighed Ronald, "so be it. May the best man win!"

"For the sake of her happiness, yes. Of the three of us, only one will suffer, unless you and I share it together; but even that is better than for her to be unhappy. I haven't a chance with you—I know I haven't; but you're my friend and—I—I love her so much, that I could give her to you, if she loved you better than she loved me."

"Rob! Rob!" cried Ronald, "you're the only friend I've got, but I don't need any more. Whatever happens, I'll hold fast to that—there'll be something left for me after all!"

# CHAPTER XV
# RIVALS

August came, but there was no sign of fighting. Beatrice was openly skeptical, and said she did not believe there had been any declaration of war, but she spent more of her time at Captain Franklin's than at home.

Forsyth and the Mackenzies missed her keenly, even though she made occasional visits across the river. Her real reason was her wish to avoid Forsyth and Ronald; but both of them went cheerfully to the Captain's on flimsy pretexts or on none at all.

Robert fell into the habit of making early morning calls on Lieutenant and Mrs. Howard. Then, when Beatrice came out of the house to sit on the porch, he could saunter over carelessly and spend an accidental hour or so with her. Ronald was more direct and never hesitated to pound vigorously at the door when he wanted to see Beatrice and had the slightest excuse for going there.

The experience was new to the Ensign, who had come unscathed through many a flirtation, and who had regarded love lightly, after the manner of his kind. He had been the master of every situation so far, but at last he had come face to face with something that made him weak and helpless—as if he had been clay in the potter's hands.

No matter how hot it was, he led Queen patiently twenty times around the Fort in the broiling sun, and never attempted to mount, even when Beatrice was in the house. Moreover, though he would have scorned to rub down his own horse, he often put finishing touches upon Queen's glossy coat after she had been groomed. This gave him an opportunity to go over to Captain Franklin's, still leading the horse, and ask Beatrice how she liked her pet's appearance. Simple and transparent as the device was, it never failed to win a smile for him, and sometimes, too, the girl would linger to feed Queen lumps of sugar and gossip with Ronald meanwhile.

She painted when she felt like it, and did a great deal of sewing, both occupations being fraught with interest to Forsyth and Ronald. Mrs. Franklin was often one of the group, and Katherine made no attempt to efface herself.

They were all sitting on the porch in front of the Captain's house one hot morning, when Ronald appeared with a bowl and a spoon. "Taste," he said, offering it to Mrs. Franklin. Katherine followed her example, then Beatrice, always eager for new sensations, helped herself rather liberally. Robert also partook of the savoury stew.

"Pretty good," he said critically; "what is it?"

"It's poor old Major," replied Ronald, sadly; "the Indians cooked him and let me have some of the remains."

Beatrice gasped and fled into the house. The other women had risen to follow her, when the situation was relieved by the appearance of Major coming across the parade-ground in full cry, with Doctor Norton in hot pursuit.

"I couldn't hold him any longer!" shouted the Doctor.

"You brute!" exclaimed Mrs. Franklin.

Katherine went into the house to relieve Beatrice's apprehensions, and they returned together to add to the torrent of reproach that assailed the Ensign's ears. He was doubled up with unseemly mirth and apparently did not hear.

"That just goes to show," he said, when the paroxysm had passed, "how the mind influences the body. I had an argument with Doc this morning, and I've proved my point. If he hadn't let Major go, you would have thought you had eaten him and been miserable accordingly. Rob said it was good, and, dog or not dog, the fact remains."

Beatrice turned pale as a horrible suspicion entered her mind. "What is it?" she asked. "Upon your word and honour, what is it?"

"It's mutton stew," replied Ronald, conclusively, "made by Mrs. Mackenzie this very morning for your own approaching dinner. She kindly gave me some of it to keep me alive till noon. In fact, I helped to make it."

"You're a wretch!" exclaimed Katherine.

"Just hear 'em, Doc," said Ronald, assuming a grieved tone.

"I'm not sure but what you deserve it," laughed Norton. "If I had known what you were going to do, I wouldn't have tried to hold the dog."

"It's really very interesting," observed the Ensign, thoughtfully. "It shows what slaves of custom we are. Major is a medium-sized, woolly animal, much better looking than a sheep, yet sheep is considered eatable and Major isn't. Then, too, we eat cattle and draw the line at horses—there must be many a good steak on Queen."

Tears came to Beatrice's eyes, but she said nothing, and Forsyth warned Ronald with a look which was not noticed.

"Not that I think of eating her," resumed George, cheerfully; "I wouldn't get any exercise if I did. I wouldn't miss leading that beast around the Fort every morning for a fortune. It's the only uninterrupted feminine society I have."

At this juncture, Beatrice went into the house and slammed the door emphatically.

"Our diet here seems to be somewhat restricted," continued Ronald, apparently unmindful of his decreasing audience,—"cow and sheep, sheep and cow, with an occasional piggy rift in the cloud. Birdie eats dog whenever he can get it, and look at him—he's got as much endurance as any five of us, and I'm not sure but what he's better put together than I am."

"Yes, he is," put in Katherine, with caustic emphasis; "and he's better company, also. Come in," she continued, to Mrs. Franklin.

Ronald gazed after the retreating figures in pained amazement. "Well, what do you think of that?" he asked mournfully. "You fellows probably don't notice it, because you're not sensitive to such things; but, to my mind, which is more finely organised, it's a delicate intimation that we're not wanted. Let's move along."

"'Delicate' is good," commented the Doctor, as they walked away. "I call it rather pointed, myself."

"Strange, isn't it," remarked Ronald, impersonally, "how some people fall into line with the expressed opinions of others!"

"Ronald," said the Doctor, with mock admiration, "I don't think I ever met a man with so much fine tact as you have. Your unerring choice of happy subjects stands by itself—alone and unapproachable."

"Run along to your medicines, you old pill-roller," retorted the Ensign; "I want to talk to my cousin Robert."

Norton laughed and turned away, but he felt his isolation keenly, none the less. Lieutenant Howard was barely civil to him, as was natural under the circumstances, and he dared not see much of Katherine. Captain Franklin was not particularly congenial, and Mrs. Franklin had a vague distrust of him. She knew nothing more about the affair than Katherine had told her in the winter, but she surmised a great deal. Ronald had been the Doctor's mainstay, but since Beatrice came to Fort Dearborn he had been conspicuous by his absence. Forsyth was busy a great deal of the time, and the Doctor was left to intermittent association with the Mackenzies and the dubious consolation of the barracks.

It was true, as he often told himself, that his nature was one of those foreordained to loneliness, but at times he hungered for the companionship of his kind. Books were few upon the frontier, and those few he knew by heart; so he scraped lint, made bandages, brewed medicines, cultivated a certain philosophical turn of mind, and wondered vaguely where and how it would end.

Ronald and Forsyth were walking aimlessly in the neighbourhood of the Fort. The rigid discipline had somewhat relaxed, but no one was permitted to pass the picket lines. The Indians only came and went as they pleased, recognising no laws but those of their own making.

Ronald appeared to have something on his mind, and made disconnected and irrelevant answers to Forsyth's observations. "Say," he interrupted, at last, "how do you suppose we're ever going to get anywhere?"

"What do you mean?" asked Robert, in astonishment.

"Why, Beatrice, you know," he said awkwardly; "you don't give me any chance."

"I don't understand you," returned the other, coolly.

"Come now," said Ronald, roughly; "you know I'm no good at words, but I don't get your idea. There's always a mob around wherever she is, and if I get her to myself a minute you prance in as if you belonged there. If you're always going to do that, we might as well hunt her up now, tell her we both want to marry her, ask her to take her pick, and end the suspense."

An amused light came into Robert's eyes. "Do you know," he replied, "it's seemed to me the same way. If I get her to myself for a minute, you make it your business to join us. This morning, now,—I was there first, wasn't I?"

The Ensign's clouded face cleared. "I guess you were," he said slowly; "honestly, do I do that?"

"I should say you did," answered Forsyth, with unexpected spirit. "Since she moved away from Aunt Eleanor's, I haven't seen her alone for ten minutes."

Ronald laughed heartily as the ludicrous element of the situation dawned upon him. "I say, old man," he began, "we'll have to fix it some way—divide her up into watches, you know, or something like that."

Forsyth did not relish the way Ronald expressed it, but he caught the idea and nodded.

"How'll we do it?" continued the Ensign. "We can't take her into our confidence."

"Don't know," returned Robert, dully. "It doesn't make any difference, really, for I haven't a chance with you."

"Cheer up—you'll never get her if you mourn all the time. A girl likes to have things lively. I know how you feel—I've often felt that way myself; but I try to keep things going just the same. You have to attract a woman's attention—it doesn't much matter how."

"I surmised you thought that this morning," remarked Forsyth, with veiled sarcasm. He failed to mention the fact that, although he loved Beatrice, her evident displeasure had made him unspeakably glad.

Ronald's face bronzed, but he seldom admitted the possibility of his making a mistake. "We'll say," he began, "for the hypothesis, that our chances are equal. Since she moved over to the Captain's you've lost your unfair advantage. She goes across the river, of course, but we'll set against that the fact that she's in the Fort the rest of the time. Now, suppose we divide the day into three parts—morning, afternoon, and evening. It's morning till noon, afternoon till six, and evening till midnight. She mustn't lose her sleep, or she'll be cross. We'll take turns. For instance, if I have the morning, you get the afternoon, and I'll take the evening. The next day it will be your turn in the morning and evening, and mine in the afternoon—see?"

"Suppose she doesn't come out?"

"That's as it may be. The fellow whose turn it is takes the risk. She can do as she pleases—we simply agree to leave the field for the other at the times specified, military and educational duties to the contrary notwithstanding. That's fair, isn't it?"

"Yes, I think it is. Anyhow, it's better than we've been doing—it will lessen the possibility of friction."

"Good thing," commented Ronald. "Many a time I've felt like taking you by the collar and shaking you as a terrier shakes a rat."

"Me, too," laughed Forsyth. "Whose turn is it this afternoon?"

"I think it's mine. We were both there this morning, but you've intimated that I didn't leave a pleasant impression, and I ought to have a chance to set myself right, don't you think?"

"As you say—it doesn't make any difference to me."

"I'll have to get out pretty early some of the time," mused Ronald, "and exercise the beast. I don't want to lose a precious hour doing that."

"We might take turns—" suggested Forsyth, tentatively.

"We will not," retorted Ronald. "That's my job—she gave it to me herself."

Forsyth went across the river and Ronald returned to the Fort. Each was relieved because the matter was settled, for, as Robert had indicated, there had been friction.

All through the long, hot afternoon Ronald kept a close watch upon Captain Franklin's door. His knock met with no response, and Katherine had long since gone home. Doctor Norton had attempted to talk with the waiting swain, but found it unsatisfactory and retired gracefully.

Just before six o'clock Beatrice emerged. Her white gown was turned in a little at the throat, and her hair hung far below her waist in a heavy, shining braid, ending in a curl. Ronald's heart gave a great leap as he went to meet her.

"Where are you going?" he asked.

"Over to Aunt Eleanor's. You spoiled my dinner and I'm hungry."

"I'm sorry," he said, with evident contrition; "will you forgive me?"

"You ought to do penance for it."

"I'll do anything you say, Miss Bee."

"Lead Queen twenty-five times around the Fort after sundown," she said. "She'll be glad to get out again, and it won't hurt you."

Ronald smiled grimly as she went away, disregarding his offer to row her across. "It's a hard service," he thought, "but I've enlisted and I'll see it through. Thorny damsel; but oh, ye gods, she's sweet!"

Forsyth had made the most elaborate toilet his circumstances permitted, and was prepared to make the best of his coming opportunity. "Did you see George this afternoon?" he asked, with feigned carelessness.

"I did not," returned Beatrice, with a toss of her head. "He nearly broke down the Captain's door, but it was locked and nobody let him in. He was talking with that precious dog of his when I came out, and he offered to row me over, but I came by myself."

"I would have gone after you," said Robert, with ill-advised eagerness.

"Thank you," she answered coolly; "but I'm not so old yet that I can't row fairly well on still water."

That evening Forsyth had the felicity of sitting on the piazza, with Beatrice beside him, while his rival dejectedly led Queen round and round the Fort. His efforts at entertainment seemed to be unusually happy and effective, though he was too obtuse to notice that she laughed only when Ronald was in sight and, presumably, within hearing.

Mackenzie sat with them for a while, but soon went in. "You take the first watch," he said to Robert, "and call Chan for the second. I've got to get up early in the morning, anyway."

"All right, sir."

"Do you think there's any use of watching?" she asked, when the trader had closed the door.

"Of course," answered Robert, promptly. "If we were all asleep, no one would hear the gun and we might all be taken prisoners before we had a chance to get to the Fort."

"Have you always watched out here?"

"Yes, a part of the night, ever since we knew war had been declared."

"It's lonely, isn't it?"

"It might be, but I always have something pleasant to think about."

Beatrice did not press the question further. "What time does the first watch end?"

"Oh, along about midnight."

"I'll stay with you," said the girl impulsively; "I had a long sleep this afternoon, and I'd love to help watch. May I?"

Robert's heart beat loudly, but he controlled his voice. "Of course you may," he said.

When Ronald's task was finished, he led Queen into the Fort. "Twenty-four," mused Beatrice. "He's skipped one, or else I didn't count right."

"Twenty-four?" repeated Robert, inquiringly.

"Yes," she said. "He had to take Queen around twenty-five times because he was bad this morning and tried to make me think I'd eaten Major. I don't like things like that."

Robert laughed happily and felt an inexplicable generosity toward Ronald. "You didn't count right," he assured her. "He never would skip."

"Perhaps not—anyhow, I'll let it go."

The hours passed as if on wings, and both were surprised when the deep-toned bell at the Fort tolled taps. The moon rose and a path of gold gleamed on the water, rippling gently with the night wind.

"See," said Beatrice, softly, "it's always seemed to me as if one might row along that path, when the moon is low, and go straight in. When I was a child I used to think that I'd do it as soon as I got old enough to manage a boat by myself. I wondered why nobody ever went to the moon when it was so close, and I thought it would be a fine thing if I could be the first one to go. I couldn't see any doors, and concluded they must be on the other side; but I was sure I could row around when I got there, and I never doubted for an instant that the moon people would be delighted to see me. What strange fancies children have!"

"You're only a child now," said Robert, huskily,—"a little, helpless child."

"Helpless?" repeated Beatrice, with an odd little cadence at the end of the rising inflection; "I've never been told that before. See how strong my hands are!"

Laughing, she offered a small, white, dimpled hand for his inspection. With an inarticulate cry he bent to kiss it, and she snatched it away, much offended.

"You presume," she said, coldly. "Perhaps you think I'm like other girls!"

"You are different from everybody in the world," he answered, in a low, tender tone. "They are clay like the rest of us, only of a finer sort, but you are a bit of priceless porcelain. You are made of flowers and stars and dreams—of sunlight and moonlight, Spring and dawn. All the beauty of the earth has gone to make you—violets for your eyes, a rose for your mouth, and white morning-glories for your hands. When you smile it is like the light of a midsummer noon; when you laugh it is the music of falling waters; when you sing to yourself it is like a bird in the wilderness, breaking one's heart with the exquisite sweetness of it. Darling! darling!" he cried, passionately; "no one in the world is like you!"

Beatrice was trembling, and for the moment was dumb. Robert stood before her with his hands outstretched in pleading until, emboldened by her silence, he leaned forward to take her into his arms, and she moved swiftly aside.

"Very pretty," she said, with an effort, and in a matter-of-fact tone, then she laughed. "I did not know you were a poet," she continued, rising and shaking out her skirts,—"the moonlight has made you mad."

"Not the moonlight, sweetheart, but you!"

"Well, the two of us, then," returned Beatrice, lightly. "It's getting late, and I must go."

"No!" he cried. "You said you would stay till the end of my watch!"

"That was before I knew you were a poet. No, I'm going back by myself— good-night, and pleasant dreams!"

He untied the pirogue for her and helped her into it, his senses reeling at the momentary touch of her hand; and when she crossed the path of gold that lay upon the water, the light shone full upon her flower-like face. The man's blood surged into his heart with rapturous pain, as, exquisite, radiant, and unattainable, she passed through the gate of the Fort and out of his sight. He stood there long after she had vanished, shaken from head to foot by a passion as pure and exalted as Sir Galahad might have felt for Elaine.

# CHAPTER XVI
# THE WORM TURNS

"Beatrice," said Mrs. Mackenzie, "what day of the month is it?"

"The eighth."

"Why, no, it isn't," put in Mackenzie; "it's the ninth—isn't it, Rob?"

"Certainly—the ninth of August."

"Have it your own way," pouted Beatrice; "what do you suppose I care?"

"There's George across the river," observed Mrs. Mackenzie. "I wonder why he doesn't come over!"

"He's busy, I guess," said Robert; "but I think he will be over this afternoon."

"How do you know?" inquired Beatrice, looking at him narrowly. "You haven't seen him to-day, have you?"

"N—no," stammered Robert, uncomfortably. "I—I just thought so." For the first time he saw how ridiculous, from one point of view, their arrangement was, and became more anxious than ever to keep Beatrice in ignorance of it. Still, it had worked well, for neither had made any evident progress and their friendship was still unbroken.

During the past week the girl had not failed to observe that she never saw Ronald and Forsyth together, except from her window, and had asked each of them in turn if there had been a quarrel. She had also noticed that her admirers were spasmodic, as it were, in their attentions, and had puzzled vainly over the fact. It seemed strange that, at the Fort, Ronald should leave her when Forsyth put in an appearance; or that when she sat on the piazza at the trading station, Forsyth should immediately find something else to do when Ronald came across the river.

The Ensign had taken Queen out for the appointed exercise and was wondering how to kill the time until noon. He was staring vacantly into space at the very moment Robert had said he was "busy," but he soon decided to wash Major in the river.

In spite of the heat the dog regarded the ceremony as a punishment rather than a luxury, and cowered as if from a blow when his master removed his coat and rolled up his sleeves. The basin of soft soap which Doctor Norton brought, in answer to a loud request from Ronald, was placed conveniently on the bank and operations began.

Beatrice was leaning on the gate, in the shade of the poplar, and chose to consider the affair as undertaken solely for her amusement. "Isn't it nice of Mr. Ronald," she said, with mock gratitude, "to wash Major where we can all see him do it! If he were selfish, he'd take him away."

Protesting barks from the victim punctuated her comment. "If he were selfish," replied Robert, pleasantly, "he wouldn't do it at all."

"I have a mind to go over there," said the girl, suddenly.

"Oh, don't!" begged Robert, with feeling.

"Why not?"

"Oh—because."

"A woman's reason," said Beatrice, scornfully. "I'm going, anyhow."

Robert was allowed to row her across, as a great favour; and Ronald, mindful of his agreement, was not particularly cordial.

"I don't believe he likes it because I've come," she said, to Doctor Norton.

"Oh, yes, he does," the Doctor assured her, gallantly.

"Do you?" she inquired, directly, of Ronald.

"Certainly."

The Ensign's face was red, partly because of his exertions and partly because of various concealed emotions. Major had been thoroughly lathered with soft soap, and was being rinsed with basin after basin of water, whining, meanwhile, because soap was in his eyes.

"There," said Ronald, when the black and white coat was thoroughly clean, "he'll be a beauty when he's dry—won't you, Major?"

The dog shook himself vigorously and sprinkled every one except Beatrice, who was out of range. "Indeed he will," she answered, with suspicious warmth. "It's strange, isn't it, how washing improves pets?"

Forsyth began to dread what was coming, but Ronald heedlessly stumbled into the snare. "Of course it improves 'em," he said. "It's worth doing, if only for artistic reasons."

Her eyes danced and the dimples came and went at the corners of her mouth. "I would like," she began demurely, "to have Queen washed."

"Lord!" muttered the Ensign, mopping his forehead with his sleeve.

"Will you do it for me, Mr. Ronald?" she continued coaxingly.

For an instant he hesitated, then the worm turned. "No," he said quietly, "I won't. You can wash your own horse."

"Will you, Cousin Rob?" she asked sweetly, turning to Forsyth.

The dull colour bronzed his face and he saw a steely glitter in Ronald's blue eyes. "No," he answered, emboldened by the other's example; "not by any means."

"I haven't any friends," remarked Beatrice, sadly, to the Doctor.

"Friends are one thing," retorted Ronald, hotly, "and body servants are another. I'm willing to lead your horse around, because it's too hot for you to ride her, and I wouldn't want to be seen riding a nag like that anyhow; but I won't bathe her nor comb her hair nor put on her shoes." He turned on his heel and walked away, the personification of offended dignity.

Beatrice laughed, while Forsyth and the Doctor looked at her in amazement. "Oh," she gasped, "isn't he—isn't he funny when he's mad!" Ronald strode into the Fort and gave no sign of having heard, save by a tell-tale redness of the ears.

Robert felt concerned in a way, but the Doctor was not. "You'll find, Miss Manning," he said judicially, "as you grow older, that there's a limit to everything and everybody."

"Of course," returned the girl, seriously; "I was just locating it."

"Shall we go back, now?" asked Robert.

"No; I'm going to see Katherine."

"Very well." He started toward the Fort with her and Norton followed them.

"What?" she asked; "are you both coming, too?"

"I'm not," said the Doctor, quietly.

"Are you, Cousin Rob?"

"Of course—I'm going wherever you do."

Ronald was talking with Mrs. Franklin, and did not seem to see the two who went to the Lieutenant's. Robert brought chairs for Mrs. Howard and Beatrice and seated himself on the upper step.

"Where's George?" asked Katherine. "Isn't he coming over?" She had grown accustomed to seeing the three together, and vaguely missed Ronald.

"He was bad," explained the girl, fanning herself with her handkerchief, "and I think he's ashamed to come."

"Bad—how?"

"He wouldn't wash Queen. I asked him to, and he said he wouldn't. Cousin Rob wouldn't, either."

"Well, I don't blame them. You seem to expect a good deal, Bee."

"Oh," laughed Beatrice, "how serious you all are! I believe Mr. Ronald and Cousin Rob thought I meant it!"

"You seemed to," put in Robert, in self-justification.

"Men are very stupid," she observed, dispassionately; "but suppose I did mean it—what then? Were you in earnest when you said you wouldn't?"

"Yes," said Robert, steadfastly; "whether you were joking or not, I was in earnest, and so was Ronald."

Hitherto, men had not openly defied the girl's imperious will, and she had the sensation of unexpectedly encountering a brick wall. "Would you mind going over after my sewing?" she asked, suddenly.

"Certainly not—where is it?"

"Aunt Eleanor knows."

"You're a sad flirt, Bee," remarked Mrs. Howard, as Forsyth went out of the Fort.

"I am not," retorted Beatrice, with spirit. "Why shouldn't he go after my sewing?"

"There's no reason why he shouldn't, if he wants to."

"Well, he wants to," replied Beatrice, "otherwise he wouldn't. That's the man of it."

"It seems strange," observed the other, meditatively, "that in a little place like this, on the very edge of the frontier, one girl can keep two men working hard all the time without half trying. On the face of it, there wouldn't seem to be enough to do."

"It requires talent," admitted Beatrice, modestly, "if not genius. Mr. Ronald!" she called.

The Ensign did not seem to hear. "Mr. Ronald!" she called again. There was no answer, though he must have heard.

"He's in the sulks," explained Beatrice, "and if he wants to stay there, he can."

"I wish you wouldn't do so, Bee," said Katherine, kindly.

"Do what?" demanded Beatrice, with her violet eyes wide open.

"You know what you're doing, and you needn't pretend that you don't."

There was a long silence, then Beatrice sighed heavily. "I think I'll move," she said. "I can go to Detroit, or Fort Mackinac, or back East."

Katherine's heart sank within her, for she knew she would miss the girl more than words could express. "You can't go," she said; "no one would go with you."

"I should hope not. Queen and I could make the trip alone. If I decide to go, why, I'll go—that's all there is about it, war or no war. I know where the pickets are and I could get through the lines without any trouble. If you miss me some morning, you'll know that I've made my escape to some peaceful spot where there is no lecturing."

She spoke with such calm assurance that Katherine was troubled. She swiftly determined to ask Captain Franklin to put an extra guard at the stables, then Beatrice laughed.

"Poor Kit," she said affectionately, "why, you look as solemn as a priest! You don't think I'd go away and leave you, do you? You're too sweet," she cooed, rubbing her soft cheek against her cousin's.

Forsyth, coming back with the sewing, was transfixed with sudden envy of Mrs. Howard. "I thought you were never coming," said the girl, smiling.

"Did it seem long?" he asked, dazed by the implied compliment, for he had been in great haste.

"Yes," said Beatrice; "but it wasn't your fault. It was because I was being lectured."

Katherine's face grew delicately pink, and she looked at Beatrice imploringly.

"Lectured!" repeated Forsyth. "Why, what for?"

"She said I flirted—with you and Mr. Ronald."

"When?"

"Oh, you goose," laughed Beatrice. "She meant I did it all the time; but you don't care, do you?"

"I don't know just what it is," said Robert, truthfully; "but if it's anything you do, I like it."

"There!" said the girl, in a tone of great satisfaction; "you see, don't you, Kit?"

"Yes," answered Mrs. Howard, "I see that you are incorrigible."

Forsyth was content to listen and to watch Beatrice as she sewed. Prosaic needles and thread assumed a mysterious charm in the dimpled hands of the girl he loved. Pretty frowns and troubled shadows flitted across her face as the thread knotted, twisted, or broke, as it frequently did, because she was not familiar with her task.

Ronald left Captain Franklin's and came across the parade-ground with a rapid stride. "Twelve o'clock!" he said, with a radiant smile. "You wouldn't think it, would you?" he added.

"I shouldn't have suspected it," answered Forsyth, with double meaning; "I must be going back."

"I'll go with you, Cousin Rob."

"Me, too," put in Ronald, joyously.

"You needn't," said the girl, coolly.

"I'd just as soon—I'm going to row you across."

"No, you're not; I came with Cousin Rob and I'm going back with him."

"Suit yourself," returned the Ensign, good-humouredly, "the river is a public highway; but I'm going over to dinner."

He was there first, and had wheedled an invitation from Mrs. Mackenzie before they got into the house. "Put me next to Beatrice, please," he said, as they came in.

During dinner every one was in high spirits except Robert, who knew that he must efface himself all the afternoon. Some way, it was harder to have Ronald there than to know that he was with her at the Fort.

However, he felt a wicked thrill of satisfaction when Beatrice pushed back her chair and began to gather up the dishes. "You needn't do that, Bee," remonstrated Mrs. Mackenzie.

"I'm going to help you, Aunty, and then I'm going to take a nap. I'm dreadfully sleepy."

Ronald's face fell. "You're lazy," he said reproachfully.

"No, I'm not," she returned; "but I have to get rested, because to-morrow I'm going to wash Queen."

"Beatrice Manning!" exclaimed Mrs. Mackenzie. "What in the world do you mean?"

"I'll tell you all about it, Aunt Eleanor." In her own mind Beatrice had determined to make a pretence at Queen's bath the next morning, in front of the Fort, and see who would offer to help her.

"I'm going to help with the dishes, too," announced Ronald.

"You needn't, George," said Mrs. Mackenzie.

"I'd rather he wouldn't," remarked Beatrice, critically, "because I don't think he's clean. He washed Major this morning."

The shaft glanced aside harmlessly, because he prided himself upon his neatness. "I got my hand in this morning," he said imperturbably, "and I've washed many a dish in this very kitchen, long before you came, Miss Bee; didn't I, Aunt Eleanor?"

"Indeed you did," answered Mrs. Mackenzie, warmly. "I don't know how I could have managed without you."

"Very well," said the girl, lightly; "as long as you're used to it, and since you insist upon doing it, I'll go and take my nap right now."

Robert, inwardly joyous, but outwardly calm, took his well-thumbed copy of Shakespeare and went out to read under the trees, while Mrs. Mackenzie and the Ensign laboured with the dishes, and Beatrice slept the sleep of the just.

It was late in the afternoon when she came out, her eyes still languorous under their drooping lids, and found Ronald sitting alone upon the piazza.

"Why, I didn't expect to see you here," she said, in a tone of pleased surprise.

"You aren't very well acquainted with me," murmured Ronald, twisting uneasily in his chair.

"I'd like to be," remarked Beatrice, with a winning smile.

"Now's your chance, then, for I'm going to stay here until six o'clock."

"That's a long time," sighed the girl, with a sidelong glance at him. "It isn't much after four now."

He cleared his throat and coloured deeply. While he was casting about for a suitable reply, Forsyth appeared with his book. "Come and read to us, Cousin Rob," said Beatrice, sweetly.

Ronald looked daggers at him when he hesitated. "Can't," he answered shortly; "I'm going to read to myself."

He went back to his place under the poplars, in sight, but not intentionally within hearing, and Ronald was unreasonably vexed with him, deeming him outside the spirit, though within the letter of the bond.

"I'm sorry he wouldn't read to us," observed Beatrice. "Cousin Rob has such a deep, melodious voice, don't you think so?"

The Ensign was writhing inwardly, but managed to say, "Yes; very deep."

Mackenzie came out and wasted half of a precious hour in talking, though Ronald answered only in monosyllables. Beatrice exerted her rarest powers of entertainment for her uncle's benefit, and he did not notice how the time passed. "Well," he said, at length, "I guess I'll go across for a bit. I want to see the Captain." Forsyth joined him at the gate, and Ronald heaved a sigh of relief when they were safely on their way to the Fort.

"Your face is red, Mr. Ronald," said Beatrice. She was rewarded by seeing the colour deepen.

"What makes it that way?" she asked, with the air of one pursuing a subject of scientific interest.

"It's the heat," explained the Ensign, miserably; "didn't you know it was hot?"

She shook her head. "I never know anything unless I'm told."

"I believe you," he growled.

"Mr. Ronald," she said, with a bewildering smile, "what makes you so cross to me?"

"I—I'm not," he answered thickly.

"Yes, you are—you're dreadfully cross to me, but you seem to get on all right with everybody else. I don't believe you like me!"

The last remnant of his self-control deserted him. "No, I don't," he said, hotly. "Good God, Beatrice, I love you—can't you see that? Why do you torture me all the time?"

Her face grew a shade paler, and her eyes refused to meet his. She knew she had been playing with fire, but none the less was surprised at the natural result, and was genuinely sorry that she had gone so far. She stared at the Fort, unseeing, and inwardly reproached herself bitterly.

"Beatrice!" he gasped. "Say something to me, can't you?"

She pointed to a cloud of dust in the south-west. "Look, some one is coming!"

"I don't care," he said, roughly, possessing himself of her hand; "you've got to say something to me!"

"I did," she returned, drawing away from him, "I told you somebody was coming. I think it's my relatives from Fort Wayne coming to take me back there."

Ronald turned away, deeply pained, and the pathetic droop in his shoulders got safely through the thorns to the girl's heart. The cloud of dust came nearer and nearer, until at last the rider turned his foam-flecked horse and dashed up the esplanade to the Fort.

Beatrice's temporary tenderness was obscured by curiosity, for the rider was an Indian, with the British flag girded at his loins.

"Why," she said, in an odd little voice, "what has happened!"

Ronald came swiftly toward her. "I don't know and I don't care," he said, in a voice she scarcely recognised; then he put his arm around her and drew her to him. "Beatrice, darling," he pleaded, "haven't you a word for me—don't you love me just the least little bit in the world?"

Then the violet eyes looked up into his and the sweet lips quivered. "I—I don't know," she whispered brokenly; "please let me go!"

His arms fell to his sides and she was free, but there was a lump in his throat and a wild hope in his heart. "My darling," he began, but she stopped him with a warning gesture.

Forsyth was pulling across the river as if his life depended upon it, and for the first time they perceived that something was wrong. With his face white and every muscle of his body tense, he ran toward them.

"What's up?" shouted Ronald.

"Orders!" cried Forsyth, gasping for breath. "Fort Mackinac has fallen and we are ordered to evacuate the post!"

# CHAPTER XVII
# A COUNCIL OF WAR

Forsyth had the second watch that night, and Mackenzie came out to join him. "I couldn't sleep," he said, in answer to Robert's question. "I don't know what we're coming to, but we mustn't frighten the women."

"Of course I don't know anything about it," Robert returned, "but I must confess that I didn't like the looks of that Indian who brought the despatches."

"He seemed fair enough, but you can't trust any of 'em and that's the whole truth of it. There's been some foul play somewhere, for he knew the purport of the order, and it strikes me that he had been a long time on the way."

"What was it that he wanted you to tell Captain Franklin?"

"He wanted me to find out whether the Captain intended to obey the order, and offered his advice to the contrary. He said the Fort was well supplied with ammunition and provisions—though it beats me to know where he found it out—and that it could be held until reinforcements arrived; but, if we decided to give up the post, it was better to go at once and leave everything standing. His idea was that the Indians would be so interested in plundering that they wouldn't follow us."

"What did Franklin say?"

"Nothing—he never says much, you know."

"Who gave the order?"

"General Hull—the Army of the North-west is at Detroit."

"Perhaps reinforcements will be sent."

"Hardly, in the face of an order to leave the post."

"Why did he wear the British flag?"

"Perhaps to secure safe passage through the country; perhaps to indicate an alliance with the enemy."

"Lieutenant Howard has said all along that the Indians were with the British and against us. It begins to look as though he were right."

"My boy," said Mackenzie, with a sigh, "wherever that flag waves, you'll find blood. The colour of it isn't an accident—it's a challenge and a warning."

"Well," returned Robert, after a silence, "we'll have to do the best we can, and that's all any one can do."

"I've wondered sometimes," said the other, thoughtfully, "if I haven't done wrong."

"How, Uncle?"

"Coming here—with Eleanor. I've brought her into danger, but God knows I haven't meant to. I've always had an adventurous spirit, and I couldn't live in the East—the hills choke me. Somebody has to blaze the trail to the new places, and I thought I might as well do it as anybody else. Things are moving westward, and some day, in this valley, there ought to be a great city about where the Fort stands now. It's the place for it—the river and the lake, with good farming country all around. I knew I couldn't live to see it, but I—I thought my children might."

The man's voice wavered, but did not break. "It's a commonplace thing to do," he went on,—"go to a new place to live,—and our people have been doing it for more than two centuries. No soldiery, no blare of trumpets, nothing to make it seem fine—only discomfort, privation, and danger. The first settlers came from across the water, and since then we've been moving along, a step or two at a time. Some day, perhaps, people will leave this place to go to another farther on, and so keep going, till we reach the ocean on the other side. I haven't done anything," he added, with a short laugh, "only what the men of our race must do for a century and more to come."

"You've done what was right, Uncle, and what seemed for the best—no one could do more. You've given Aunt Eleanor and the children a good home—shelter, warmth, food, and clothing. You've given your children sound minds, sound bodies, free air to breathe, and you're giving them an education. You'll find danger anywhere and everywhere—life hangs by a thread at its best. If it comes to a fight, we have arms and ammunition and fifty men, as strong and true as steel. We have modern weapons against arrows and tomahawks, military skill against savage instincts; and as for the British, why, I have my grandfather's sword, that fought them once at Lexington. They tried it and they failed—they'll fail again; but I say, let them come!"

"God bless you, boy; you put new courage into me!"

Soft darkness lay upon the earth, and pale stars shone fitfully from behind the clouds as slowly the night passed by. Across the river, with measured tread, the sentries kept guard at the Fort. Through one watch and well into another the two men sat there talking, with their voices lowered, lest the sleepers in the house should wake, and from each other taking heart for the morrow.

The spirit of his dead fathers lived again in Forsyth; the blood that burned at Lexington took fire once more at Fort Dearborn. His heart beat high with that resolute courage which sees the end only, with no thought of the possible cost—it was as though Victory, in passing, to hover just beyond him, had brushed his face with her blood-stained wings.

131

In the first light of morning, Beatrice came across the river from the Fort. Whether she knew of the impending danger or not, she showed no signs of fear. "Well," she said, "it was only yesterday that I told Kit I thought I'd move, and here's a military order to make it practicable. We're going with the soldiers— Queen and I."

Forsyth smiled, but made no other answer, and she went on into the house. Mrs. Mackenzie did not appear, having passed a sleepless night; so Beatrice presided over the coffee-pot and made breakfast a gay affair. She revelled in her new authority, and took advantage of her position to tease the children.

"Maria Indiana," she said, with mock severity, "you'll have to behave yourself better from now out, because I'm your mother."

The child's eyes filled and a big tear rolled down one cheek. She slid out of her chair and instinctively went to Robert, as one who might be trusted. "Is Tuzzin Bee my muzzer?" she asked plaintively.

"No, dear," he laughed, taking her up in his arms.

"Give her to me!" cried Beatrice, snatching her away from him. "You darling," she said tenderly, as another tear followed the first one; "I'm not your 'muzzer,'—I'm only your 'Tuzzin Bee.'"

"She's too little to joke with," said Forsyth, in an aside.

"And I'm too big to be lectured," replied Beatrice, with a saucy smile. "We get on all right, don't we, baby?"

Something in the girl's attitude, as she held the child in her arms, reminded Forsyth of a picture of the Madonna, and an unreasoning giddiness took possession of his senses. With a blind impulse to get away, he went out on the piazza, but Beatrice followed him.

"Cousin Rob," she said, in a low tone, "please tell me the truth—is there danger?"

There was no denial of that look in the eyes of the girl he loved, no chance to conceal the truth. He drew a quick inward breath as he thought, for the first time, what danger might mean to her. "Yes," he said, in a voice that was scarcely audible; "I am afraid there is."

In a flash he saw that she had misunderstood him, but it was too late to explain. The colour flamed into her cheeks, and she held her head high. "I'm sorry you're afraid," she said, scornfully, "I'm not!"

He looked after her helplessly as she went into the house, dazed by the consciousness that he had lost her forever. He knew then that she had never forgotten his failure to go up-stream with Ronald the night the Indians had been at Lee's, even though she had asked him to forgive her.

"I have lost her," he said to himself, over and over again,—"I have lost her." Second thought convinced him that he had had no chance from the beginning—since the night he leaned on his musket in the shelter of the Fort; confused past the power of action, when the Ensign asked for volunteers.

"Want to go over, Rob?" It was Mackenzie who asked the question, and Forsyth gladly welcomed the respite from his torturing thoughts.

At the Fort all was changed, for the order had been read that morning on parade, and the men stood about in little groups earnestly discussing it. Mrs. Franklin and Katherine were on the porch at the Lieutenant's, and Robert went there, feeling that their society would be more bearable than that of the men.

"If we go," said Katherine, "there'll be very little we can take with us."

"If we go!" snapped Mrs. Franklin. "Do you think for a minute we're not going? A soldier's first duty is to obey orders!"

Katherine turned a shade paler as she welcomed Forsyth. "Have you packed your belongings?" she asked.

"Not yet," he answered, with a hollow laugh. The impending danger was obscured, in his mind, by something of infinitely more moment. "When do we start?" he inquired of Mrs. Franklin.

"I don't know—Wallace hasn't decided. But we'll start when he says we will, and nobody need think we won't!"

"Kit," said Mackenzie, as he joined the group, "I wish you'd go over to your mother—she isn't well. Bee is with her, but perhaps you could do something."

"I'll go at once," replied Katherine.

"And I must go home," said Mrs. Franklin. "If I can do anything, just let me know."

Ronald and Lieutenant Howard were standing near the gate, and Forsyth stopped there when Mackenzie and Katherine went on home. "It's usual in such circumstances," Ronald was saying, bitterly, "to call a council of war."

"And by the Lord," flashed the Lieutenant, "there shall be a council of war! What are we—children, or fools?"

Ronald put a friendly arm across Forsyth's shoulders. "What do you think about it, old man?"

"I haven't thought about it. I'm not a soldier, you know, and I'm not supposed to think. Of course, I'll obey orders, and if it comes to trouble, here's one more man to fight—I'm with you to the last."

"Bully for you!" said Ronald. "If the Captain would listen to reason, there wouldn't be any trouble; but he won't—I know him too well."

"He is only one man," put in the Lieutenant, with sinister significance.

"And he is our superior officer," concluded Ronald. "Hello, Norton!"

The Doctor and the Lieutenant exchanged cool salutations. The faces of the others were clouded, but the Doctor was as serene as the clear blue sky overhead. "Haven't you heard?" asked Forsyth, in astonishment.

"What's the odds?" queried Norton, with a cynical shrug of his broad shoulders. "So far, we have one life and one death; at the end of one we meet the other—how does it matter, when or which way?"

"It matters to me," said Ronald, huskily, "whether I die like a soldier or like a beast."

"'Imperial Cæsar, dead and turned to clay,'" quoted Norton, suggestively. "Clay we were in the beginning and clay we shall be at the end. 'Dust thou art; to dust shalt thou return.'"

Lieutenant Howard's white teeth showed in a sarcastic smile, but he said nothing. He seemed interested and even amused by the surgeon's point of view.

"That's all very well for you," retorted Ronald, "because you're a selfish brute, with water in your veins instead of a man's blood. If you loved a woman——"

The Lieutenant instantly stiffened. His smile disappeared, leaving a frown in its place, and Norton's face changed, almost imperceptibly. "If I loved a woman," he said, "I would protect her at the risk of my own life, my own happiness, my own soul. If need be, I would protect her even from herself. If I loved a woman she should think of me in just one way—as her shield."

For the sheerest fraction of an instant his eyes met Howard's, openly and unashamed; then, with another shrug of his shoulders, he turned away, saying, "I must go back to my lint and my bandages—we may need them before long."

Forsyth went back to the trading station, and the other two continued their uneasy march around the parade-ground. "I think," said the Lieutenant, "that the sane, reasoning men in the settlement, outside the ranks, ought to get together and talk to the Captain."

"It won't do any good," replied Ronald, dubiously.

"No? Perhaps not, but there's nothing like trying. We don't have to go, you know—it's not compulsory. The boys would be with us, and, as I said before, he's only one man."

Ronald recoiled as if from a blow. "God, man," he said, thickly, "don't make me forget I'm a soldier!" He swallowed hard, and it was some time before he spoke again. "I don't mind telling you, privately, that I don't think much of Captain Franklin, nor," he added, as an afterthought, "of General Hull; but, in one sense at least, they're my superior officers. I don't know what's going to happen to me in the next world, nor even if there is any next world; but I'll march to the end of my enlistment with my soldier's honour still unstained."

The Lieutenant gnawed his mustache in silence while Ronald walked beside him, breathing heavily. "It's madness," said the Ensign; "we all know that. The North-western Army is at Detroit, and the British are at Fort Mackinac—unless they've already started down here. Meanwhile, the Indians, leagued to a man with the enemy, are waiting for us to set foot outside the Fort. That fellow that brought the despatches dared to inquire what we were going to do—so the tribes could act in harmony, I suppose! Of course, it's possible that we can get through to Fort Wayne in safety, and go on to Detroit with a force large enough to clear our path—but I doubt it."

"Well," said Howard, "let's have a try at it. Let's call a council of war."

"All right—I'll go across for Mackenzie and Forsyth, while you get Norton."

The Lieutenant waited until he saw the others coming before he delivered the message. The two men stood facing each other for a moment after the salute.

"Doctor Norton," said Howard, stiffly, "we have called a council of war at Captain Franklin's, immediately. Will you be present?"

"Yes; if you wish it, I will."

"I do wish it," answered the Lieutenant, clearing his throat.

Captain Franklin himself opened the door to the five men, and there was no trace of agitation in his manner as he welcomed them and bade them be seated. "To what do I owe the honour of this visit?" he inquired, after an awkward silence.

"We have come for a word with you, Captain," replied Lieutenant Howard. "In effect, this is a council of war."

"One moment please." The Captain went to the door, summoned his orderly, and gave him a whispered message. "Now, then, I am ready to listen."

"Do you intend to obey this order from General Hull's headquarters?"

"Certainly—why not?"

"Captain," said Ronald, "we appreciate your position, but you must see that it is highly improbable that we should ever reach Detroit, or even Fort Wayne, in safety. Since war was declared against England, the Indians have been openly hostile. The country through which we must pass is infested with them, and they are in league with our enemies. For what reason do the English pay an annual tribute to the Indians, at the same time searching our ships on the high seas? Do you remember, before war was declared, two of the Calumet chiefs told you that our women would soon be hoeing in their corn-fields? If you need further proof, consider for a moment that the Indian who brought the despatches wore the blood-red flag of our enemy.

"Captain, our march must be slow. We have women and children to protect, and feeble men of seventy and more in our own ranks. We have only a few horses, scarcely enough for the women, and about fifty fighting men. If General Hull had been acquainted with the conditions, he would not have given the order. As it is, we must act upon our own judgment, and, short of suicide, only one course seems to be open."

"Is this your opinion also, Lieutenant Howard?"

"It is."

"Doctor Norton?"

"I am not a military man, but I agree in substance with what has been said."

"Mr. Mackenzie?"

"I'm no soldier, either," said the trader, "but I think the proper course has been described. Of course, if we go, I'll lose everything I've got in the world; but I don't care for that, if we only do what's best."

"Mr. Forsyth?"

"Like my uncle, I'm no soldier, but I agree with Ensign Ronald. Still, I will do what seems best, obey whatever orders may be given by those in authority, and if you wish to send a messenger to Detroit I am at your service. I will take my horse and start at once."

"Gentlemen," said the Captain, ignoring the suggestion, "I appreciate the spirit in which you have come to me, but it is impossible to disobey orders. A soldier's obedience is paramount to all other considerations. Special orders have been issued by the War Department that no post is to be surrendered without battle having been given. Our force is inadequate to cope with either Indians or British, and I should be severely censured for remaining, if not court-martialed.

"On the other hand, even if the Indians are in league with the enemy because of the yearly distribution of presents, we have weapons of the same kind in our hands, and I shall not hesitate to use them. There is a prospect of a safe march through, and I propose to ally the Indians, temporarily at least, with us."

Here the orderly entered, bringing with him Black Partridge.

"Say to him," said Franklin to Mackenzie, "that the White Father bids him assemble his people from the four quarters of the earth before noon of to-morrow's sun." The trader translated rapidly as the Captain spoke.

"Tell him that we have long dwelt side by side in peace and content, except when our brother, Black Partridge, was away from us, and the Winnebagoes, fearing nothing because our protectors were gone, fell upon us to kill.

"Say that our Great White Father in Washington has bidden us to assemble at another place, even as he will bid his people to assemble here, and that, while our hearts are torn with sorrow, we must obey the command. Tell him that we wish him and his people to see us start upon our journey, and that our cattle and our provisions, our clothing and our supplies, at present in the storehouses of the Great White Father, will be given to him and his people as a parting gift. Tell him all this and ask him if he understands."

Mackenzie was translating, sentence by sentence, and all eyes were turned upon Black Partridge. The Indian stood as calm and as immovable as stone, listening intently, with only the glitter of his eyes betraying any interest whatsoever.

"Tell him that long shall remain in our hearts the memory of the kindness received at the hands of our brethren the Pottawattomies, and the wise counsel of the Great Chief who rules them. Some day, when other suns have run their course, and the Great White Father gives us permission, we shall return to live in peace once more with our brethren, the Pottawattomies, and their Great Chief, Black Partridge, who is our brother and our friend. Ask him if he understands."

The harsh gutturals of the question fell upon the ears of the bronze statue, and, for the moment, there was a tense stillness in the room. Then the Indian signified that he understood, and withdrew as silently and as sinuously as a snake in the grass.

# CHAPTER XVIII
## "IF I WERE IN COMMAND"

Long before the word had been given, the Indians were coming in. Winnebagoes, Ottawas, Chippewas, and Pottawattomies, from north, south, and west, were gathering in the woods around Fort Dearborn. Like the rattlesnake coiled to strike, like vultures drawn to a battlefield, silent, sinister, and deadly, the lines were closing in.

Noon was the hour appointed for the council, and at that time Black Partridge, through Mackenzie, made known to Captain Franklin that it would be another day before all the Pottawattomies could be assembled. "Till noon of tomorrow's sun," said the Captain, sternly; "not one moment more."

Beatrice, from the window of the trading station, saw innumerable Indians, dressed and painted in the manner of other tribes, carefully inspecting the house and barn as if appraising their value. The Agency building was haunted by others, who peered in furtively at the windows, hoping for an early look at the goods which were to be distributed among the tribes.

Mrs. Mackenzie had recovered from the first shock and went about the house as usual, quiet yet cheerful, and patient with the children and her manifold household tasks. To Beatrice only she admitted her fear.

"Don't talk about it, Aunt Eleanor—we must all try to think about something else."

"Yes," sighed Mrs. Mackenzie, "we must not fret away the strength we will need for the journey. Your uncle has slept scarcely an hour since the news came."

"I know, Aunt Eleanor, I know."

"You must help me be brave, dear. Someway, of late, I have felt myself a coward, and it has made me ashamed. Not for myself alone, but for the children——"

The sweet voice quivered, then broke; and for the moment Beatrice's eyes were dim, but she swiftly put the weakness from her.

"There's nothing to be afraid of, Aunt Eleanor. The British haven't come, and as for the Indians, why, they wouldn't dare to attack the soldiers. We'll get to Fort Wayne, safe and sound, and perhaps the whole army will go on to Detroit with us. I wonder what my aunt and uncle will say when they see me riding Queen into Fort Wayne at the head of the troops!"

Mrs. Mackenzie laughed in spite of herself. "I hope you're right, Bee."

Forsyth and Ronald were walking back and forth in front of the Fort, talking earnestly. A little apart stood Mackenzie and Captain Franklin, while Indians went in and out of the stockade, apparently at pleasure.

"Aunt Eleanor," said Beatrice, thoughtfully, "I read a story once about a girl. There were two men who—who—well, they liked her, you know. They were both good, but there was a difference. One always teased her and tormented her and made her feel at odds with herself, even though she knew he was just in fun.

"The other always rested her. No matter how tired she was, or how much out of sorts she happened to be, it always made her feel better to be with him. He was quiet and his ways were gentle, and he knew more about—about books and things, you know. The other one was a soldier, and this one was a student, but he—he wasn't brave. He couldn't help it, but he was afraid."

"A woman never could love a man who wasn't brave," said Mrs. Mackenzie.

"No, of course she couldn't."

"And if a man always teased and tormented a woman, and made her feel irritable, she would never be happy with him."

"No; she couldn't expect to be."

"Perhaps she had made a mistake about the other one—perhaps he really was brave."

"No; because she saw him twice when she knew he was afraid."

"Then she shouldn't marry either one."

"That's what I thought," said Beatrice.

"Which one did she marry?"

"Who, Aunt Eleanor?"

"Why, the girl in the story?"

"Oh," answered Beatrice, colouring; "why, I—I've forgotten. It's queer, isn't it, how people forget things?"

"What book was it in?"

"I—I don't remember. My memory is poor, Aunt Eleanor. I'm going to my room, now, if you don't want me, and pack up some of my things."

Red and white clover blossomed in the yard, where the children were playing, and a butterfly winged its way through the open window, then flew swiftly out again. Mrs. Mackenzie sat by the table with her face hidden in her hands, while childish voices came to her ears in laughing cadence and filled her heart with fear and pain. Then there was a touch upon her shoulder.

"Eleanor!"

"Why," she said, looking up, "I didn't hear you, John."

Her clear eyes revealed a sadness beyond tears. "Eleanor," said her husband, with the muscles working about his mouth, "I can't bear for you to feel so."

"I—I'm all right, John. Don't fret about me."

"No, you ain't all right—don't you think I know? I've brought you into danger, Eleanor—I see it now, and that's the thing that hurts me most of all. It's nothing to lose all I've got, for that's happened to me before, and I'm only fifty—I can get it all back again, but I can't ever change the fact that I've brought you into danger. I promised before God that I'd protect you, and I haven't done it. I've taken you to a place where it ain't safe."

The man's distress was pitiful. His gigantic frame was bent like an oak in the path of a furious storm and every line on his haggard face was distinct, as if it had been cut. His dark eyes, under their bushy brows, were utterly despairing; he was like one whose hope is dead and buried past the power of resurrection.

"John, dear——" she began, with her hand on his bowed head.

"I've brought you into danger," he said helplessly, "I've brought you into danger, you and—" A lump in his throat put an end to speech, and with his hand he indicated the children.

"John, dear, don't talk so. I—I can't help feeling anxious, but I'm not afraid. In all the nine years we've lived here, the Indians have been our friends. There isn't one who would lift his hand against you or yours."

"They ain't all our friends, Eleanor. There's hundreds and hundreds of them coming in, even from as far away as the Wabash. How should they know that we are their friends? I've brought you into danger," he repeated. "I can't ever forget that."

"My husband," she said, and the tone was a caress, "we promised each other for better or for worse. 'Where thou goest, I will go, thy people shall be my people, and—' I forget the rest.

"If we've come to danger, we'll meet it together, side by side. When I promised to marry you, I didn't mean it just for the smooth places, I meant it for all. In all these twelve years you've shielded me—whatever you could do to make things easier for me, you've done, and all that love and care has been in vain if I am not strong enough to do my part now.

"There's never been a harsh word between us, John; we've never fussed and quarrelled as some married people do, and we never will. The road has been long, and sometimes it's been dusty and hot, but we've never walked on thorns, and whatever we've come to, you've always helped me through it.

"If this is the end, why, there's nothing to look back on to make either of us ashamed, nothing to regret, not a word to be sorry for, not a single thing for which either of us should say 'Forgive me.' If this is death, we'll face it as I have dreamed we should, if God were good to us; we'll face it as I've prayed we might—hand in hand!"

"Eleanor!" he cried, clasping her in his arms. "Brave heart, you give me faith! True soul, you make me strong!" His trembling lips sought hers, then on her face she felt his tears.

"Well, upon my word!" said Beatrice, from the doorway. "I hope I don't interrupt?"

Blushing like a schoolgirl, Mrs. Mackenzie released herself and the trader laughed mirthlessly. "You're a saucy minx, Bee," he said, with a little catch in his voice. Then the primitive masculine impulse asserted itself and he went out, covered with confusion.

"What have you been doing, Bee?"

"Nothing much. How pretty you are, Aunt Eleanor! I haven't seen your cheeks so pink for many a day."

The deep colour mantled Mrs. Mackenzie's fair face. "Where's Robert?" she asked hastily.

"Don't know," murmured Beatrice, instantly beating a retreat. "See, Aunt Eleanor."

Out of the mysterious recesses of her pocket, she drew a bag, made of gay calico, with a long string attached to it.

"Very pretty—what is it for, dear?"

"It's for cartridges," laughed Beatrice. "If I ride with the soldiers, I have to bear arms. I've got my pistol—the one Mr. Ronald gave me the day after I came here, and I'm going over to the Fort now, after ammunition."

She seemed to be in high spirits as she pirouetted around the room, but there was an undertone of sadness, even in her laugh. She was half-way to the door when she turned, moved by a sudden tenderness, and came back.

"Dear, sweet Aunt Eleanor," she said, rubbing her cheek against Mrs. Mackenzie's, "you've always been so good to me. Perhaps you've thought me ungrateful, but truly I'm not, and I want to thank you now."

"You've been like a second daughter to me, dear," said the other, a little unsteadily, "you've done more for me than I ever could do for you."

Ronald was waiting for Beatrice on the other side of the river while she was pulling across, and she waved her bright coloured bag at him in gay fashion. "You gave me a gun," she said, "but you didn't give me anything to put in it. I want cartridges."

"How many?" he asked, smiling.

"As many as the bag will hold."

"Foolish child, you never can carry all those."

"Oh, but I can—you don't know how strong I am! I'm going to tie it around my waist, you know."

"Happy bag," said Ronald, as he took it from her. "I'll get them for you," he continued, seriously.

"One thing more," she said, with lowered voice. "If—if—well, the Indians will never get me. And they shall not have Queen. Where shall I shoot?"

"Fire at the exact centre of the line between Queen's eyes."

In spite of herself the girl shuddered. "And—and—?" she asked, looking up into his face.

"The right temple," answered Ronald, huskily. "Heart's Desire, you are a mate for a king!"

Forsyth passed them on his way to the entrance of the Fort, and Beatrice put out a restraining hand. "Where are you going, Cousin Rob?"

"Home—to open school."

"I thought this was vacation?"

"It is, but it is better for the children, under the circumstances, to have their minds occupied."

The oars splashed in the water, and Ronald turned to her again. "Darling—"

"Look," interrupted Beatrice, "there's the Lieutenant." She hailed him merrily. "Cousin Ralph, is Katherine at home?"

"I believe so," he answered, coming toward them; "if not, she's at Mrs. Franklin's."

"I'm going to find her." She made an elaborate courtesy to each of them, and departed.

"Ronald," said the Lieutenant, "this is absolute foolishness, and something has got to bedone. How many hundred Indians do you suppose have already gathered here—and Black Partridge postponing the council till the rest get in—any fool can see what it means!"

"Yes, any fool but the Captain," said the Ensign, bitterly.

The parade-ground was deserted, for the August heats beat fiercely upon the land. Stray Indians went in and out, and the sentinel, with his musket over his shoulder, paced round and round the Fort. Lieutenant Howard cleared his throat.

"The lives of the women and children are in our hands," he said, in a low tone. "I'm not speaking for ourselves, now. If Franklin is still set on this mad course, there's only one thing to do." His face and voice were eloquent with sinister meaning.

The flag hung like a limp rag at the masthead and the long droning notes of the locusts sounded loudly in the tense stillness. "Murder," whispered Ronald, with his face white.

"Yes, murder, if you will have so. It's a harsh word, but I don't quibble at the term. 'Cæsar had his Brutus, King Charles his Cromwell, and——'"

Ronald's head was bowed and his hands were tightly clenched. Sharp, hissing breaths came and went between his set teeth and the Lieutenant put his hand upon his shoulder.

"Boy," he said, in a softer tone, "I'm a soldier, like you. So far, I've marched as you have, true to my colours, but of late, I've been wondering if it wasn't time to turn. Since the first soldiers marched against the enemy, there has been a false worship of orders—we have regarded the dictum of a commander as equivalent to a fiat of God.

"Good men and true have gone to a needless death, because the commander was a fool. You know what we're coming to. You can see it, plain as day. Do you remember, up at Lee's that night, you felt the mutilated bodies of those two men, and came back, with your hands stained with their blood? Our boys will be treated worse than that, if the Captain has his way."

"If you were in command—" said Ronald, thickly.

"If I were in command, that order should be torn to bits and scattered to the four winds. Every ounce of food in the Agency storehouse, every pound of powder and shot, every musket, every rifle, and every pistol, should be brought into the Fort.

"I would drive the cattle inside the enclosure, keep a few in the stables, kill the rest, salt down the meat, and preserve it. A cellar should be prepared for the women and children, a hospital corps drilled, the cannon in the blockhouses manned, and the gates of the Fort closed.

"If I were in command there should be no needless slaughter, no torture of women and children, no disembowelling of our soldiers, no cutting our hearts out while we are still alive. No! We'd fight like soldiers, die like men; we'd hold the Fort till the flag was shot to pieces and not a man stood among its ashes to defend it, if I were in command!"

"If you were in command—" muttered Ronald.

"If I were in command, Fort Dearborn should go down to history with honour, not shame. Water and food are assured. What if the British with all their forces were hammering at our gates, allied with the red devils as they are! We have the Fort at our backs—they have the river and the open prairie. We could hold it for six months, if necessary. The War Department says: 'No post shall be surrendered without battle having been given,' and, by the Lord, we'd give a battle that would fill hell with our enemies. One stroke will do it—one bullet from our precious store of ammunition—one man brave enough to strike; but it must be done to-night—now!"

The Ensign's face was ghastly. "Think what it means to you," whispered the Lieutenant. "Think of the woman you love! Oh, I know—I have not been blind. Would you see her put to the torture, stripped, violated, torn limb from limb by those fiends that even now are watching the Fort?

"Think of their bloody, cruel hands upon her soft flesh—think of the torture—eyes burned out with charred sticks—finger-nails split off backward—things that there are no words to name, while Beatrice cries to you!

"Boy, think of the woman you love, with her big childish eyes,—shall the savages burn them out? Her dimpled hands—shall her fingers be torn out, one by one? Her sweet voice—shall it cry to you in vain? Think of her fair white body, at the mercy of two thousand fiends! Think what she means to you—her beauty and her laughter—her tenderness and her thorns—then think of this! One man—one bullet—one moment—to-night—now!"

His voice died into a hoarse whisper and Ronald writhed in anguish. For an instant, only, the scales hung in the balance, then he turned and faced him.

"No!" he roared, "by God, no! I'll protect the woman I love while a drop of blood is left in my body—as long as this sword has a hand behind it to fight. If I am powerless to save her, she shall die at my hands, but I'll be no beast!

"I'll not commit murder like a Brutus or a Cromwell. I'll not strike down my Captain like a thief in the night! I'll stab no man in the back—I'll meet him face to face in fair and open fight, and may the best man win!

"Ralph, you're beside yourself—you don't know what you're saying. You're a soldier, man, you're not a brute! Stand fast to your soldier's honour, and let God do as He will!

"We're all against him—officers and men. Perhaps there's not a man in barracks who would hesitate at what you ask—mutiny and insurrection stalk abroad in our midst, but, by the Lord, I'll obey my orders! Strike the blow if you will—go like a coward and a thief to take the life of a brave man, who is doing what seems to him his duty—hire your contemptible assassin if you choose, but remember this—the man who touches one hair of my Captain's head, answers for it—to me!"

# CHAPTER XIX
## SAVED FROM HIMSELF

The morning of August twelfth dawned with burning heat. The lake lay as smooth as a sea of glass and from the south-west came the dreaded wind of the prairies, hot as a blast from a furnace and laden with dust. The sun blazed pitilessly in a cloudless sky and countless Indians patrolled the Fort, the Agency House, and the trading station.

The newcomers were alive with curiosity. Many of them had never seen the Fort before, and they swarmed in and out unceasingly. Through the wicket gate and the main entrance, past the soldiers' barracks, guard-house, hospital, storehouse, magazine, and contractor's store, back and forth between the officers' barracks, the Indians continually passed. They lay down on their faces to smell of the drain, muttered unintelligibly when they came to the subterranean passage, and wondered at the flag, with its fifteen stripes and fifteen stars, that hung limply at the staff.

They openly defied the sentinels at the gate, climbed into the blockhouses, where they surreptitiously felt of the cannon and peered furtively into the muzzles, and even went into the officers' quarters. It was the kind of a visit that one makes to an occupied house, on the eve of taking possession.

"Wallace," said Mrs. Franklin, "isn't there any way to keep these people out of the Fort?"

"Why, I hadn't thought about it," returned the Captain, absently. "They're not doing any harm, are they?"

"They haven't as yet," retorted Mrs. Franklin, with spirit, "but they're likely to at any moment. I don't want them in my house, and I won't have them here!"

"Tell them so," laughed the Captain. "I have no doubt of the effectiveness of your request."

"Don't make fun of me."

"I'm not making fun of you, dear, but it is of the utmost importance that we do nothing to excite the Indians. If they think we are unfriendly, mischief may easily result. I suppose our houses and the Fort have the same interest for them that their wigwams and blankets had for us, when we first saw Indians. Personally, I have no objection whatever to their examining our weapons of offence and defence."

Mrs. Franklin sighed. "When do we go?" she asked.

"As soon as possible after the council, which will be held this afternoon. It takes time, however, to prepare sixty or seventy people for a long overland journey."

"I wish we had boats."

"So do I, but we haven't. Still, I don't know that we'd be any better off, at the mouth of the St. Joseph River, without guides, than we are here. There may be a trail from the river across to Detroit, but I don't know anything about it. Lieutenant Swearingen marched his company around by land, when the Fort was built. When we get to Fort Wayne, we'll either stay there, or go on to Detroit with a larger force. It depends upon the movements of the British."

"Some way, Wallace, I'm afraid of trouble—I don't know why."

"I don't think there'll be any trouble, dear, but the idea that it would be right and proper to disobey the order appears to be spreading. Mackenzie is at the bottom of it, of course, and I don't know that we should blame him, for it means heavy financial loss to him. Yet he never could have established himself here if it had not been for the Fort, and it is his place to uphold the military, rather than to work against it; but there's no accounting for the vagaries of the human mind. All of his work here has been contingent upon the protection of the Fort; when that is withdrawn, he has no right to complain. Civilians seem to think that an order doesn't mean anything in particular—it's to be obeyed or not, as suits their erratic fancy. A soldier is a man who obeys orders—when he is no longer willing to do that he should get a discharge."

"Do you think the Indians will destroy this house, after we leave?"

"Probably, and the Fort also. Quarrels are bound to occur among the different tribes before long, and while they are settling their disputes in their own way, we'll get well on to Fort Wayne."

"I've thought," said Mrs. Franklin, slowly, "that Lieutenant Howard was inclined to make trouble. I haven't had any reason to think so, but I can't get it out of my head."

"It's quite possible," returned the Captain, with a significant shrug of his shoulders, "for he is one of the men who are always against everything they do not originate. He's been chafing at his bit all along because he isn't in command. If he were Captain, he'd want to be a step higher—I suppose he thinks himself capable of handling the whole army. But don't bother yourself about it, dear—we'll get through some way. I must go, now—I've got things to see to."

In and out of the stockade, parties of Indians were still passing, braves and squaws, who took great interest in their new surroundings. Mrs. Franklin locked her door, but savage faces continually appeared at the windows and at last she determined to go out upon the parade-ground and find a soldier or two to protect her.

When she opened the door, she started violently, and put her hand upon her heart.

"I'm sorry I frightened you," said Katherine. "I'm frightened myself. I don't like to have those Indians running in and out. Four squaws just came into my house and began to look around, just as if I had something that belonged to them. I don't know what they're doing now—they're still there. Can't we get some of the boys to drive them out and shut the gates?"

Before there was time for an answer, three braves and two squaws entered the Captain's house and began to inspect the furnishings of the room. Katherine was stiff with terror, but Mrs. Franklin was angry. She held her peace, however, until one of the warriors took down a musket from the wall, aimed it at the ceiling, and fired.

In an instant the Captain's wife was on her feet. Her husband's rifle was on the table behind her, and quick as a flash, she levelled it at the intruders. "Out of my house, you dogs!" she cried, and the Indians retreated, pausing outside just long enough to make savage grimaces at the women.

The report of the musket brought Ronald and some soldiers to the rescue. "What's up?" he asked, looking from one to the other.

It was Katherine who explained, for Mrs. Franklin's courage had deserted her, and she was trembling so she could not speak. "Cheer up, Mamie," said the Ensign—"I'll see to it."

Upon his own responsibility, he cleared the Fort of the intruders, closed the south gate, and put a double line of armed sentinels at the north entrance.

No sooner was it accomplished than Captain Franklin came out of the offices. "May I ask," he sarcastically inquired of Ronald, "by whose authority you have done this?"

The Ensign saluted. "By the authority of a Second Lieutenant who sees the wife of his Captain in danger," he answered stiffly, then turned on his heel and walked away.

The two women were sitting on the piazza and the Captain did not share Ronald's fears for their safety. Mackenzie and Black Partridge passed through the line of sentinels and he went to meet them.

"He says," began the trader, indicating the chief, "that noon of the sun is too early for the council, but that at the second hour after noon, he and his people will be assembled upon the esplanade, to await the pleasure of the White Father."

"Very well," said the Captain, carelessly.

Black Partridge went out and the Indians at once began to rally around him. At least a thousand, including the squaws, came out of the woods and were assigned to different stations, according to their rank. The chiefs of the several branches of the Pottawattomies and the chiefs of allied tribes, had places of honour in the front ranks. The braves and young warriors came next, and the squaws were grouped a little way off, by themselves.

For fully an hour before the appointed time, the solid phalanx waited in the broiling sun. Some of the squaws sat upon the hot ground, but the braves stood, silent and statuesque, with grim fortitude. The Ensign went to the gate of the Fort and took a long look at the assembly, frankly admitting to himself that he did not like the appearance of it.

When he had turned back and had passed the sentinels, Doctor Norton stopped him. "Ronald," he said, in a low tone, "the boys are talking mutiny."

The Ensign considered a moment. "How do you know?"

"Well, I've overheard two or three significant remarks that seemed to point in the same direction."

"Who began it?"

"It seems to have started in about fifty places at once."

"Do you know the names of the men?"

"No, I do not." Ronald knew that the Doctor lied, and respected him for it.

"Do you think the boys thought of it by themselves?"

"I should judge so—I didn't hear any references to the officers."

Ronald looked at him quickly but he appeared unconscious. "I just thought I'd tell you," he continued. "Of course, it's none of my affair."

"All right—much obliged to you."

The Doctor went away and Ronald went immediately to his superior officer. "Lieutenant Howard," he demanded sternly, "have you been talking mutiny to the men?"

Howard's eyes met his squarely. "No," he said sharply, "have you?"

Ronald retreated, shamefaced and ill at ease. "I—I beg your pardon."

"The boys aren't fools," laughed the Lieutenant. "They can see farther than some. I've spoken to no one but you, but if mutiny arises, I'll let it take its rightful course."

"Well, I won't. Remember what I said."

"I can't remember all your valuable utterances. Don't cast your pearls before swine, but reserve them for—for a more appreciative audience."

Stung to the quick by the insult, Ronald instinctively put his hand on his sword. Then both saw the Captain coming swiftly toward them, and waited.

"It is time for the council," he said.

"Well?" queried the Lieutenant, after an awkward pause.

"Are you going with me?"

Silence.

"Lieutenant Howard and Ensign Ronald, it is time for the council I have appointed with the Indians. Are you going with me?"

"An order, Captain?" inquired Ronald.

"Neither an order nor a request—not even a suggestion. It is an opportunity, to be taken or not, as you choose."

"Speaking for myself," said Ronald, "I do not see what we could accomplish by going. You are the army and the officers of it."

"As you pay no attention to our suggestions," remarked the Lieutenant, "I prefer to remain here."

"Very well." The Captain and Mackenzie went out alone.

"Better go to the blockhouse, hadn't we?" asked Ronald. "There may be trouble."

"I hope there will be," answered Howard. "Let Franklin fight it out alone with his precious Indians. Providence may yet intervene and give me the command."

Ronald went to the blockhouse alone, trained the cannon at the port-holes, and watched the Indians. After the first formal greetings were exchanged, the business of the afternoon began. Franklin spoke to Mackenzie, who translated for the benefit of Black Partridge, and he, in turn, conveyed the message to the assembly.

"We come for the last time," said Captain Franklin, "to speak with our brothers, the red men. Your Great Chief has told you how our Great Chief has bidden us to assemble at another place and how, though our hearts are torn with sorrow, we must obey the command. We have sent swift messengers a day's journey and more on every side, that we might say farewell to those with whom we have so long dwelt in peace. The goods in yonder storehouse, by the mandate of the Great White Father, are to be given to our brothers as a parting gift, that they may long hold us in kindly remembrance, as we shall them.

"We ask, however, a favour in return. We ask that some of our noble brothers, such as it may please, shall escort us to Fort Wayne, the place of our first assembly, and long known to the red men, who have many friends there. We ask that our brothers shall aid us in protecting our women and children from the dangers of the trail. If any are graciously inclined to do this kindness for us, we shall press upon them still other gifts when we reach our destination."

Black Partridge, in a loud voice, repeated the speech in the Indian tongue. Each of the chiefs in the front rank then expressed an opinion upon the subject, as he was asked by the spokesman. Then Black Partridge spoke apart with Mackenzie.

"They say," said the interpreter, "that it is well. They will joyously receive the goods in the storehouse as a parting gift from their white brothers, beside whom they have so long dwelt in peace. The plains will be lonely and the river sad without the palefaces. The houses of the Great White Father will be desolate when the friends of the red men are gone, but as it is written, so must it be. The bravest of the warriors will attend on the trail to Fort Wayne and safely shield the friends of the red men from savages and wild beasts. From all that stalks abroad with intent to slay, the friends of the palefaces will guard them. Let the children of the Great White Father have no fear. All shall be well. Side by side shall they journey with their brothers, the Pottawattomies and the allied tribes. In three moons, or perhaps two, if the Great Spirit is kind, the palefaces will return to dwell with their brothers once more, when their assembly is over and the Great White Father has made known unto them his commands."

"Tell them," said Captain Franklin, "that at the same hour of to-morrow's sun, the presents shall be given them. They shall have blankets, prints, calicoes, broadcloths, and adornments for their women and their papooses. For the Great Chiefs there will be tobacco, war paints, cunning contrivances for the sharpening of weapons, and provisions against the long cold Winter when the hunting grounds are barren, which is but four moons away. Say that the Great White Father will be pleased when he learns how the Great Chiefs, with their fearless braves and warriors, have safely guided his children unto the place of assembly."

"They say it is well," said Mackenzie, after the speech and its answer had been duly made, "and that at the same hour of to-morrow's sun they will assemble here, to receive the parting tokens of the Great White Father."

With much ceremony, the council was concluded and the Indians dispersed. Black Partridge lingered to express his pleasure because all had gone well, then he, too, went along the river bank to the woods where the Indians were gathered.

"Captain," said Mackenzie, "I want to talk to you a bit."

"All right—let's go back to the Fort, where it's cooler."

Ronald came down from the blockhouse as they entered the stockade and went across the river, where Beatrice was visible at a shaded window.

"How about the ammunition and liquor?" asked the trader. "Are you going to include that in the distribution?"

"I hadn't thought about it—why?"

"It's risky," said Mackenzie. "We don't want to furnish them with weapons to use against us. Arm those seven hundred Indians with muskets, give them powder and shot, fill them up with liquor, and where would we be?"

"It might amuse them," replied the Captain, thoughtfully. "If there was whiskey enough in the storehouse to get every man of them dead drunk, except our guides, it might be the best thing to do."

"Unfortunately, we can't force the proper quantity down the throat of each one. Some are wiser than the rest and they wouldn't drink."

"Well, suppose they had the muskets—wouldn't they use them against each other?"

"No," said the trader, conclusively, "they wouldn't. They'd turn against us."

"I hardly think that any of them will go with us, except Black Partridge and a few of his friends. By to-morrow, numerous fights will have started, and they'll be too busy to notice our departure. Besides, they have promised."

"Captain Franklin, the promise of an Indian is absolutely worthless, as you must know by this time. Since the troubles on the Wabash, the general trend of feeling toward us has been hostile. Their tomahawks are bad enough—they don't need our own weapons. When I got as far as De Charme's, last Fall, on my way to Detroit, and heard of the battle of Tippecanoe, I turned back immediately to Fort Dearborn and sent messengers to the outer trading posts with positive orders to furnish neither ammunition nor liquor to the Indians. Do you remember?"

"Yes, I remember. Perhaps it would be as well to keep back the liquor and ammunition, but in that case, they must not know we have them. How can we manage?"

"Bring everything into the Fort secretly, by night, and destroy it."

"Very well," said the Captain, after a silence; "you have had better opportunities than I have had to gain an intimate knowledge of the Indians. To-night and to-morrow night, as secretly as may be, I will have the goods brought in and destroyed."

After Mackenzie went home, the Captain went out to walk back and forth on the prairie near the Fort. His head was bowed and his arms were folded. In spite of General Hull's order and the friendly professions of the Indians, he felt the situation keenly. His responsibility sat heavily upon him, for he knew his officers were opposed to him and had begun to suspect that the men were disaffected. He would not have been surprised at a mutiny, feeling, as he did, that it was a case of one man against the world.

From a window, Katherine saw him walking to and fro, and at first she thought it was her husband, but a second look convinced her of her mistake. She was about to turn away when something arrested her attention.

On the Captain's right, and at some little distance from him, an Indian was moving stealthily toward the Fort. On his left, and still farther away from him, another was doing the same thing.

The Captain turned to the right, and instantly the Indian on that side dropped full length on the grass, while the other moved more quickly toward the Fort. When the Captain turned to the left the manoeuvre was repeated, but it was some time before she grasped the horrid significance of their actions.

When she perceived that both Indians were endeavouring to get between the Captain and the Fort, the blood froze in her veins. The parade-ground was deserted, and the long, droning notes of the locusts were the only sound she heard. She screamed, but the Captain did not turn, and no one seemed to hear. At the gate the sentinel leaned on his musket, unconscious of danger. She screamed again, but could not hear her own voice.

Then the springs of action threw off their lethargy. She dashed out of the house and flew over the parade-ground, with the taste of hot blood in her mouth and a heavy weight upon her breast. Trembling in every nerve, she climbed the ladder that led to the blockhouse, and entered, flushed and gasping. She was dimly conscious that she was not alone, but there was no time to waste.

Praying that she might not be too late, she seized a loaded musket, aimed through the porthole, and fired. It seemed an age before she saw the Captain through the smoke, running back to the Fort, and the two Indians making for the woods.

"Thank God!" she breathed, "thank God!" Then she turned—and faced her husband, his face so ghastly that she scarcely knew him.

"Ralph!" she whispered, hoarsely. "Ralph!"

His eyes refused to meet hers, and a tumult surged in her brain. Detached pictures of her childhood, confused and unrelated memories, and a thousand trivial things passed swiftly before her mental vision. Then, as if by magic, there was a clearing—all things gave way to the horrible knowledge that he had seen—and had failed to warn.

"Ralph! Ralph! My husband!"

The blood beat hard in her pulses and her lips curled in scorn. Then her unspeakable contempt melted to pity, as she saw how the man was suffering. Like an avenging angel she stood before him, confronting him mutely with his sin.

Captain Franklin came into the Fort. As the Lieutenant saw him safe and sound, he groaned deeply, like one whose suspense is ended. Then he raised his eyes to the face of his wife.

"I thank you, Katherine," he said, gravely; "you have saved me from myself."

# CHAPTER XX
# RECONCILIATION

That night, while the sentries kept guard, Lieutenant Howard paced to and fro, as sleepless and as vigilant as they. Now and then parties of soldiers came through the gates with ammunition or liquor from the Agency, and piled it in front of the storehouse to await the Captain's orders. Throughout the night the contraband goods were transported, as quietly as possible, in order that the suspicions of the Indians might not be aroused.

The Second in Command was in the midst of that battle with self which every man fights at least once in his life. The events of the past few days and his own part in them confronted him with persistent accusation. The prairie beyond the Fort and the figure of the Captain were etched upon his mental vision with the acid of relentless memory.

The scales fell from his eyes at last, and he saw himself clearly—mutinous, insubordinate, unworthy of his office; distrusting his wife and alienating his friends. Conscience, too long asleep, awoke to demand such reparation as lay in his power to make.

Ten minutes more and it would have been too late. Ten minutes more and the deadly tomahawk of an unseen foe would have been buried in the Captain's brain. That little space of time was all that stood between him and the command of Fort Dearborn—a command which he had planned to use in open rebellion against the orders of his superior officer.

Cold sweat stood out upon his forehead, and his clenched hands trembled. Ten minutes more and he would have been a murderer in deed as well as in thought, though his hands would not have been stained and there would have been no proof of his guilt. The pine knots blazed fitfully in the crevices of the stockade, turning to a ghastly glare as daylight came on. "A murderer!" he said to himself over and over again; "a murderer!" He was like one who wakes from some horrible nightmare with the spell of it still upon him, and wondering yet if it is not true.

Behind it all was a new emotion,—a new feeling for Katherine. Her hand had saved him. She had drawn him back from the brink of the abyss even as the ground was crumbling beneath his feet—Katherine, his wife, whom he had sworn to love and to cherish, and whom he had made miserable instead. To-morrow, or at most the day after, would see the end of it all. Two days remained in which to make atonement—two days, snatched from the past, to fulfil the promise of the future that once had seemed so fair.

"All in, sir," said a soldier. "Not a box nor a barrel is left at the Agency. It's all there." He pointed to a pyramid in front of the storehouse, which was almost as high as the building itself.

"No one saw you?" queried the Lieutenant.

"No, sir; no one saw. One of the pickets has just come in, and he says, sir, that every blamed Injun is up in the north woods. There's been a dance going on all night."

"Very well," answered the Lieutenant, carelessly; but his heart sank within him.

"Mad Margaret was there, too, sir—she was havin' one of her spells."

"Well," said the Lieutenant, sharply, "what of it?"

"Nothing, sir—excuse me, sir." The soldier saluted and went away.

The night wind died down and the sun rose in a fury of heat. No clouds softened the hard, metallic sky—it was like a concave mirror on which the sun beat pitilessly.

The guard was changed, and presently Doctor Norton came out on the parade-ground. When he saw who was there, he turned to go back, then waited, for the Lieutenant was coming swiftly toward him.

They faced each other for a moment, like adversaries measuring the opposing strength, then Norton smiled. "Well?" he asked calmly.

"I have not come to you," said the Lieutenant, thickly, "as you have doubtless expected me to. We have no time to cherish any sort of a grudge when, in two days at least, we start for Fort Wayne. You know what awaits us on the way, and if worst comes to worst, and I can no longer protect her, I ask you to make Mrs. Howard your especial care."

Schooled as he was in self-control, the Doctor started, and the expression of his face changed as he looked keenly at the Lieutenant.

"What!" cried the other, scornfully, "are you not willing to do that much for her?"

"Lieutenant Howard, as you say, it is no time to cherish a grudge. What you have asked of me would be an honour at any time, but I will not accept the trust until you know from me how I stand. I love your wife with all my heart and soul."

"Have you told her so?" asked Howard, quickly.

"In words, no—but I think she understands—in fact, I hope and believe that she understands."

The silence was tense, and Lieutenant Howard gnawed his mustache nervously. His hand went to his belt instinctively, then dropped to his side.

"I fear you have misjudged her," the Doctor continued. "A purer, truer woman never drew the breath of life. In word or act or thought she has never been disloyal to you. I said a moment ago that I loved her, but it is more than that—it is the worship that a man gives to a woman as far above him as the stars."

"In that case," said Howard, in a hoarse whisper, "you are well fitted to protect her."

"You still offer me that trust?" asked the other, eagerly.

The answer was scarcely audible. "I do."

Their eyes met in a long look of keen scrutiny on one side, and of fearless honesty upon the other. Then Norton extended his hand. The Lieutenant grasped it, caught his breath quickly, then turned away, for once the master of himself.

Beatrice came out of the Captain's house and smiled at him as he stood there with his head bowed. "You're—you're out early," he said, with an effort.

"I couldn't sleep. It was hot, and—Cousin Ralph, you must tell me. I am not a child, to be kept in the dark. What is this horrible thing that seems to be hovering over us? Uncle John does not speak to any one; twice yesterday I found Aunt Eleanor crying; Cousin Rob and Mr. Ronald are not in the least like themselves; Kit and Mrs. Franklin are as pale as ghosts, and you—I saw you walking here all night. What does it mean? Tell me!"

"We fear attack," he answered sharply.

"Indians or British?"

"Indians—under British orders."

For a moment the girl stared at him as if she did not believe what he said. "Would they—would they—" she gasped, "turn those fiends upon us?"

"Yes," he cried, "they would! They have done so in times past and they will do so again! They—I beg your pardon—I have forgotten myself—I—I—"

"Cousin Ralph, you are not well. You have walked all night, and you need rest. I understand your anxiety, your fears for us, but you need not be alarmed. We are women, but we are weak only in body—at heart we are soldiers like you, and, like you, we will obey orders. Cousin Ralph! You are ill! Come!"

He staggered, but did not fall. Beatrice put her arm around him and helped him home. "Don't be frightened, Kit," she said, when the door was opened; "he's just tired. He's been up all night and sleep will bring him to himself again."

"Can I help?" asked Forsyth, anxiously. He had come to ask Beatrice if she would not breakfast at home.

"Yes, please," said Mrs. Howard, quietly. "Help me get him into bed. He has been under a great nervous strain."

Beatrice sat on the piazza and waited. She had said she was not weak, but she was suffering keenly, none the less. After a little Robert came back. "He went to sleep immediately," he said; "but Mrs. Howard prefers to stay with him."

"Then we'll go home," she sighed. Together they went out of the stockade into the merciless heat that already had set shimmering waves to vibrating in the air. She drooped like a broken lily—her strength was gone.

Robert's heart went out to her in pity, and something more. When they reached the piazza he put his hand upon her arm. "Beatrice, dear," he said, softly, "lean on me. I cannot bear to see you so—my darling, let me help you!"

His voice shook, but she did not seem to hear. "I'm tired," she answered dully; "I—I didn't sleep." She put him away from her very gently. "I—I'm so tired," she repeated, with an hysterical laugh that sounded like a sob. "I don't want any breakfast—I just want to lie down and rest. Don't let Aunt Eleanor worry."

She went down the passage unsteadily, and he watched her until she was safely within her own room. He quieted Mrs. Mackenzie's fears as best he could, and managed to eat a part of his breakfast, though it was as dust and ashes in his mouth.

"Rob," said the trader, "can you help me to-day?"

"Certainly, Uncle."

"We've got to get all the goods out of here and out of the Agency, and divide them into lots of equal value. Black Partridge says seven hundred of his people are entitled to the gifts. The Captain and I decided last night to put the things out behind the Fort, send the Indians by in single file, and let each one choose as he will. Black Partridge agreed to the plan. He will form the line himself, so there's no chance for trouble."

The bateau was put into service, and Chandonnais was instructed to carry all the stores from the trading station to the esplanade, where two of the soldiers kept guard. Mackenzie and Forsyth, with the aid of a number of soldiers, carried out nearly all the stores from the Agency House, reserving only the provisions needed for the march.

Mackenzie had made out lists the night before from his inventory, so the task was not as difficult as it first appeared. As the men brought out the goods, articles of a kind were grouped together, so, with the aid of his note-book, the lots were quickly formed.

Had it not been for the heat, the task would have been finished by noon; but two o'clock found the tired men still at work and the long line of Indians waiting impatiently, kept back by the pickets on guard and the commands of their chief.

"Why," said Mackenzie, in surprise, "the things aren't all here. Three blankets are missing, two hams, a side of bacon, some calico, and I don't know what all."

"Haven't you made a mistake, Uncle?"

"No, I'm sure I haven't. Somebody must have stolen them, but I don't know how nor when it could have happened. Go up to the Fort, Rob, and get all the blankets they can spare—I can even up while you're gone."

The Indians were waiting with ill-concealed eagerness, and in half an hour more the word was given. Each went in turn to the wide stretch of prairie where the piles of merchandise were placed, and where sentinels were stationed to prevent stealing. When one started back with his goods, another went, and so on, until late in the afternoon.

On account of the great number of Indians and the reservation of provisions for the march, as well as four months' depletion of the stores, the portion of each one was small; but there were no signs of discontent until the distribution was over and the last Indian gathered up the single pile that was left and went back to his place at the foot of the line.

Then Black Partridge called Mackenzie and said he wished to speak to Captain Franklin.

"The goods of the White Father have been given to his children, the red men," translated Mackenzie. "We have received the blankets, calicoes, prints, paints, broadcloths, and the tobacco that the White Father promised us at the second hour after noon of yesterday's sun. All is as it was written. But where is the powder and shot of the Great White Father? Where are the muskets that were in the storehouse? Why can we not have weapons for our hunting during the long Winter that is but four moons away?

"The feet of the palefaces have a strange tread. They have frightened away the deer, the wolves, and the foxes that the Great Spirit has placed in the forest for his children to slay. Where is the firewater that strengthens the arm and the heart of the red man—the firewater which is the best gift of the Great White Father? Much of it was in the storehouse—we have seen it with our own eyes, but now it is gone."

"Say to him," said the Captain, "that when the strange tread of the palefaces has died away on the trail, the forest will once more fill with the wolves and the deer and the foxes that the Great Spirit has given for his children to kill. In the meantime, we leave our cattle for our brothers, the Pottawattomies, beside whom we have so long dwelt in peace. The grass is green upon the plains and there is water for all. When the long Winter night comes upon them, the hay that we have stacked in the fields will sustain the cattle until the Great Spirit once more sends the sun. There are roots in our storehouses with which they may do as they please, and they will not miss the deer and the wolves and the foxes that the palefaces have frightened away.

"The firewater which our brothers think they have seen in our storehouses was not firewater, but only empty casks. The red man is brave, and it has been written by the Great White Father that he needs no firewater to strengthen his arm and his heart. It is for women and for children and for men who are not strong, as the medicine man of the Pottawattomies has told them many times. It would be displeasing to the Great White Father should we take away the firewater from the palefaces who need it, for the sake of the red men who need it not.

"We have given to our brothers freely all that we have to give. It is a sorrow in our hearts that there is not more, but our storehouses are empty, as they must see, and other gifts are promised at the place of our assembly.

"When other moons have waxed and waned, and when the Great White Father has made known unto us his commands, we shall return once more to the river and the plains to dwell by the Great Blue Water with our brothers, the Pottawattomies, whose kindness and whose wise counsels are forever written in our hearts."

"They say it is well," said Mackenzie, when the long speech and its brief answer had been translated; "and that they will pray unceasingly to the Great Spirit that the moons may be few ere the friends of the red men return."

Forsyth and Mackenzie went home thoroughly exhausted. Night brought no relief from the intense heat, and the guards paced listlessly to and fro. Under cover of the darkness a small company of soldiers, under Ronald's orders, broke up the muskets and flint-locks, wet down the powder, put the shot into the well in the sally-port, and knocked in the heads of the barrels containing liquor.

Careful as they were, noise was inevitable. Barrel after barrel was rolled to the river bank and its contents poured into the stream. A cask of alcohol shared the same fate, and the peculiar, pungent odour filled the air.

"It's too late, sir," said a soldier, when he came in, rolling the last empty barrel before him.

"What do you mean?" demanded Ronald.

"The Indians, sir. Three of them are lying in the grass downstream, drinking the river water for the sake of the grog."

"Where are the rest?"

"In the woods, sir, dancing, same as last night. The northern pickets told me, sir."

A long, low whistle came from the Ensign's lips. "If I might be so bold, sir," continued the man, in a low tone, "some of the boys have thought as how you weren't falling in with this order of the Cap'n's. Orders is orders—we know that—but the boys are with you, to a man. We'll do whatever you say, sir."

In spite of the threat which the words veiled, Ronald was deeply touched by the devotion of the barracks. He laid his hand on the man's shoulders before speaking.

"To be with me is to be with the Captain," he said. "It is one and the same. Trying times must come to all of us, and for a soldier there can be no nobler end than to die fighting for his country. Captain Franklin will ask no one of us to go where he would not go himself. Tell the boys that, and that to stand by the Captain is to stand by me."

"All right, sir. And the barrels isn't all emptied. There's a cask over in the barracks. The boys thought it might hearten 'em up a bit, and they said, sir, that you wouldn't care."

"You are welcome to it," answered Ronald, absently, "but make a good use of it. We'll need a steady hand, each and every man of us, when we start out on the march."

The night sentinels came on and the soldier went on to the barracks, where his comrades were making merry with the wine. "I wonder," said Ronald to himself, "what would have happened if he had said that to—to another?"

Even in his thought he did not name the Lieutenant, but, as he passed the house, he saw Katherine moving back and forth before the open window. "Poor girl," he said aloud. "Poor girl!"

Katherine had had a hard day, even though her husband had slept without a break since Forsyth helped her get him into bed. At first she thought he had been drinking, though she knew he was not in the habit of it. Mrs. Franklin had been over and had been told indifferently that the Lieutenant was tired out and was resting.

It was late when he awoke, rubbed his eyes, and sat up in bed. Katherine went to him and put her cool hand upon his hot face. "Are you better, dear?" she asked.

"Yes," he sighed; "I'm all right. It's hot, isn't it?"

She sat down on the bed beside him and talked to him soothingly, as if he were a tired child. She told him everything that had occurred during the day, and said she was glad he could rest. She got him a glass of water, then bathed his flushed face with a soft cloth and stroked his hands gently with her cool fingers.

For a long time he watched her as she ministered to him with unfailing gentleness. Her straight shoulders were bent a little and there were lines upon her face; but the ashen gold of her hair and the deep blue of her eyes were the same as when he first loved her—so long ago. He remembered the mad joy that possessed him when his lips first touched hers, and the crushing sorrow of their bereavement, which should have drawn them closer together, but instead had driven them apart. He knew that another man loved her and that she knew it also, yet she had been loyal.

As she went out, he wondered whether another woman in her place would have been true to him. With a swift searching of self he tried to remember some tender word that he had said to her, but it was all blotted out, as if darkness had come between them. For the first time he looked at their life together from her point of view, and shuddered as he saw how she might think of him. Her silence and her patience were evident to him, as they had not been before. Many a time he had seen the blue eyes fill and the sweet mouth tremble at some careless word of his, and often, too, he had seen her shut her teeth together hard when some shaft was meant to sting.

Two days were left—no, only one—for it was night now. One day in which to atone for the countless hurts of the past four years. The dominant self melted into unwonted tenderness as she came back into the room.

"I was gone too long," she said quickly; "but I didn't mean to be."

"Katherine!" he said in a new voice.

"Yes, dear; what is it?" She sat down beside him once more and looked anxiously into his face, fearing that he was ill.

"What is it, dear?" she asked again.

"Nothing," he said huskily; "only that I love you and I want you to forgive me."

"Ralph! Ralph!" she cried, sinking into his arms, "there's nothing to forgive; but I've prayed so long that I might hear you say it!"

"Will you?" he pleaded, with his face hidden against her breast.

"Yes," she cried, "a thousand times, yes! I've wanted you to love me as I've never wanted anything else in the world!"

"I love you with all my soul," he said simply. "I——" A catch in his throat put an end to speech, for her love-lit face, wet with tears, was very near to his. His arms closed hungrily around her, and the lips that but a moment before were quivering with sobs, were crushed in eternal pardon against his own.

---

# CHAPTER XXI
# THE LAST DAY IN THE FORT

"Sir," said a soldier; "some one is coming!"

"From which way?" asked the Captain.

"South, sir."

Captain Franklin climbed the ladder that led into the blockhouse at the south-east corner of the stockade, wondering whether it was friend or foe who approached. Dim upon the far horizon was a single rider, who moved slowly, as if his horse were tired. Behind him marched a small company of Indians.

"What do you make of it, sir?" asked the guard in the blockhouse, anxiously.

"He bears no flag," answered the Captain. "Train the guns and wait for a signal."

Only the north gate of the Fort was open, and, as always of late, it was well protected; but, none the less, the Captain's heart was heavy. He strained his eyes toward the rider, far across the sun-baked prairie, and the minutes seemed like hours. The man sat his horse like an Indian, yet, someway, even at the distance, conveyed the impression that he was a white man.

The news quickly spread, and the soldiers who were off duty mounted the stockade. As the company came nearer, the rider waved his hat, but the men at the Fort made no answer until one soldier, with keener eyes than the rest, shouted joyously, "Captain Wells!"

"Captain Wells! Captain Wells!" The parade-ground rang with the cry. The two fifes and two drums struck up a military air, and a small escort marched to meet him.

"Captain Wells!" The shout brought every soldier to the front, and even the women, smiling, waited for him at the gate. The escort turned back, and, swiftly upon the sound of the music, the cannon boomed a welcome.

When the travel-stained rider dismounted, Captain Franklin wrung his hand as if he never would let it go. "God bless you," he cried; "what brought you here?"

"Orders from General Hull," answered Captain Wells. "I have brought thirty faithful Miami Indians to escort your command to Fort Wayne."

Beatrice, Forsyth, the Mackenzies and their children, as well as every one at the Fort, gave Captain Wells a warm reception. "Come to our house," said Katherine.

"He's not going to your house," answered Mrs. Franklin. "He's my uncle, and he's coming to mine."

It was some time before the Indian escort was taken care of, and Wells and Franklin had an opportunity to discuss the situation.

"How are things with you?" asked Wells, anxiously.

"All right, I guess; I've been doing the best I can. On the ninth I received orders from General Hull to evacuate the post and proceed with my command to Detroit by land, leaving it to my discretion to dispose of the public property as I thought proper. The Indians got the information as early as I did, and they have come from all quarters to receive the gifts. I asked Black Partridge to summon his people, but I don't believe all the Indians here are Pottawattomies. I have given them all the goods in the factory store, and all the provisions which we cannot take with us. I have destroyed the surplus arms and ammunition, fearing they would make a bad use of it, and I have also destroyed all the liquor."

"Do the Indians seem friendly?"

"Yes—of course they wanted the ammunition and liquor, but I explained that. There has been some friction here at the post. The Mackenzies, of course, are opposed to going, and the feeling has affected others. There does not seem to be much danger, though, unless the British come down from Fort Mackinac, which seems hardly possible. The Indians have promised to see us safely to Fort Wayne, but then—what's the promise of an Indian?"

"Not much, I admit," answered Wells; "but I'm here to stand by you. If worst comes to worst, here's one more man to fight. I'm with you to the last."

"It is a great relief to me," said Franklin, after an eloquent silence, "for I have felt myself alone—one man against the world."

"I'd do all I could for your wife's sake, if for no other reason. Call an Indian council this afternoon and let me talk to them."

Franklin's face brightened. "The very thing!" he cried. "I'll give the order at once." Then he grasped the other's hand and said again, "God bless you!"

At the appointed hour in the afternoon the entire company of Indians assembled upon the esplanade. After ceremonious greetings were exchanged with the chiefs, Captain Wells turned to the others.

"A good day to you, my brothers," he said. "The time has seemed long indeed since we parted. I see among you many new faces from the far country, and I am rejoiced to learn that you have promised to accompany the White Father and his people to the assembling place. Had I known of this I should not have come, but should have trusted wholly to my brothers.

"However, it is a happiness to me to see my friends once more. Although I am a white man, I have been brought up like one of you. I have learned the secrets of the forest and the trail and I have fought side by side with the red men. For many of you I have sad news. The Great Chief, Little Turtle, whose daughter I have taken in marriage, went to the happy hunting grounds on the fourteenth day of the last moon.

"Were he alive he would send his greetings to his brothers who are here assembled. Thirty of his people have come with me to lead the Americans safely upon the trail. For three or more days must we journey, since the feet of the palefaces are slow, but we have no fears. From the dangers of the day and the night, from wild beasts, from every creature that stalks abroad with intent to slay; from the unlearned tribes who are unfriendly to the whites, and from the warriors of another White Chief, who may be known by their red coats, we will protect our friends. It has been written by the Great White Father that after we have led his people safely to the assembling place, many gifts shall be distributed among us there. My brothers, I bid you farewell."

Silently the Indians went back to the woods. No answer was made to the speech except that it was good, and that all should be as it was written.

"Franklin," said Wells, when they were again alone, "everything seems to be all right, and yet I scent trouble. Do you suppose they have received orders from the British to cut us off?"

"I wish I knew," answered Franklin, sadly; "and yet what could I do?"

"We must get out of here as quickly as possible. How much ammunition have you reserved?"

"Twenty-five rounds per man."

"How about provisions?"

"We have enough for a long march. We'll take all we can, and give the remainder to the Indians on reaching Fort Wayne."

"How many horses have you?"

"Enough for the officers and the women, as well as for the waggons. The children can go in the waggons."

"Things are better than I feared," said Wells. "I hope we'll get through all right—at any rate we'll do our best."

Orders were given for an early start on the following morning, and the baggage of each person was limited to the absolute essentials. The day passed in active preparations for departure, and the appearance of Captain Wells, with the guard, had lightened the situation considerably.

All of the pine knots that were left were fastened between the bars of the stockade, as the soldiers had determined to illuminate in honour of Captain Wells. The day had promised to be a little cooler, but the lake breeze of early morning soon retreated before the onslaught of the south-west wind.

The women had packed up their toilet articles and a few little trinkets valued for their associations, and the kit of every soldier was in readiness. Forsyth made a belt for his sword, pistol, and cartridges, which looked oddly enough when it was fastened over his suit of rusty black. Beatrice had recovered her spirit enough to laugh heartily at the picture he presented.

All save Ronald were more cheerful than they had been for many a day. He walked about as if he were in a trance, and when he was spoken to he did not seem to hear. More than once he was seen staring into space with a glassy look in his eyes.

In the evening the Mackenzies became sad at the prospect of leaving their old home, as they sat before the desolate hearth, side by side, for the last time. For a little while Beatrice sat there with them. The children were asleep, Robert was finishing his packing, and she felt herself an intruder, so at last she stole away and went over to the Fort, where the pine knots blazed with a lurid light and cast shadows afar.

Lieutenant Howard and Katherine were on the piazza at Franklin's, where Captain Wells sat with his hosts. Under cover of the darkness the Lieutenant was holding Katherine's hand, and Captain Franklin sat with his arm over the back of his wife's chair.

"See what it is to be a spinster," laughed Beatrice, as she approached. "Captain Wells, would you mind holding my hand?"

Wells stammered an excuse, for he was unused to the ways of women, and Beatrice made him the subject of her playful scorn. "Am I so unattractive, then?" she queried, looking sideways at the discomfited Captain from under her drooping lids.

"N—no," answered Wells, miserably; "but—" He floundered into helpless silence, not at all relieved by the laughter of the others.

That evening, if at no other time, Beatrice was beautiful. Her high colour had faded to a languorous paleness, and the harshness of her manner was gone. Her trailing white gown was turned in a little at her round, white throat, and her long, shining hair hung far below her waist in a heavy braid.

"Ronald," called the Lieutenant, "come here!"

The Ensign came slowly across the parade-ground. His shoulders drooped and his face was very pale. "What is it?" he asked.

The tone was unlike Ronald. "Nothing," replied the Lieutenant, "except that Beatrice wants somebody to hold her hand and Captain Wells won't. He's too bashful, and the rest of us are occupied."

"It's too hot," sighed the Ensign. He sat down on the piazza, near Beatrice, and fanned himself with his cap; but he took no part in the conversation, and did not even answer Katherine's "good-night" when her husband took her home.

"I'm going in, too," said Mrs. Franklin, "if nobody minds. I'm very tired."

Franklin and Wells talked listlessly, feeling the restraint of the others' presence. "Come out for a little while," said Ronald to Beatrice. "I don't think they want us here."

The full moon was low in the heavens and the lake was calm. They went out of the Fort and down near the water, but still he did not speak. Then Beatrice put her hand on his arm. "What's wrong with you?" she asked softly; "can't you tell me?"

His breath came quickly at her touch and he swallowed hard. "Heart's Desire," he said huskily, "I die to-morrow—will you tell me you love me to-night?"

"Die!" cried Beatrice. "What do you mean?"

"Sweet, the death watch ticked last night—Norton and I heard it and most of the men. To-night, while I have eyes to see and ears to hear, let me dream that you are kind. Since that first day, when I saw you across the river, I have hungered for you; yes, I have thirsted for you like a man in the desert who sees the blessed, life-giving water just beyond his reach. My arms have ached to hold you close—my rose, my star, my very soul!"

"All my life has been lived only for this; to find you and to tell you what I tell you now. I have no gift of words—I'm only an awkward soldier, but with all my life I love you. Poets may find new words for it, but there is nothing else for a man to say. Just those three words, 'I love you,' to hold the universe and to measure it, for there is nothing else worth keeping in all the world!"

Shaken by his passion, he stood before her with the moonlight full upon his face. His shoulders were straight once more, but his eyes were misty and he breathed hard, like a man in pain.

The girl was sobbing, and very gently he put his arm around her. "Heart's Desire," he said again, "I die to-morrow—will you tell me you love me to-night?"

"I do—I do," she cried, as he drew her closer; "but, oh, you must not talk so! You cannot die to-morrow—you are young—you are strong! Don't! Don't! I must not let you misunderstand! It is not what you think!"

His cry of joy changed to an inarticulate murmur, and his arms stiffened about her as she stood with her face against his breast. "I must be a stone," she sobbed, "or I would care. Don't think I haven't known, for I have; but I've been afraid—I've always been afraid to care, and now I've grown so hard I can't! Pity me—be kind to me—I cannot care, and on my soul I wish I could!"

His arms fell to his sides and she was free. Half fearfully she lifted her lovely, tear-stained face to his. "I wish I could!" she sobbed. "Believe me, upon my soul, I wish I could!"

"Heart's Desire, I would have no words of mine bring tears to your dear eyes. To see you so is worse than death to me. I was a fool and a brute to speak, but the words would come. I have known you were not for me. I have walked in the mire, and you are a star; but sometimes men dream that even a star may descend to lift one up. Forget it, Sweet, forget that I was mad, and if you can, forgive me!"

"I never shall forget," she answered, with her lips still quivering, "for it is the sweetest thing God has yet given to me. But all my life I have been afraid to trust, afraid to yield, and now, when I would, I cannot. It is my punishment, and even though I hurt you, I must be honest with you."

"Sweetheart, the hurt is naught—it is a kindness since it comes from you. I ask your pardon, and remember I shall never speak of it again. Others, perhaps, would say I have had enough—my youth, my strength, and all that makes life fair. I have served my country well and to-morrow I die fighting, as soldiers pray that they may. Women have loved me, and yet— My darling, I die to-morrow—ah, kiss me just once for to-night!"

She was very near him, but she turned her face away. "No," she whispered, "I can't. I will give you nothing unless I give you all."

"So let it be," he sighed. He put his arm around her again, and she tried to move away, but he held her fast. "Don't be afraid of me," he said. "Dear Heart, can't you trust me? You might lay your sweet lips full on mine, and yet mine would not answer unless you said they might. I just want to tell you this. I can see no farther than to-morrow, and after that—I do not know. But I'm not afraid of death, nor hell, nor of God Himself, because I take with me these two things. I think all else will be forgiven, Sweet, because I have served my country well and I have been man enough to love you."

"Oh," cried Beatrice, with the tears raining down her face, "I can bear it no longer—let me go home!"

She went across the river alone, and the sound of her sobbing came through the darkness and cut into his heart like a knife. The dull stupor of the day gave place to keenest pain. He was alive to the degree that no man knows till he is wounded past all healing. Every sense was eager for its final hurt. "How shall I live!" he muttered. "How shall I live until to-morrow, when I die!"

He went back into the Fort with his head bowed upon his breast. As in a dream he saw Wells and Franklin sitting by a table in the Captain's house. The single tallow dip, with its tiny star of flame, was almost too much light for his eyes to bear. The pine knots in the crevices of the stockade filled the place with a lurid glare that seemed like the blaze of a noonday sun.

---

He sat alone in a dark corner, muttering, "How shall I live! How shall I live until to-morrow, when I die!" Lieutenant Howard passed him, but did not see him. Then Doctor Norton called out, "Do you know where Ronald is?"—but the Lieutenant did not know.

There was a stir at the gate and Mackenzie came in, accompanied by Black Partridge. They went straight to the Captain's quarters and were admitted at once. Mackenzie's face was grey and haggard, but the Indian was as stolid as ever, save that his eyes glittered cruelly. Wells and Franklin felt an instant alarm. "What is it?" asked Franklin, hurriedly.

Black Partridge took off the silver medal which Captain Wells had given to him and laid it on the table. The light of the tallow dip shone strangely on the metal, and picked out the figures upon it in significant relief. Then he spoke rapidly, and Mackenzie translated.

"Father, I come to deliver up to you the medal I wear. It was given me by the Americans, and I have long worn it in token of our mutual friendship. But our young men are resolved to bury their hands in the blood of the whites. I cannot restrain them, and I will not wear a token of peace while I am compelled to act as an enemy."

"Captain," cried a soldier, rushing in, "the Indians are having a war dance in the hollow!"

"Close the gates," commanded Franklin, "and call the pickets in." He was outwardly calm, though cold sweat stood out upon his forehead, and Captain Wells stood by in silent distress. Before any one had time to speak, Black Partridge was gone. He passed through the gates almost at the moment they rumbled into place, and fled like a deer to join his people.

"I suppose," said the trader, "that in the face of this you will not march to-morrow."

"Yes," cried the Captain, in a voice that rang; "we march to-morrow in spite of hell!"

Beside himself with fear, anger, and pain, Mackenzie rushed out and told the first soldier he met all that had passed. In an instant there was the sound of hurrying feet and the Fort was aflame with rebellion. "Wells," said Franklin, quietly, "I wish you'd go to the barracks. You may be needed there."

But the barracks were empty. As the guns thundered the signal for the pickets to return, the men gathered around Ronald. Instinctively, in times of trouble, they looked to him.

"Go to the barracks, boys," he said, in a low tone, "and wait for me there. I'll do what I can."

A white figure appeared at a window and the Lieutenant went in to speak to Katherine. Doctor Norton went straight to the Captain.

Franklin's eyes were blazing and his body was tense. The martial spirit of the frontier had set his blood aflame. His fingers fairly itched for his sword, and his hands were clenched. "Captain," said the Doctor, calmly, "is there no other way?"

"No," cried Franklin; "there is no other way! Are you a coward that you ask me this?"

The Doctor laughed unpleasantly, and went out without another word. Hardly had his footsteps died away before Lieutenant Howard came in, white to the lips with wrath.

"Is this true?" he shouted. "Do we march to-morrow, with our women and children, when the Indians have declared war?"

"Yes," said Franklin, meeting his gaze steadily, "we do."

"Captain, this is madness. The men will never go. It is certain death to leave the Fort. Your orders will not be obeyed, if it comes to that."

"Lieutenant Howard, my orders will be obeyed. The man who refuses will be shot."

"Captain, can't you listen to reason? Our force is small. We never can cope with those fiends that even now are having their war-dance in the hollow. I said it was certain death, but death in itself is nothing to fear. Torture waits for us—for our women and children. Captain, change the order—stay!"

"Sir, I have my orders."

The Lieutenant turned away. "Stop!" commanded the Captain. "You need not go to the men. I am in command of this Fort and I will have no mutiny. The soldier who attempts to disobey my orders will be shot down like a dog, be he officer or man. We march to-morrow, if I go alone!"

The Lieutenant staggered out and almost into the Ensign's arms. "Ronald," he pleaded thickly, "go to the Captain. See if you cannot do something to save us all. Don't ask for ourselves—he is pitiless there—but the women and the children—" His voice broke at the words, but he kept on. "Ronald, for God's sake, go!"

The thought of Beatrice's danger stirred the Ensign's blood to fever heat, and he rushed into the house like a madman. "Captain!" he cried.

There was an instant of tense silence. A torrent of words was on Ronald's lips, but the Captain raised his hand. "I suppose," he said coolly, "that you are merely following the general tendency. Mackenzie, Norton, and the Lieutenant have all been here to suggest that I disobey my orders. Is that your purpose, also?"

"Yes," shouted Ronald, "it is!"

"By what right do you presume to offer unasked advice to your superior officer?"

"By the right of one who has kept your men from mutiny!"

The Captain cleared his throat. "Well?"

"I have no plea to make for myself, Captain. I have come to ask at your hands the lives of the women and children who are under our protection—to ask you not to betray the most sacred trust that can be given to man. You speak of orders. As I understand it, no time was set for the evacuation of the Fort?"

"We have delayed too long already."

"Suppose the British army was at our gates—would those orders hold good?"

"Sir, you are impertinent!"

"Captain, that medal which Black Partridge returned to you to-night was equivalent to a declaration of war. If you are not willing to act upon your own responsibility, send Captain Wells and his Indians to General Hull to ask for reinforcements. If Captain Wells is not willing to go, I am. I know the provisions have been given to the Indians, but we have the cattle and perhaps enough else to last the garrison two weeks or more. With reinforcements we can hold the Fort against any force that may be brought against it. Captain—let me go!"

"Sir, I have my orders."

"Orders be damned!"

"At West Point," asked the Captain, hoarsely, "were you taught to speak to your superior officer in that way?"

"Captain, I speak to you not as my superior officer, but as man to man. Our force is small, some of our boys are too old to fight, and we have women and children to protect. I ask nothing for myself, nor for men like me—we are soldiers. I plead for the helpless ones under our care. I ask you only to wait, not to disobey. I beg you to save the women and children from torture—from cutting their flesh to ribbons while they still live—from things that one man cannot look another in the face and name."

Franklin turned away, his muscles rigid as steel.

"You have a wife, Captain—a tender, loving, helpless woman. Are you willing to give her to the Indians and let them do as they please with her? Suppose you had a child, just old enough to walk—a little daughter, whose flesh was so soft that you almost feared to touch her—a child who loved you, trusted you, and leaned upon you, knowing that you would risk your life to save her from the slightest hurt. Suppose two thousand Indians in their war-paint were pounding at the gates of the Fort, and the knife and the stake were waiting for their victims—would you stand upon the stockade and throw that child to those beasts?

"That is what you are going to do to-morrow. You will sacrifice your own wife, the wife of every man at the post, and every little child, but it touches you only at one point. In the name of the woman who loves you—in the name of the children who might have called you father—Captain—in God's name—stay!"

The Captain's face was ashen, but his voice was clear. "Sir, I am a soldier—I have my orders!"

With a muttered curse, Ronald flung himself out of the room. He staggered to the parade-ground blindly, gasping with every breath. Then the door opened softly and a white figure, barefooted, came quietly into the room.

"What!" cried the Captain; "you, too?"

Her gown was no whiter than her face, but she came to him steadily. "Wallace," she said, "you are a soldier, and I am a soldier's wife. I could not help hearing what they said. Don't think I blame you—I know you will do what is right. Captain Wells and I will stand by you!"

He took her into his arms, and then a hoarse murmur came to their ears. She started away from him in fear. "What is it?" she cried.

"It's only the barracks," he answered, trying to smile. "Come, dear, come!"

When Ronald opened the door, where the men were drinking heavily, the confusion was heard to the farthest limits of the Fort. "Boys," he cried, "it's all over—there's nothing any one of us can do!" Lieutenant Howard, the Doctor, and Captain Wells were standing together near the door, but he did not seem to see them.

Straight to the middle of the room he went, and a soldier filled his glass. "Make merry while you can, my brave boys," he shouted, "for this is the last of life for us! To-night we are men—to-morrow we are food for the vultures! To-night we are soldiers—to-morrow we are clay! To-night we may sleep—to-morrow we wake to the knife, the scourge, and the flames! To-night, for the last time, we stand side by side—to-morrow we fight a merciless foe of ten times our strength!

"If you have neither wife nor child, thank God that you stand alone. If you have, load your muskets and strike them down at sunrise to-morrow,—yes, stain your hands with their innocent blood that you may save them from something worse. Twelve hours of life remains—waste none of it in sleep! Fill your glasses to the brim and drink till the night is past. Pray that your senses may leave you—that your reason may be replaced by the madness of beasts! Pray for strong arms to-morrow—pray for a soldier's fate! Drink while the stakes are being put in place for us—drink to your ashes and the fall of Fort Dearborn—drink, boys—to Death!"

The room had been deadly still while he was speaking, but now the cry rang to the rafters,—"To Death!"

"Again," shouted Ronald, "fill your glasses once more! To the strong arm and the fearless heart—to the torture that waits for us to-morrow—to the red spawn of hell that is grinning at our gates—a toast to Death!"

The door opened and Captain Franklin came into the room. Every man turned accusing eyes upon him save one. "To the Captain!" cried Wells, lifting his glass.

He drank alone, since, for the moment, no one else moved. Then, with one accord, the wine was thrown to the floor and the sharp crash of glass followed it, as the deep-throated bell sounded taps—for the last time.

# CHAPTER XXII
# THE RED DEATH

"Attention! Forward—march!"

To the music of the Dead March the column swung into line and turned southward from the Fort. At the head rode Captain Wells, who, after an Indian custom, had blackened his face with wet gunpowder in token of approaching death. Half of the Miami escort followed him, then came the regulars, accompanied by the women, all of whom were mounted; then the three waggons, and the remainder of the Miami escort.

Mrs. Mackenzie and her four children were in the bateau, with their clothing and a limited amount of supplies. Chandonnais and a friendly Indian were at the oars. Black Partridge had appeared at the trading station before daylight, to ask Mackenzie and his family to go in the boat. The trader refused, saying he would march with the soldiers; and Robert also declined the opportunity. Both Mackenzie and his wife insisted that Beatrice should take the safer course, but it was useless.

"What?" she asked, "and leave Queen? Not I! We're going with the soldiers!"

The other children at the post, eleven or twelve in all, were in the first waggon, which was driven by a soldier. The second waggon contained the supplies for the march; and in the third, where the ammunition was stored, sat Mad Margaret. She had come very early in the morning, with a small bundle, ready for departure.

The day was intensely hot, and the lake was like a sea of glass. The line of march was along the water's edge, where sand hills intervened between the beach and the prairie. The Pottawattomies, more than six hundred strong, kept behind the sand hills and were seldom visible.

As the little company proceeded toward Fort Wayne, heavy hearts grew lighter and anxious faces became peaceful. No Indians were in sight save the Miami escort at front and rear. The music of the Dead March ceased, and then upon the silence came Mad Margaret's voice, as she croaked dismally, "I see blood— much blood, then fire, and afterward peace."

Beatrice was riding with Robert, a little way behind Ronald. That morning she had seen Mad Margaret for the first time. "Listen," she said, as she leaned forward to stroke Queen's glossy neck, "doesn't that sound like a raven in the woods? She's a bird of evil omen, but, just as we were starting, she told me I should find my heart's desire to-day."

"I trust you may," said Robert, gravely. Then he called to Ronald, but the Ensign did not hear. He had begun the day in the dull stupor of yesterday.

At the mouth of the river a Pottawattomie chief crept up behind the column and signalled to the Indian in the bateau to stop rowing. He did so, and the company went on a little way without missing the boat.

They were about a mile and a half from the Fort when Captain Wells came riding back furiously. "They are about to attack us," he shouted. "Turn and charge!"

Captain Franklin and his company dashed up a sand hill,—a veteran of seventy falling by the way,—and were greeted with a volley at the top. In an instant the massacre was on. Under cover of the sand hills a part of the Pottawattomies had reached the front, and now surrounded them at every point. The Miamis fled to a safe place when the first shot was fired.

Captain Franklin endeavoured to mass the waggons upon the shore, but it was useless, for dire confusion was in the ranks and each man fought for himself as best he could. Behind them lay the lake—at the right and left and in front of them were six hundred savages, armed with arrows, muskets, and tomahawks. The plain rang with the war-whoop and the cries of the victims, while shrill and clear above the clamour came Mad Margaret's voice, shrieking, "The time of the blood is at hand!"

At the first alarm, Chandonnais leaped out of the bateau, swam ashore and ran to join the troops, leaving Mrs. Mackenzie and the children alone with the Indian. He made his way through the left line of the savages with incredible quickness, fighting as he went with the ferocity of a beast. A painted warrior raised his weapon to strike, but the half-breed, cursing, snatched it away from him and laid him low with his own tomahawk.

Now and then Captain Franklin's voice could be heard giving orders. His plan was to break through the line, turn, and close in, but the attempt failed and was fraught with heavy loss.

Beatrice was a little way off, partially sheltered by a sand hill. Her eyes were wide and staring, and the blood was frozen in her veins. Even in dreams she had not thought it could be like this. Queen snorted and pawed the ground impatiently, but the hands on the bridle were numb, and there was no chance to escape.

The exultant cries of the Indians beat upon her ears with physical pain. The early goldenrod, in full flower on the prairie, was broken down as by some terrible storm. She saw Mackenzie repeatedly fire his musket, and always effectively, in spite of warning shouts from the enemy. Lieutenant Howard was wounded in the shoulder, but was still fighting gallantly; and Ronald, in the front rank, seemed possessed of the strength of a madman.

Robert was nowhere to be seen, and even then Beatrice's lip curled contemptuously. Mrs. Franklin, separated from her husband, turned blindly back toward the Fort, but two warriors overtook her, pulled her down from her horse, and carried her away screaming.

Katherine dashed by, toward the thickest of the fight, for her horse was maddened and utterly beyond control. Doctor Norton was beside her, his face streaming with blood, and he was making desperate efforts to reach the dangling bridle rein.

Beatrice laughed hysterically. After they were out of sight, a deadened auditory nerve resumed its functions, and she heard Katherine's voice saying, hoarsely, "You were right—I am glad I have lost my boy!" The power of thought came back to the girl by slow degrees. She must get away—but how?

Far out on the lake and a little to the rear was the bateau, where Mrs. Mackenzie sat as if she were made of stone, with the children huddled about her. Beatrice dismounted, and climbed, gasping, part way up the sand hill that sheltered her, then looked to see if the trail were clear, but the battle seemed to be thickest there. Isolated upon a low mound, far across the plain, she saw Captain Franklin and half a dozen men. Fifty or more Indians, with yells of fiendish glee, were running toward them, and Beatrice slipped back, down the incline of burning sand, afraid to look a moment longer.

She thought if she could attract Mrs. Mackenzie's attention, the boat might be brought near enough to shore for Queen to reach it safely, but the flutter of her handkerchief was not even seen, much less understood. If she could not get to the boat there was only one other way—to watch for an opening and ride like mad to Fort Wayne, trusting to Queen's speed for her safety. It seemed hardly possible that she could hide among the sand hills till dark, or even until there was an opportunity to try the last desperate plan.

Then out upon that plain of death danced Mad Margaret, with her white hair hanging loosely about her. "I see blood!" she shrieked. "The time of the blood is at hand!"

A tomahawk gleamed in the air, but fell harmlessly beyond her, and there was a murmur of horror in the ranks of the Indians. She went straight toward them, and they fell back, afraid of her and of her alone. Doctor Norton saw what she intended to do, and, with his hand on the bridle of Katherine's horse, kept behind her and out of range.

Step by step, with demoniac laughter and unintelligible cries, with every muscle of her frail body tense, Mad Margaret forced the Indians back. One, bolder than the rest, and drunk with blood, stole up behind her with his tomahawk upraised.

"*Mère! Ma mère!*" cried Chandonnais, darting out of the ranks. In a flash he had wrenched the weapon away from the Indian and started toward Margaret, hacking at those who opposed him.

A savage cry rang at his right, and Margaret turned. She saw the danger and retreated, then ran like a deer between the Indian and Chandonnais. "*Mère! Ma mère!*" the half-breed cried again, as the tomahawk intended for him sank into her darkened brain. With the tears raining down his face he caught her to him, and went backward, step by step, toward the place where the others were fighting, with the dead body of his mother in his arms.

Instinctively the soldiers drew near him, but kept to the rear. The Indians were advancing, but no one of them was bold enough to touch the man who held Mad Margaret. A moment more and the gap would have been closed, with that frail body forming a powerful defence; but a warrior, maddened by the loss of his friends, crept in behind Chandonnais and struck him down.

Then the battle took a new lease of life. In the midst of the smoke Norton saw Katherine's strained, white face close to his. They were surrounded, and a company of Indians, brandishing their war clubs, were racing toward them. Every avenue of escape was cut off. "Death comes," said the Doctor, quietly, wiping the blood from his face; "and here and now I dare to tell you what you must have known, that I——"

He was wrenched from his horse and his scalp lifted off at a single blow. Katherine turned, and in an instant she was in the grasp of an Indian. With desperate strength she tried to get possession of the scalping knife that hung about his neck, but in the moment that she had her hand upon it she was seized by another Indian, who lifted her bodily and carried her to the lake.

Mrs. Mackenzie saw the painted savage with the body of her daughter in his arms, then merciful unconsciousness blinded her.

Captain Wells was in the midst of the battle, fighting with musket and sword. In and out of the Indian ranks he sped, wreaking vengeance upon his foes. His hand was steady and his aim was sure. Warrior after warrior fell before him, and as yet he was but slightly wounded.

A young Indian entered the covered waggon where the frightened children were huddled together, and emerged at the other end with his tomahawk dripping and a look of fiendish satisfaction upon his painted face.

"Is that their game?" cried Wells; "butchering women and children! Then I will kill, too!"

He wheeled and turned toward the Indian settlement, mad with the desire for revenge. "Tell my wife," he shouted to some one, "that I died fighting like a soldier, and that I killed at least seven red devils!" Then his horse was shot under him, and in the fall he was pinioned so that he could not escape.

With wild laughter the savages gathered around him, hacking at him with their knives. "Don't kill him," muttered one of them, in the Indian tongue, "but keep him for the festival to-morrow!"

"Squaws!" cried Wells. "Women! Papooses! Eight against one, and you dare not strike to kill! Squaws!" The taunt went home, as he intended it should, and a tomahawk put a merciful end to his suffering. Then with one accord the savages fell upon the body, cut out the brave heart and ate it, hoping to gain his fearless strength.

One of them passed very near Beatrice's hiding-place with a bloody scalp in his hand. By the black ribbon that dangled from the queue, she knew that Captain Wells had met the fate he feared. For a moment horror paralysed her, and the metallic taste of blood was in her mouth.

Queen was standing as quietly as if she were in her stall, but her nostrils quivered with excitement. "In a moment, Beauty," whispered the girl, "we'll make a run for life." There was a muffled step, then around the base of the hill came Ronald, followed by his faithful dog.

The blood was streaming from a deep wound in his breast, and he was plainly done for; but he smiled when he saw her, then reeled, and would have fallen had it not been for the horse. Beatrice took hold of him, and, gasping, he sank to the ground at her feet.

The sand formed a hollow where they were, with the hill on one side of it and the lake on the other. Drifted ridges of sand still further screened them, and it was not likely that they would be seen.

"Poor old Major," said Ronald, with long pauses between the words; "poor—old—boy!" With trembling hands he loaded his pistol, and, before she knew what he was going to do, he had shot the dog.

"They'd—hurt him," he explained, with a feeble wave of his hand. "They're all—over there. The Captain has surrendered, but—Wells and Norton are dead—and most of the boys. The squaws are on the field with—with the others. They're opening up the wounds with—with pitchforks!"

His face whitened. Beatrice put her arm around his shoulders, and he leaned heavily upon her breast. "It's worth while—to die—" he gasped—"for this!"

"You're not going to die, dear. We'll stay here till night, then we'll go on to Fort Wayne. You can ride Queen."

Hurt as he was, Ronald smiled. "I—I wouldn't ride that—that gun carriage," he said with something of his old spirit. "Heart's Desire, you must not stay. At the first chance, go—ride like mad to—to Fort Wayne—if you are pursued or surrounded—you know what to do!"

His dimming eyes wandered to the bag of cartridges and the pistol at her belt.

"Yes," she said steadily, "I know what to do."

"Go!" he whispered.

Beatrice left him for a moment and went up the sand hill to reconnoitre. Peeping over the top of it, she saw that the Indians were all north of them, except a few, and that the trail was clear.

"I can't," she lied, when she came back. "There's hundreds of them in the south."

The cry of a wounded horse came from the field, and Queen started in terror. Beatrice quieted her, then knelt down beside Ronald. A look of ineffable happiness came into his eyes and his lips moved, but she put a warning hand upon his face. "Hush—you mustn't talk—lie still!"

"It seems like heaven," he breathed, "to have you—near me—and to have you—kind!"

The hot tears came to her eyes. "Don't!" she pleaded. "Dear boy, can't you forgive me?"

"Sweet, there is naught to forgive. I would live it all—to have you near me—to have you kind."

"Oh," she sobbed, "you break my heart!"

His hand closed limply over hers. "You must not stay—go—go—to Fort Wayne!"

"I shall never leave you," said Beatrice, simply.

"Dear Heart, you must—there is no other way. When you are gone—I—I——"

He looked her full in the face for a moment before she understood. "No!" she cried in anguish; "you shall not!"

"It is best," he said. "I am hurt—even past your healing—it is better than—the torture—and—and—if you are followed, you must do the same. Promise me you will!"

"I promise," she answered, but she hardly knew her own voice.

"They were—in the north," he went on. "To the southward—all is clear. If it were not for me—you would go."

He fumbled around in the sand until he found the pistol and loaded it once more, though his hands shook. Beatrice tried to take it from him, but very gently he put her away.

"It is time," he breathed. "Taps have sounded for me. I said I would not—not speak of it again—but you—you will grant me pardon—I love you—so much that death will make—no difference—I love you—with all—my soul!" With a trembling hand he put the muzzle against his right temple, and looked up into her face with the ghost of a smile. His eyes asked mutely for something more.

Then Beatrice bent over him, and the kiss for which he had vainly pleaded was laid full upon his lips. He caught his breath quickly, with a gasp of pain. "God is very good to me," he said unsteadily. "It was in my dream—but I did not dare—and now—Heart's Desire—good-bye!"

He closed his eyes. There was a sharp crack, a puff of smoke, and the boy was dead; but the supreme exaltation of a man's soul was frozen in his face.

For a long time Beatrice sat there, sobbing helplessly, with his cold hand in hers. It was nine o'clock when they started, and now the sun blazed at the zenith. Mrs. Mackenzie and the children were nowhere in sight—the boat was gone. Beatrice was as absolutely alone as if she had been in a desert. "Oh, if it were dark!" she thought, and then she prayed, in a shrill whisper: "Dear God, make it dark now!"

She felt her reason slipping from her and knew that she must get away. Blinded by her tears, she climbed to the top of the sand hill once more, and saw, dimly, that the coast was clear. A few Indians still moved about among the dead, but there was no firing, and the garrison horses, riderless and blood-spattered, stood quietly here and there, apparently heedless of the burning heat.

With the start she had, she was sure she could get away safely. Once on the trail, and then——

She saw that saddle and bridle were right in every detail, and mounted. "For life," she whispered to the horse; "for your life and mine!" She cautiously guided Queen in and out among the sand hills until she came to the open prairie. Before her lay the trail and hovering beyond it in her distorted vision, like a mirage glimmering in the desert, she saw the flag flying from the ramparts of Fort Wayne.

"Now then, Beauty—fly!"

Like an arrow shot from a bow, Queen sped across the plain, but there was a war-whoop just behind them and Beatrice knew she had been seen. The cry came nearer and she looked back. Fifteen or twenty Indians were in full pursuit and others, mounted, were following them.

The girl's heart rose in her throat. "On!" she breathed—"on!"

---

The unintelligible cries of the savages echoed and re-echoed in her ears, becoming perceptibly fainter as she rode on. Then there was an exultant yell and she turned quickly in her saddle. The mounted Indians had overtaken the others and seemed to be gaining upon her, but with a sudden spurt, Queen left them far in the rear.

Beatrice laughed hysterically and the sickening taste of hot blood was in her mouth. Those on foot had given up the chase and one of the horses had fallen, but well in the lead, with his sides bleeding cruelly, Ronald's big bay charger thundered down the trail.

An arrow sang past her, then another just missed her, and she leaned forward, close to the horse. Queen plunged on, then suddenly snorted and reared as an arrow struck her flank.

Beatrice managed to loosen the barb and pull it out, hurting the horse badly as she did so, and in the meantime the enemy gained upon her. Another arrow, shot from the right, pierced Queen's quivering side, and Beatrice, hopeless and despairing, reined in long enough to tear it out. She was sick at the sight of Queen's blood-stained body and the savage who rode Ronald's horse was almost within range.

She turned, held her pistol steadily, and waited. Queen was almost exhausted and breathed heavily. Spurred on to new effort, the other Indians emerged from a cloud of dust and galloped toward their leader.

A tomahawk whizzed past her and sank into the sand. Then she fired, and with a cry of pain, the Indian dropped from his horse.

Without waiting for the word, Queen started on at a furious pace, but in spite of it, Beatrice managed to load her pistol again. She looked back only once, for she could hear the hoof-beats behind her. Ronald's horse, with a new rider, was again in the lead, and the rest were close upon his heels.

Inch by inch they gained upon her and mutterings of hideous portent reached her ears. Queen's strength was rapidly failing, and when an arrow struck her in the leg, the gallant little horse stumbled and fell. A tomahawk gleamed just beyond them and at the same instant an arrow grazed the girl's left arm.

Blind with pain, she staggered to her feet, put the muzzle between Queen's pleading, agonized eyes, and fired. The horse rolled over, dead, and Beatrice loaded once more, thinking grimly, as she did so, that there was just time.

She raised the pistol, felt the burning circle of the muzzle against her temple, and turned for one last look at the world that once had seemed so fair. The Indians were almost upon her, but far out on the plain was a man with neither hat nor coat, riding furiously, and the pistol fell from her nerveless hand.

"Robert!" she cried, as if he could hear. "Go back!"

All at once she saw what he meant to do. Already he had turned a little toward the lake, hoping to cut them off.

"Oh God!" breathed Beatrice. "And I called him a coward!"

The Indians now were not more than three hundred feet away, but when they saw him coming they swerved away from Beatrice and rode toward him. Robert turned straight east at a plunging gallop, then there was a sharp report from his musket and a savage fell dead.

Then he threw away the musket, pulled out his pistol, fired and wounded another. A tomahawk grazed his head and the blood dyed his face, but he kept on.

From where she stood, she saw it all. Hand to hand, almost—yes, they were upon him now, but there was a gleam of silver in the sun and two of them fell back, wounded.

"Lexington!" she cried. "His grandfather's sword!"

All but four retreated, though his horse was hurt and well-nigh spent. His next shot missed fire and his pistol was snatched out of his hand, but the keen blade shone once more and another was dismounted.

The blood streamed from his wound as he dashed toward her, gaining upon the two who were pursuing him. All at once he stopped in his mad pace, turned, and with a single swift cut struck down the one nearest him. With a wild war-whoop the second Indian signalled to another who stood beside his dead horse, far out on the plain, but there was no answer. Quick as a flash Beatrice ran toward them, aimed steadily, fired, and the last Indian fell, mortally wounded.

"Thank God!" cried Robert, as he fell from his horse. "You are safe!"

They stood alone upon the desolate plain, looking into each other's eyes. Robert's clothes were torn and cut, and his face was black with blood and dust, but he seemed like a god to her.

"You saved me," she murmured, with parched lips. "How did you save me?"

"You were like another Beatrice," he whispered,—"you led me through hell!"

Face to face at last, after all the misunderstandings, Beatrice saw him as he was. The terrors of the day were temporarily forgotten, as when one wakes from a horrible dream to a new joy. Something stirred in the girl's heart and sprang, full-fledged, into exultant being. The light in her eyes confused him, and he turned his face away.

"It was nothing," he said diffidently,—"only a running fight—that's all. When the history of to-day is written, it will be a single paragraph—no more. Two officers and thirty-six regulars killed in action, two women and twelve children—a mere handful. No one will know that a civilian was so fortunate as to save the woman he loved. It is a common thing—not worth the writing."

Beatrice, still transfigured, put her hands upon his shoulders; but, though he trembled at her touch, he kept his face turned away.

"Don't thank me," he said unsteadily. "I can't bear it. It is nothing. Perhaps I've proved that I'm not——"

The girl put her fingers on his lips. "You shall not say it!" she cried. "With all my heart I ask you to forgive me—you have covered me with shame."

He turned and looked down into her eyes. "Shame," he repeated; "no, not you. Forget it, Bee; it is nothing. A single paragraph, that is all—which has to do with the soldiers, not with me."

"My soldier!" she said in a new voice, "my captain—my king—listen! No better, braver fight was ever made. The thirty-six who were killed in action have done no more than you; and some day, when they write it all, they will say a civilian fought like a soldier to save the life of the woman who loved him!"

# CHAPTER XXIII
# RESCUE

After the first part of the battle was over, the bateau in which Mrs. Mackenzie and the children sat was brought near the shore at the mouth of the river. When Mrs. Franklin was taken from her horse, an Indian carried her to the boat, laid her in the bottom of it, signed to her to keep quiet, and covered her with a blanket. She was badly wounded, and her position was well-nigh intolerable, but she was afraid to move.

Two warriors soon approached and demanded the prisoners which they said were concealed under the luggage, but the Indian at the oars assured them that the bateau contained only the family of Shaw-ne-aw-kee, and they went away apparently satisfied.

Katherine had fainted when she found herself in the arms of a painted savage. When she came to her senses she was in the deep water, and the Indian still held her in a firm grasp. She struggled until her strength was almost gone, but then perceived that her captor did not intend to drown her. Long and earnestly she looked into his face, and at length, in spite of the hideous disguise of his war-paint, she recognised Black Partridge.

Another brave joined him, and after a long conversation between them she was left to the care of the second Indian. Black Partridge went back to the battlefield, received Captain Franklin's surrender, through an interpreter, and then returned to Mrs. Howard.

When the firing had ceased, she was lifted out of the water and carried to the shore. Black Partridge took her by the arm and led her northward along the beach. She was drenched through, and her clothes were heavy with water. A squaw had stolen her shoes, and the long march upon the burning sand was exceedingly painful; but when they came near the Fort and she saw her mother upon the piazza at the trading station, she went on with new courage.

In the dismantled home the survivors were gathered. Captain and Mrs. Franklin, both wounded; Lieutenant Howard, also wounded; the Mackenzies, their children, and a few of the soldiers were all that remained of the company that had fared forth so gallantly only a few hours before.

When Katherine staggered in, her husband caught her in his arms, and his hot tears fell upon her face when he stooped to kiss her. "I thought you were dead!" he cried. "I never knew till now how much I love you!"

A radiant smile illumined her white face. "I thought you were dead, too," she whispered, "and I did not care to live. I wanted to be with you, wherever you might be."

One after another described what he had seen, and the melancholy details of the battle were soon told. It was stipulated in the terms of the surrender that the lives of the prisoners should be spared; but the Indians considered the wounded exempt from that provision, and horrible things were done upon the field.

Doctor Norton's heroic efforts to save Katherine, the valiant death of Captain Wells, Mad Margaret's fearless dash against the enemy, the half-breed's gallant fight, and the courage of the soldier's wife, who let herself be literally hacked to pieces rather than be taken prisoner—these things and many others were sadly recounted.

Captain Franklin assured them that Ensign Ronald was dead, and they were glad to believe him; but no one knew what had become of Robert and Beatrice. "Forsyth fought beside me for a while," said the Captain.

"And with me, also," added the Lieutenant, "on another part of the field."

"Where is my Tuzzin Bee?" asked Maria Indiana, plaintively. "I want my Tuzzin Bee!"

At this they all broke down, and even the men were not ashamed of their tears. Beatrice, the merry-hearted, whose birdlike laughter still seemed to linger in the desolate home—where was she? "Oh, God," sobbed Mrs. Mackenzie, "if we only knew that she was dead!"

"We'll hope she is," said the trader, brokenly. "She must be, or she'd be here!" He tried to speak as if he were sure, but his face belied his words.

Outside, groups of Indians moved about restlessly. From sheer savage wantonness they had killed the cattle that were left to them, as the troops turned away from the Fort. The houses had all been plundered, and incongruous articles were strewn all over the plain. The finery of the women had been divided, and the savage who had Captain Wells's scalp at his belt wore Katherine's bonnet upon his head.

Mackenzie, with his penknife, had removed two bullets from Mrs. Franklin's arm, and had improvised a bandage from some old linen he found in the house. Katherine was badly wounded in the shoulder, where the tomahawk meant for her had struck when Black Partridge snatched her away. Lieutenant Howard had several cuts upon his body and Captain Franklin and Mackenzie were each wounded in the thigh.

As some of them had suspected from the first, they were British prisoners, and were to be taken to Fort Mackinac or Detroit very soon. "To-morrow," answered the Indian chief whom Mackenzie asked, "or perhaps the next day. No stay here long."

Black Partridge had vanished as completely as if the earth had swallowed him up. The Mackenzies looked for him anxiously among the Indians who patrolled the Fort and the river bank. In spite of the surrender, his presence was the only assurance of safety they had.

An animated discussion was going on in front of the house, for a party of Indians, evidently from the Wabash, had just arrived. There was much loud talking and many gestures, and the bleeding scalps were fingered with admiring curiosity. Mrs. Mackenzie sat near the window, sheltered by a curtain, hoping and yet fearing to seeBeatrice's beautiful hair ornamenting the belt of some savage.

The mutterings outside grew louder, and hostile glances were turned upon the trading station. "Mackenzie," said the Captain, "have we any means of defence?"

"Not even a musket," answered the trader, bitterly; "and that door wouldn't hold more than two minutes."

Even as he spoke a company of Indians came up the path. "Quick, Katherine," commanded Mrs. Mackenzie—"here!" She pushed her on to the bed in the next room and covered her with the feather-bed, fearing that her light hair and fair skin would betray her as a newcomer to the more remote Indians.

With supreme self-command Mrs. Mackenzie sat on the bed beside her and sorted out a bag of patchwork pieces, humming as she did so, in a voice she scarcely knew.

The intruders entered and went through the house, peering into every nook and corner. When they were in the next room, Katherine whispered to her mother: "Oh, let me go! This is unbearable, and I can die but once—let them have me!"

"Hush," sang Mrs. Mackenzie, to a faltering tune. "Don't move and they will go away. If you stir it means the death of us all!" She went on with her work, scattering the gay pieces all over the bed and the floor, but the Indians did not go.

They grouped themselves about the doors and windows, effectually cutting off escape. Every one of them was heavily armed, and their faces were sullen and revengeful. They began to mutter to each other and exchange significant glances. All hope was lost, when the door was pushed open and Black Partridge came into the room.

"How now, my friends," he said. "A good day to you. I was told that there were enemies here, but I am glad to find only friends. Why have you blackened your faces? Is it that you are mourning for the friends you have lost in battle? Or is it that you are fasting? If so, ask our friend here and he will give you to eat. He is the Indians' friend, and never yet refused them what they had need of."

Thus shamed, the spokesman of the party explained that they had come for some white cotton cloth in which to wrap their dead. This was given them and they went away peaceably.

Then Mackenzie had a long talk with the chief and told him of their anxiety for Robert and Beatrice. The others, guessing at the subject, pressed close around them. "What does he say?" asked Katherine, anxiously; but the trader made no answer until the Indian had gone.

"He says he will put a strong guard of his own people all around the house and that we will be safe here, but we must strike no lights and make no noise, because some of the Indians from the far country do not know that we are their friends. He says the big soldier is dead, from a tomahawk that struck him in the breast, and that the little black horse is also dead on the plains far south of here; but neither the scalp of the paleface nor that of her lover are among those his braves have taken. He bids us to be quiet and to wait for news."

"To wait," sighed Mrs. Mackenzie—"to wait for news! It is the hardest thing in the world!"

The heat of the afternoon was sickening, so the curtains were closely drawn, and the little company huddled together, scarcely daring to speak above a whisper, but gathering human comfort and new courage from the mere sight of each other, wounded though they were.

Maria Indiana and the baby were put to bed for their regular afternoon nap, and some of the comforts of life were still left in the house. So the day passed on, with a double line of Indians around the house, and the hum and whir of midsummer coming to their ears from the fields beyond them, as if there had been no massacre and there was no such thing as death.

Robert and Beatrice were in the shade of a sand hill, nearly five miles south of the Fort. When his horse had rested a little, he assisted her to mount, and walked by her side until they reached the only shelter that was available. The sun was approaching the west, and the mound kept off the direct rays, as well as the south-west wind. They were faint from hunger, and both were slightly wounded, but otherwise they were quite comfortable. In front of them lay the lake, serene and smooth, with not a ripple upon its glassy surface, and no reflection of the conflict that had just been waged was mirrored upon its waters. Robert was one who recovered his strength quickly, and as the afternoon wore on he began to feel like himself. After reaching the sand hill, his first act had been to cut open the sleeve of the girl's dress and apply his lips to her wound.

"Why?" she asked. "Why do you do that?"

"Because the arrow may have been poisoned, dear."

"Then you'll be poisoned, too," she said, drawing away from him.

"No, I won't."

In spite of her protests, he drew the blood until no more came, then bathed the wound with water from the lake, and bandaged it with a clean handkerchief he happened to have in his pocket. Afterward, lover-like, he kissed the fair, smooth arm from shoulder to wrist, with an exquisite sense of possession.

"What are we going to do?" asked Beatrice, after a little.

"We can do nothing until night. Then I'll cover you with sand—all but your head, and go back to the waggons for food and ammunition. I'll get another horse, too, if I can find one, and then we'll go to Fort Wayne."

"And if you can't find another horse?"

"You'll ride this one, and I'll lead him. I'll get your saddle if I can."

"We'll never make it," she said sadly.

"Yes, we will—I'm sure of it. Life means too much to us, darling, to give it up without a fight."

The deep crimson dyed her white face. "I—I had to tell you," she whispered, "or you never would have known."

A long shadow appeared upon the sand, and Robert saw the unmistakable outlines of a feather head-dress. Beatrice was nestled in his arms, with her face against his breast. His pistol was at his belt, loaded, and his sword lay near him. "Is your pistol loaded, dear?" he asked, very softly.

She started away from him in terror. "Yes," she cried; "but why?"

"Hush!" He pointed to the shadow on the sand, which stealthily approached.

"Oh!" she moaned; "after all this!"

Robert rose to his feet and went noiselessly toward the southern side of the sand hill. Beatrice stood just behind him, white as death. Then Black Partridge appeared before them, with something very like a smile upon his face. "How!" he grunted cordially.

The conversation which followed was a veritable "confusion of tongues." Robert knew about as much of the Indian language as the other did of English; but, after some little time, he was made to understand that they were British prisoners, and that, for the present, they were safe.

"Ask him about Aunt Eleanor and the others," said Beatrice.

There was another long colloquy. "They are all safe," Robert explained, finally; "the White Father and his wife, the other White Father and his fair-skinned wife, and the family of Shaw-nee-aw-kee. They have been anxious about us, and when he goes back he will tell them that we are all right."

---

By signs and broken speech Black Partridge made it evident that they could not stay where they were, and ordered them to follow him. Robert demurred, but the chief frowned upon him so fiercely that he dared not disobey. From a voluble speech in the Indian tongue, Robert gathered that Black Partridge had not forgotten his promise—that the memory of the picture was still warm in his heart, and that he was the faithful friend of the paleface and her lover.

Beatrice smiled when Robert told her what he had said. "He knew, didn't he?" she asked shyly.

They began their long march northward upon the sand. Beatrice was mounted, and Robert walked beside her. Straight as an arrow and as tireless as an eagle, the Indian went swiftly in front of them, looking back, now and then, to see if they were following.

It was a hard journey for Beatrice, since the dead lay all around her. Even the Indians Robert had killed seemed to distress her, and when she passed the spot where Queen lay she could not keep back her tears. Vultures, with slow-beating wings, were silhouetted now and then against the setting sun, as they went from one grewsome feast to another.

"What are those birds?" asked the girl. "I never saw them before."

"I do not know," lied Robert. "I have never seen them, either."

The wind had covered Ronald's body with drifted sand, and she was spared the bitterness of that; but the plain of death, with its burden of mangled bodies, would have touched a harder heart than hers.

"Don't look, darling," he pleaded, and, obediently, she turned her face away, but the tears fell fast, none the less, and she could not repress her sobs.

"Sweetheart," said Forsyth, coming closer to her side, "I can bear anything but that. Your tears make me weak—your grief unmans me."

She hid her face in her hands and struggled hard for self-control. Then he went around to the other side of the horse. "Look at the lake, dear," he said; "or look at me and forget what lies beyond."

So they marched, in the full glare of the afternoon sun. The pitiless heat burned into the sand and was thrown back into their faces. But Beatrice did not once turn her head to the left, and Robert, looking past her, was thankful that she did not. Chandonnais and his mother were side by side, locked in each other's arms. Their bodies had not been touched, but others near them had been stripped and mutilated beyond all recognition.

When they came to the bank of the river, they looked anxiously toward the Fort and the trading station, but saw only Indians. A young warrior met Black Partridge here, and Beatrice was told to dismount. She did so, thinking that in a few minutes more she would be at home again, but when she saw that they were not going up the river she could not keep back a cry of pain.

The chief turned upon her fiercely, and muttered angrily to Robert. "Hush, dear!" he said to Beatrice, but his face was very pale.

They stood there for some time, and at length a large canoe was brought downstream. "Oh, where are we going!" she moaned.

"I don't know, dearest," answered Robert, in a low tone; "but wherever it is, we're going together." His fingers tightened upon his sword, that still hung at his side.

They got into the canoe, Beatrice at the bow and Robert at the stern. Black Partridge took the paddle, and with swift, sure strokes they shot out into the lake and then turned north. After some time Robert ventured to ask a question, but received no answer except a meaningless grunt.

The last light lay upon the water and touched it to exceeding beauty. The lake seemed like a great turquoise, deepening slowly to sapphire. Sunset colours flamed upon the clouds near the horizon, but their hearts were heavy, and they did not see.

As twilight approached, the canoe moved even more swiftly and Black Partridge never faltered at his task. Robert began to wonder if they were going to Fort Mackinac, and laughed at himself for the thought.

Now and then, after a sudden spurt ahead, the Indian anxiously scanned the shore, as if he were looking for a landmark. At last they turned in. With a grating of the keel the canoe grounded on the beach, and they got out, still wondering, still afraid, and completely at the Indian's mercy.

He signed to them to follow him, and they went up the steep bank as best they could, catching at saplings and undergrowth to keep their footing sure.

Once on the bluff they turned northward again, and Beatrice, utterly weary and hopeless, leaned heavily upon Robert's arm. Some way, the ground was familiar to him, but he could not have told where they were.

It was almost dusk when Black Partridge stopped and waited for them. They followed him down a little incline, which was smooth and well worn. "Why!" said Beatrice, in astonishment.

They were at the door of the little house in the woods that they had discovered so long ago; and over the doorway the silver cross still hung, its gleam hidden in the darkness.

The Indian spoke to Robert, repeating each sentence slowly, until he understood. Then Robert shook hands with him, and the Indian plunged down the bluff, ran along the beach to his canoe, and went south.

With a soft, rhythmic sound the splash of the paddle died into a murmur, then into silence. "What was it?" asked the girl, still afraid.

"We are to stay here to-night and perhaps longer—we are to wait until he comes for us. He says this is Mad Margaret's cabin, and that no one will dare to molest us here. The Great Spirit is already displeased, because by an accident she was killed. It is not good to touch her nor anything that belongs to her."

"Are we safe?" asked Beatrice, in low, moved tones. "Can it be that we are safe at last?"

Robert took her into his arms and kissed her twice. "My sweetheart," he said, "my own brave girl, we are safe at last, and we are together for always. Nothing but death can part us now!"

# CHAPTER XXIV
# THE REPRIEVE

Beatrice looked around the cabin curiously, though its aspect was very little changed from her memory of it. The rude, narrow bed at the farther end was still covered with the blue-and-white patchwork quilt which Mrs. Mackenzie had so strangely lost. The furniture, as before, consisted of rough chairs and tables made from boxes and barrels by an inexperienced hand. New shelves had been added, and these were filled with provisions in the familiar guise of the trading station.

A bolt of calico, some warm winter clothing, and countless articles of necessity and comfort were all neatly put away. Chandonnais had evidently pilfered from his employer constantly and systematically. Whatever he saw that seemed desirable for his mother's use, he had plainly taken at the first opportunity. Even the children'splaythings had been brought there to amuse Mad Margaret.

Beatrice pulled aside a cotton curtain that had been fastened across one corner, and was not a little surprised to find her own pink calico gown, which she had made early in the summer. Robert was as interested as she was, though the light was rapidly failing. He had found a tallow dip and kept it within easy reach, though he had his doubts as to the wisdom of a light.

With an exclamation of astonishment, he stooped and picked up a pair of moccasins—small, dainty, and heavily beaded—the very pair he had lost.

"See, dearest," he said, "these are the moccasins I had for your birthday. I told you they had been stolen, don't you remember?"

The girl turned her sweet face to his. "I'm going to thank you for them now."

"I don't deserve it, sweetheart, and I'll tell you why. I wanted to tell you then, but, someway, I didn't have the courage. I didn't know it was your birthday—I'd had the moccasins a long time, but I didn't want George to get the better of me, and so I let you think I knew."

The mention of Ronald's name brought tears to her eyes. "I have a confession to make," she said. "Come here." She put her arm around his neck and drew his head down, then whispered to him.

"My darling!" he replied, brokenly, "did you think me beast enough to grudge him that? I'm glad you did it and I always will be. Poor lad, he couldn't have you, and you are mine for always."

"I know," she sighed; "but I like to think that I made him happy—that he was happy when he died."

"He loved you, Bee—almost as much as I do."

"He couldn't," she said softly, "for nobody ever loved anybody else as much as you love me"; and he was quite willing to have it so.

Shortly afterward he came to an active realisation of the fact that neither of them had eaten anything since morning. He lighted the tallow dip and searched the cabin until he found a generous supply of the plain fare to which they were accustomed. He wanted to build a fire and make some tea for Beatrice, but she refused, and asked for water instead. He went down the bluff and brought her some, but it was so warm as to be almost insipid.

After they had eaten, the inevitable reaction came to Beatrice. The high nervous tension of the past week suddenly snapped and left her as helpless as a child. "Oh!" she moaned, "the heat is unbearable—why doesn't it get cool!"

She threw herself upon the narrow bed, utterly exhausted. With a clumsy, but gentle touch, he took the pins out of her hair and unfastened her shoes. Beatrice suddenly sat up and threw her shoes into the farthest corner of the cabin. Then a small, soft, indistinct bundle was pushed to the floor.

Robert laughed and brought the moccasins. "Will you let me put them on?" he asked. Without waiting for an answer he slipped them on her bare feet, not at all surprised to find that they fitted perfectly. "The little feet," he said, tenderly; "the bare, soft, dimpled things!"

"The moccasins are softer," she answered, in a matter-of-fact tone, "and I think I'm going to sleep now."

For a long time he sat beside her, holding her hand in his. They talked of the thousand things which had suddenly become important—their first meeting, their individual impressions of it, and of everything that had happened since. With some trepidation he told her that he was mainly responsible for the poem which accompanied the Indian basket.

"It was a very bad poem," she observed.

"Yes," answered Robert, with a new note of happy laughter in his voice; "it was an unspeakable poem."

Then he described the arrangement which he and Ronald had made "to lessen the friction," as he said, and she smiled in the midst of her tears. "Poor lad!" she sighed.

"Poor lad!" he repeated; and then, after a long silence, "true lover and true friend."

The intervals between question and answer lengthened insensibly, and at last Beatrice slept. He stole away from her on tiptoe and went out in front of the cabin, where there was only a narrow ledge upon the bluff. He sat down in the doorway, where he could hear the slightest sound, and deliberately set himself to watch out the night.

He was physically exhausted, but his mind was strangely active. For the first time he was in a position to review the events of his stay at Fort Dearborn, from the night of his arrival, when Mad Margaret had appeared at the trading station, to the present hour, when he sat in her pathetic little cabin, with the girl he loved so near him that he could hear her deep breathing as she slept.

"What has it done for me?" he thought—"what has it brought me?" The answer was "Beatrice," which came with a passionate uplifting of soul. With a certain boyish idea of knight-errantry, he had kept his hands and his heart clean, and, in consequence, love brought to him at last an exquisite fineness of joy. In that hour of close self-communion, his deepest satisfaction was this—that in all the years, in spite of frequent temptation, there was nothing of which he need to be ashamed—nothing to remember with a pang of bitterness, when Beatrice lifted her innocent eyes to his.

"Sir Galahad," some of his friends had called him, jeeringly, and, before, it had never failed to bring the colour to his face; but now the words rang through his consciousness like a trumpet-blast of victory. He was spared that inner knowledge of shame and unworthiness which lies, like bitter lees, in the wine of man's love.

"Beatrice! Beatrice!" Like another of her name she had led him through hell, and he saw now a certain sweet slavery in prospect. Wherever his thoughts might wander, she would always be with him, like the golden thread which runs through a dull tapestry, in and out of the design, sometimes hidden for an instant, but never lost.

Aunt Eleanor and Uncle John—they had been like father and mother to him, and he loved the children as though they were his own. The plaintive lisps of the little girl came back to his memory with remorseful tenderness, and he smiled as he wondered, dreamily, what Beatrice might have been at four or five. Swiftly upon the thought came another, which set the blood to singing in his veins, and which he put from him quickly, as one retreats before something too beautiful and too delicate to touch.

Captain Wells and Doctor Norton—they were dead. And Ronald—a lump came into his throat which he could not keep down, for, of all the men in the world, the blue-eyed soldier was best fitted to be his friend. They supplemented one another perfectly, each having what the other lacked, and enough in common to make firm neutral ground whereupon friendship might safely stand.

Of his other friends at the Fort he thought idly, since he had not known them so well, but he was genuinely glad that they had survived the horrors of the day.

As night wore on, the battle assumed indistinct and indefinite phases. Here and there some incident stood out vividly; unrelated and detached. He had spoken truly when he told Beatrice that "a mere handful" had been lost. What, indeed, did such things matter in the face of history?

It was but the price of a new country, which courageous souls had been paying for two centuries and more, and which some must continue to pay until——

Like a lightning flash came sudden breadth of view. What if a thousand had died instead of fifty; how could it change the meaning? Broad and beautiful, from the Atlantic to the unknown shore unmeasured leagues away, stretched a new country, vast beyond the dreams of empire, which belonged to his race for the asking.

Something stirred in his pulses, uncertain but vital; so strangely elemental that it seemed one with the reaches of water that lay just beyond him. Here, at the head of Lake Michigan, some day there must be—what?

There was a rustle beside him, but it was only a leaf. In the stillness it seemed as if it must wake Beatrice. Another near it fluttered idly, and a white birch trembled. A sudden coolness came into the air, then out of the lake rose the blessed north-east wind, with life and healing upon its grey wings.

He went into the cabin to put a blanket over Beatrice. Her face was turned toward the door, that her wounded arm might be uppermost, and something in her attitude of childish helplessness brought the mist to his eyes. The white, soft arm, with the bandage upon it, had its own irresistible appeal. Half fearing to wake her, he stooped to kiss it softly, thrilled with a tenderness so great that his love was almost pain.

He went back to the cabin door, where the wind was rioting amid the saplings, and sat down again. Already there was a hushed murmur upon the shore, and when the late moon rose, full and golden, from the mysterious vault beyond the horizon, the lake was white with tossing plumes—the manes of the plunging steeds that lead the legions of the sea.

Far out upon the water was a path of beaten gold—that fairy path which the little Beatrice had thought to take when she went to visit the moon people. The memory of that night came back with rapturous pain—when he had found the words to tell her what she was and what she meant to him, as far as words could express the sacred emotion that was kindled upon the altars of his inmost soul.

The moonlight shone into the cabin and full upon the girl's face. The childish sweetness, the womanly softness of her as she lay there came to him like the breath of a rose. A thread of light went higher and touched the silver cross to lambent flame. Beyond it, over the cabin, was——

He sprang to his feet and ran up the little incline to the bluff. In spite of the thick woods he could see the ominous glare upon the clouds in the south-west, and knew only too well what it portended. "Cowards! Dogs!" he muttered. "They are burning the Fort!"

His hands shut and opened nervously, and the nails cut deep into the flesh. A savage impulse to wrest every foot of soil from the Indians shook him from head to foot. Here, at the head of Lake Michigan—then the dream came upon him with the claim of mastery. "The baseless fabric of this vision.... The cloud-capped towers and gorgeous palaces...." His thought swiftly framed the words, then he laughed shortly, and turned away.

But, all at once, he knew what he must do. He saw himself clearly in the van of that humble army, which has no trappings of soldiery or state, but only the weapons of peace, by which, from the beginning, all men have ultimately conquered. The plough and the harrow, the spade and the pruning knife, the steady toil with hand and brain—here and now.

Step by step he saw the savages forced backward, their arrows met with muskets and the ring of steel—back to the farthest limits of the civilisation which at last should sweep them from the face of the earth. It was the dominant race beating back the opposition; the conquest of the wilderness by those fitted to rule.

Fired with purpose and ambition, he stood there until the lurid light in the south-west began to fade. Not one life, but the many—not the reaping, but the planting—he did not know it, but strong upon him had come the spirit of the pioneer.

The moon rose high in the heavens and from the zenith sent stray lines of light to touch the cross, where the figure of the Christ, wondrously moulded, was eloquent with voiceless appeal. The stars faded, as if blown out by the wind, and then there was a soft voice at his side: "Have I been asleep, dear?"

"You sweet girl," he laughed, taking her into his arms; "you've slept all night—it's nearly time for sunrise, now."

"I didn't know. You'll go to sleep now, won't you?"

"No, dearest—I'm not sleepy."

"Neither am I, so I'm going to stay with you."

In the doorway of the cabin, with their arms around each other, they sat while the darkness waned. The wind lifted her magnificent hair in long, slender strands, and now and then, when a heavy tress touched his face caressingly, Beatrice laughed and pulled it away.

"Don't!" he said.

"You dear, silly boy, you don't want my hair in your face."

"Yes, I do."

"Why?"

"Because I love you, from the crown of your head to your dimpled foot, with all the strength of my soul."

There was a long silence, then the girl sighed contentedly. "I never thought love was anything like this, did you?"

"No, dear—I didn't know what it was."

"I didn't, either, but, of course, I wondered. From all I had heard and read I was afraid of it, and I thought it would make me unhappy, but it doesn't. I can't tell you how it makes me feel. It seems as if God made us for each other in the beginning, but kept us apart, and even after we met it wasn't much better until all at once there was a light, and then we knew. It seems as if I never could be miserable or out of sorts again; as if everything was right and always would be; that whatever came to me you'd help me bear it, and always you'd be my shield."

"Sweetheart," he answered, deeply touched, "I trust I may be. It would be my greatest happiness to bear your pain for you."

Far in the east there was a faint colour upon the clouds. "See," she said, "it is day." He drew her closer, and she went on,—"Think what it means to go away forever from all this horror—to go back to the hills!"

Robert swallowed hard, then said thickly, "Heart of Mine, I would die to shield you, but Destiny calls us here."

With a cry the girl started to her feet. "Here!" she gasped. "Robert, what do you mean!"

In an instant he was beside her, with her cold hand in his. "What do you mean!" she cried.

"Listen, dear; I am asking nothing of you—it is for you to say. To-morrow we will be taken to Detroit as British prisoners—for how long we do not know. The Indians have burned the Fort, but some day, when the war is over, we must come here to live, for to go back is to acknowledge defeat."

The word stung her pride. "Defeat!" she said; "and why? Why are we defeated if we choose to live in a safe place instead of in danger—in peace rather than in the fear of massacre? Yesterday, did you not see? Only by the merest chance I am not among them—and yet you ask me to go back!"

Her voice vibrated with feeling, and her breast heaved. Even in the dim, purple light of early morning he could see the suffering in her face, and it struck him like a blow.

"My darling, listen—let me tell you what I mean. We will go wherever you say. If it pleases you to live in France or England, we will go there—it is for you to decide, not for me. Do you understand?"

"Yes," she answered dully. "Go on."

Robert's dream was dim and the fire of his ambition had dwindled, but he went on bravely. "We are at the very edge of civilisation, dear, and it must go on beyond us. The tide is moving westward, and we must either go with it or against it. We must go forward or retreat, there is no standing still. Yesterday a battle was fought, which, in its essence, was for the possession of the frontier. We have surrendered, but we have not given up. If we retreat, it must be fought again. From shore to shore of this great country there must be one flag and one law. Here, where the ashes of the Fort now lie, some day a city must stand."

"So," said the girl, with a harsh laugh, "and you would build a city from dreams?"

The tone hurt him to the quick. "Yes," he answered steadfastly, "I would. Nothing in the world was ever built without a dream at the beginning."

"Well," she said, after a silence—"what then?"

"Sweetheart," he cried, "you make it hard!"

Upon the purple light in the east came gold and crimson, touched here and there with deep sapphire blue. Little by little a glorious fabric was woven upon the vast looms of dawn. Beatrice saw his face, strained and anxious, and knew in her heart that she would yield. What Katherine had said came back to her— "When you find your mate, you have to go—there is no other way."

"To-morrow we go," he was saying, "back to the hills, but that is not the end— it is only the reprieve. We must come back here to fight it out, to finish the task we have begun, to hold our place in the face of all odds. We must stand in the front rank of civilisation, make our footing steady and sure, carry the flag westward into the stronghold of the wilderness—make a city, if you will, from dreams.

"Beatrice, this is the last time—I shall never ask you again. We will do as you will—this is my only plea. I ask you now, with the horrors of yesterday still alive in your heart, with your wound still open and sore, to come back here with me, when the Fort is rebuilt, and fight it out by my side.

"It must be done—by others if not by us, and if we retreat we are shamed. God knows I love you, or I would not ask you this. God knows I would shield you, and yet I would not have you shamed. Wherever there is human life, there is also danger, but we must make a place where our children and our children's children may live without fear. Heart of Mine, so strong and brave, you are not the one to falter—my Life, my Queen," he cried, in a voice that rang, "are you not a mate for a man?"

Prismatic colours lay on the water and the sunrise stained her face. Far across the pearly reaches a new day was dawning, and she looked at him steadily, as if her eyes would search his inmost soul.

"Once more," he said huskily, "will you come and do your part? Will you fight it out with me?"

Love and pain were in his voice—his body was tense and eager, like one who pleads for his utmost joy. Beatrice felt his courage, his passionate uplifting, and it stirred her pulses sharply, like a bugle call. Caught on that wave of absolute surrender, seeking only for the ultimate good, the girl's soul rose superbly to meet his own.

The first ray of sun leaped across the water, to touch her face with transfiguring light, and there was a gleam from the cross above her, where the splendour of the morning was turned back toward the altars from whence it came. Her fear fell from her like a garment, the horrors of the past were forgotten, and she saw herself one with him, on whatever height he might choose to stand.

Her burnished hair was like an aureole about her, and in her eyes was the fire of victory. Mate for a man she was in that exalted moment, when she leaned toward him with her lips parted and her soul aflame with high resolve. The eastern heavens illumined with a flood of white light that seemed like a challenge.

"Once more, sweetheart—will you come?"

She smiled and her sweet lips trembled as if already she felt his kiss, then clear and strong as the note of a silver trumpet came the girl's triumphant answer. "Yes," she cried, "I will!"

# The End

www.ingramcontent.com/pod-product-compliance
Lightning Source LLC
Chambersburg PA
CBHW070901290526
45795CB00001B/199